Cycle of the Seasons

A New England Year

Eric M. Howe

Illustrations by Sarah Howe

ISBN-13: 978-1542381000
ISBN-10: 1542381002

Introduction

Several years ago I kept a daily handwritten journal of the small things that characterize the natural and physical world of the changing seasons in the little town of Paxton, Massachusetts.

Three years later I did the same and discovered, with great comfort, that the beautiful patterns of life here are much the same. There is something deeply rewarding in this awareness, this cycle of the seasons.

This book contains my observations and reflections of those things worth seeing and the belief that they will continue from one year to the next.

Spring

Awakening

March 20

Today, we naturally consider things in heavenly terms, for it is the equinox and as such the celestial beginning of our spring here in the northern hemisphere. This is a welcome milestone for us New Englanders, who've suffered through what has seemed at times to be endless stretches of darkness, cold and snow. The beauty of those early crystalline snowfalls in December had given way to a grudging defeat as we settled in for the long haul of January and February.

There isn't anything notably unique about this day, apart that we regard it reverently as our own right of passage. We've gained more sunlight these past few weeks, and today signifies that transitional time when the amount of daylight wins out over our darkness, becoming increasingly dominant as this season progresses into the next. Still, it's difficult to celebrate just yet. It feels decadent, even though the sunset is now after 7:00 pm and getting later by leaps and bounds. Perhaps we feel the punishment of winter too dearly; we need no reminder of the shortest day not long ago. This transition is an ephemeral thing; the warm day of tomorrow will undoubtedly be followed by a cold snap, and we are unsure whether or not to let our breath relax in acknowledgement that winter is indeed over or keep cautiously to our resolve that some day it will end, but just not today.

It is close now, the coming of our true spring, when the grass greens fully and the daffodils burst forth, when the street sweeper makes its annual pass down the road to collect the cast off sand and debris, and the orioles return to find the wedge of orange we've placed in the wire next to the big maple. We will feel it when it has finally arrived. There will be no emotional ebb and flow. It will simply be.

Today is the first day of spring. Tonight, we are due to get several inches of snow. Sigh.

March 21

The snow arrived last evening at midnight while we were sleeping and accumulated four inches by daybreak. What was the turning green of yesterday has been instantly transformed to the winter landscape of only a few short weeks ago. Such is the nature of early spring, where the norm is often one step forward and two steps backward.

The birds are in a frenzy this morning by the side feeders. I count a dozen juncos, four red-winged blackbirds, two mourning doves, three blue jays, one cardinal, one red-bellied woodpecker, and a half dozen house finches. There is no open spot at any of the tubes for the birds that take their fill upon the perch. Two chickadees and a titmouse just arrived, flapping near the feeders and causing the house finches to relinquish their spots in fright. This agitates the whole thing so, causing seed to fall from the openings to the ground below, where the juncos and doves are all too happy to receive fresh manna from above.

The only consolation is that the snow is falling lightly now, and descending straight down from the skies in only the most gently breeze. It is quite pretty, seeing the arbor vitae, spruce and pine boughs fill with snow and watching their branches bend slowly until some breaking force causes a plume to release downward, cascading in a gentle fall of snow and spray.

March 22

The afternoon sunshine is notably brighter and less golden than it was just a couple of weeks ago. Even in today's 31 degrees, the strength of the rays is enough to quickly melt the several inches of snow from yesterday. Thankfully, such is the reward of a spring snowstorm.

The dogs and I took a walk down the access road toward Asnebumskit Pond. In the shaded domain of the old trail, there were still a few inches of dense snow, and they enjoyed bobbing up and down one in front of the other as they made their way through the woods and toward the berm that buttresses the pond. As we emerged and climbed the embankment, Asnebumskit stretched out before us, glittering brilliantly against the clear blue of the afternoon sky and surrounding trees. Exposed as the berm was, the melt had hastened to the point that there were only patches of snow here in there in small depressions. The rest had reverted to the muted greens of grasses that have yet to rejuvenate.

It occurred to me standing there how simply beautiful this place can be. The wind cast shifting patterns of movement across the expanse, and there were sounds of melting snow dropping from the limbs of trees in the woods behind, making wooden tinkling noises like bamboo chimes as they released and cascaded on the way to the forest floor. Titmice were calling to one another from within the fen, and in the occasional stillness when the breeze relaxed, the sun warmed my face just so, set with my eyes closed and facing toward the sun.

March 23

Amy from down the street stopped us in the road this evening. Evidently on her drive home last night, she turned the corner on Pond and nearly collided with our area moose, who seemed as startled by the encounter as did she. There is something ungainly about a moose to begin with, considering its lumbering head and body atop the comparatively spindly and unsure looking legs. Imagine a moose that has been startled by an unexpected car and tries desperately to make for the side of the road, legs going in several different directions at once.

Sometimes we will come upon its tracks in the snow or mud and know of its recent passage, though we've only actually seen it once. It was in the early spring, a couple of years ago, and we were outside in the front tidying up the knot garden of the deadfall leaves of the previous autumn, admiring the emergence of the spring flowers that had broken through the exposed soil in desperation. Our son John rather casually said, "Guys, there's a moose coming up the driveway," in a tone that you'd normally associate with someone remarking about something as mundane as a passing car.

We looked up, just as casually, and stared in disbelief as the lumbering giant came strolling without a care right up the driveway, paused not ten feet from where we stood, then continued onward toward the side woods and beyond.

It's shoulders were nearly six feet high, and its head extended outward and upward another two feet. It was enormous and utterly unconcerned about our presence (not that we could do much to affect it).

March 24

The stars were brilliant early this morning after the moon set and a small squall came through that cleaned the atmosphere of the humidity left over from the low of the past few days. Venus departed as our morning "star" over a month ago, and Jupiter has taken her place as the brightest object in our predawn view. It sits off to the west now, nearly ten degrees above the horizon at five o'clock.

Venus completes her yearly orbit of the sun in approximately nine of our earth months, and the time between her transition as the evening star to the morning star is shorter yet – only several months until she reemerges here on the verge of setting in the evening sky and climbing steadily each night to her prominent position. She will swing back and forth between evening to morning as she continues from one year to the next.

Jupiter progresses in a statelier pace. I recall distinctly it resting just over the left shoulder (Betelgeuse) of the constellation Orion only two years ago, and now it resides roughly two large hand widths away to the left. Jupiter's orbit is large by comparison, taking nearly 12 of our own years to complete one revolution around the sun. The means Jupiter travels nearly 30 degrees of sky per year (360 divided by 12), which is somewhat slow (at least in terms of our own Earthly perspective). Jupiter won't return to the constellation of Orion for another 10 years. It's a little misleading to express it this way. Perhaps better put that we won't see Orion in the background of Jupiter's orbit for another 10 years. Either way, chances are still fair that I will be around to see it there again.

March 25

The grass is showing more green in places and looks comparably alive to what it was only a couple weeks ago. In another few, it will be remarkable. We pleasantly forget how explosive the vibrancy of spring colors can be, in the carpet of new growth in the lawns and roadsides where emergent grasses give life to the earthy browns that have predominated since December. Our own lawn is nothing to boast of, with a patchwork of grass mixtures and perennial weeds. The latter have been increasing these past several years, and I have neglected the evidence of what must be the changing soil acidity in the lawn.

Among the grasses that have new growth, where emerald green blades lie interspersed with the faded yellow of the dormant lot, there are more patches of invaders. Wild strawberry, cinquefoil, wood sorrel and violets are beginning to take over giving our lawn the appearance of a fodder field rather than the cultivated look that so many strive to achieve. In truth, we dislike the monoculture frontage, where homeowners evidently put down copious fertilizer and weed killer to achieve the perfect uniformity of blade after blade of blight free grass. This degree of control seems unnatural. In fact, it is unnatural! Ours looks a bit ragged, but the mixture of small strawberry flowers and purple blossoms of the violets, both which will explode in another month, are quite pretty against the remaining greens of the grasses that shoot up in earnest.

It's more field than lawn at this point. We've learned to live with it.

March 26

A warm front came through this afternoon, clearing away the cold morning fog that seemed to linger closely. One minute the temperature was a damp 41 degrees, and the next it shot to 60 as breaks of sunshine peaked in through cloud layers that moved by swiftly from the south. As the mist vanished and the warmth returned, the crocuses opened slowly as if to welcome the change, becoming full in less than an hour and inviting the bees to visit. All this took place in the late afternoon, and despite the lowering sun overhead it was warm enough to remind us that spring sunshine gives that much more heat than only a few weeks ago.

Sarah and I sat on the driveway in a dry spot where the sun's rays had done their job. We were simply content to allow the sunshine to fall upon our faces and to feel the warmth of the afternoon mix with the emergent sounds of bees and birds coming alive in the background. Overhead, there was a parallax of wonder, as lower clouds only a hundred feet up or so were moving rapidly by, while another layer far higher seemed to parade from the south at a more leisurely pace. It was a little disorienting to observe.

March 27

The Worm moon came last night, full and notably bright following the clearing sky of yesterday. It rose beautifully through the forest of the lower woods, casting the leafless hardwoods in a diffuse backlight and making the landscape almost glow with its soft incandescence.

The worms are indeed turning in the yard, evident in the numerous castings that are deposited on the surface, resembling small piles of dark wet sand. Their action is welcome now, as they aerate the soil so that water and air can more easily penetrate to the grass roots below. They also serve to decompose the organic matter of the upper layers, taking in microscopic bits of leaf fall and dead material that has mixed within these past several years and excreting their inorganic wastes in the castings. These will serve as needed nutrients to the soil below, dissolving in the rains and mixing within.

This is early spring. It is a season of transition, begun in the preparation for things that will explode in growth shortly. There is wonder even in the simplest things like the turning of the worm or the rising of the moon.

March 28

At the bottom of the hill where Crowningshield Road
descends and just before it angles off to the left, there is a
small creek that runs underneath through a culvert and
outward toward one of the Kettlebrook Reservoirs not one
hundred yards away yet hidden by the thick woods. On
the eastern side, the creek empties briefly into a small
pond before continuing onward through the trees. The
pond is swollen this year, and there is evidence of a new
beaver dam on its far side.

I know this, because I happened to walk by early this
morning as daybreak was revealing the outline of the
surrounding woods and the early spring birdsong was
tentatively beginning. The only other sounds came from
the low chorus of grey tree frogs and spring peepers – not
yet the cacophony that we will hear when the later spring
arrives but pleasant all the same.

The reverie was interrupted when I passed, as my
presence startled the unseen beaver, which then forcefully
slapped the water with its tail before making a hasty
retreat to the far side of the pond. I nearly jumped out of
my skin in fright, which I suppose is the intended
outcome.

March 29

We've begun the annual chore of cleaning the buffer
spaces that border the yard and extend into the woods.
Here is where the leaves from last autumn were hastily
raked or the deadfall sticks were thrown. Here is where
the advancing multiflora rose or bittersweet is now clearly
visible, when soon enough the emergent leaves will hide
their advance. I don't mind this work all that much,

though it's defeating to make much progress against the bindweed and bittersweet.

A small patch of briars has taken hold in the access road that runs beside the property. I know this, because I dragged a small deadfall branch directly through them and cursed that I was wearing short pants. Between the thorns of the multiflora rose and the evil weapons of the briars, my legs looked like I was attacked by an angry cat, sporting raking lines of red scratches in several places.

To make matters worse, I fell at least a dozen times while trying to pull the bittersweet vines out from the soil. It's incredible how profuse their orange roots penetrate, reaching in lengthy branches beneath the soil as a testament to their ability to spread. So it was "yank, yank, fall (on my backside)."

An hour's worth of yanking, scratching and falling. On second thought, I do mind this spring chore.

March 30

We had four gray squirrels congregating at the bottom of the feeder pole this afternoon. Three seemed suited to each other's temperament, and I suspect they may be siblings or such. The fourth was clearly an outsider, both in appearance and personality. It would approach the pole tentatively to dig through the seed cast off on the ground and be summarily chided by the others; they would bite and claw as the outsider fled in a panic to the large maple that sits beyond. A chase would ensue, as the outsider would spiral upward and around the base of the tree, followed closely from behind by one of the attackers, until both revolved frantically at least a dozen times around the maple and vanished above into the upper branches.

A few minutes later the chaser would return, resuming beneath the pole as if nothing had transpired. Shortly, the outsider would peak around the base and hop gingerly toward the others, and the whole cycle would begin anew.

March 31

March is at its end – not as a lamb or as a lion but rather somewhere in between. The weather has been the typical rollercoaster of warms and colds, sunshine and rain, with some snow thrown in for good measure (and to remind us that New England spring really is an ephemeral thing). In past years, I've sometimes been happy to bid March farewell, and in others less so. This has been a fairly temperate version of the month, which makes the transition to April seem less urgent or desperate.

There is so much to anticipate in the coming weeks, and I feel remiss to look forward so at the expense of not appreciating the month that just passed. We tend to do this all too often – to anticipate what is over the next horizon in favor of simply reflecting on the wonders that have been. One consolation is that soon the leaves will emerge within the next month, and the explosion of growth within the forests will lessen our vistas.

Winter is a contrast this way. The loss of leaves reveals more of the landscape beyond, and our vision can see the line of the hillside beyond to where the gentle slope of the distant hill rises to meet another. In this sense, winter expands our horizons, though the lengthy darkness and difficult cold makes us turn inward to hearth and home.

Spring brings its own similar contrast, as our spirit becomes desperate to seek the solace of the natural world that is returning in abundance, its very growth closes our vistas to those places we have viewed from afar these past few months.

April

April 1

A warm air mass from the south moved through during the evening, pushing the temperatures well into the high fifties over night. By morning, it was strangely colder in the house than outside, and the sunroom windows fogged when we opened the door to smell the humid air and hear the chorus of frogs from down below. It won't be for a couple of months that we are able to simply use the screen door as our barrier to the outside, and by then we will be accustomed to this privilege. To do so today feels decadent and improper after so many months of being closed up against the elements.

At daybreak I took the dogs for a morning walk down Grove, past Robinsons and onward to the lowland just before the road turns on Pond Street. There in the shoulder, where only a couple of weeks ago shown the promise of green shoots, lay a patch of blooming Coltsfoot. I couldn't help but smile, relieved to see one of the first colorful wildflowers return. As the day brightened, I noticed that several of the daffodil buds in various yards, those that had been swelling in anticipation the past week, have burst forth in full blossom overnight. Soon enough we will have dozens decorating the landscape – another sure sign that the change is at hand.

Wood frogs, gray tree frogs, and spring peepers are all now calling – made more urgent by the warm morning so that the lowland woods and wet bogs come alive with their music. Only yesterday the mornings were silent, save for any wind that came through the branches of the dormant trees or the sound of snow melting off the pines and falling to the ground in cascades. Even the resident crows and chickadees of the forest had been particularly quiet, almost as if they were in rest and awaiting the explosion of renewal that was close at hand. Now there is no silence, with birds calling to one another from afar mixed with the sounds of life desperate to take a foothold and grow into this thing we call spring.

April 2

Just like that the tide of spring recedes, allowing late winter to gain an upper hand. This change was forecasted, though we irrationally hoped that the coming front would divert at the last minute. By eight o'clock this morning, the wind shifted from the south to the west, and the old barometer that hangs on the office wall started dropping steadily. By eleven o'clock, the temperatures had dropped from the mid fifties to the lower thirties, reaching the mid twenties by the afternoon with leaden skies that gave flurries.

All the spring calls of yesterday ended, save for the chattering of the birds at the feeder who were desperate in their attempt to gather as much seed as possible while the snow began to accumulate on the greening yard. Such is New England, and though we are accustomed to this ebb and flow of the oncoming of the vernal season, it is still difficult to tolerate as we begin April.

The only consolation is that the red maples have been producing their crimson flowers in full profusion. The trees are new tinged in a reddish glow, which is cast in sharp relief against the dusting of white upon the forest floor and hillsides. Were we not so far past the beginning of the year, I'd be more happy to observe that the landscape looks remarkably festive with the greens of the pine boughs, the reds of the maples and the clean white of the dusty snow.

Spring snows are ephemeral things thank goodness. The ground is warm enough from the stored heat of the past two weeks that it won't be long before this accumulation melts away, and we will return to the reverie of our needed spring once more.

April 3

The low pressure of yesterday was replaced with an approaching high, bringing fierce winds from the northwest that blew steadily the entire day. Across the road the spruce line, still laden with the burden of heavy, wet snow from the storm, swayed violently in the gale. These trees were planted nearly 70 years ago by the elder Cournoyer as a break between the homes on Grove Street and the line of sight to the fields just beyond. Though they may have served to hide the workings of the farm some decades ago, the trees have grown to maturity, and the lower branches have long since been absent any boughs of needles. In truth, we prefer it this way, so that we may enjoy the rhythms of the farm life throughout the seasons.

Now those mature trees are struggling in the violent tempest. Each year, we typically lose one or two to the throes of the winter gales, where age and weight conspire to topple them leeward toward the road. Today was just the case, as one of the more scraggly elders uprooted in the wind and came down hard across the road, partially hitting the electrical wire on its fall and disrupting the power.

In short order the town was alerted, sending the workers to come with chain saws to cut away the tree and linesmen to reestablish the grid. In their wake, we were left with another gap in the line, where before there was our familiar spread of large trunks and rising boughs. Now, there is a place where our view is unobstructed to the field and horizon, and it feels at once liberating and inappropriate somehow.

April 4

The Juncos have remained longer than usual, perhaps because of the lingering cold and snow, which they seem to prefer. Just now there are nearly fourteen of them beneath the tube feeder working frantically to dig through the few inches of powdery white in order to locate the cast off sunflower seed beneath. They are comical birds, though not as curious as the chickadees nor possessing quite the attitude as does the nuthatch, both of which are presently sharing the side yard with the Juncos. The only other visitors are a pair of mourning doves who descended rather abruptly in their typical way, landing with no semblance of grace near the base of the pole. The Juncos don't seem overly bothered by any of the traffic.

April 5

The town saw fit to deposit a fresh spread of blue salt crystals early this morning, despite that the temperatures were to rise well above freezing by midday. Even by nine o'clock the residual heat of the roadbed was enough to combine with the action of the pellets to create a blue slurry of mush, and shortly there were small rivulets of tainted blue runoff headed down hill on the sides of the street.

It wasn't too long ago that towns used sand, and while this wasn't as effective at ridding the surface of the perils of ice and snow, at least it provided enough traction to aid driving enough. They haven't sanded in years, preferring now to coat the road with some derivative of salt, the latest as calcium chloride I'm told, which is supposed to be more "environmentally friendly" and less corrosive to the undersides of our cars.

The switch to more salt usage happened roughly eight years ago.

Within the past several years, we've noticed an increase in browned foliage of those trees that border the roadsides, particularly the evergreens such as cedars, white pines and spruces, though even the deciduous trees such as oaks and maples seem sensitive to something deposited nearby.

This is a lesson in correlation. It may be a lesson in causation.

April 6

Even though the temperature never rose out of the thirties, the angle of the sun has risen enough so the more direct rays melted the snow from portions of the front yard, revealing the greening grass once again. The sun is as strong now as it was last September, and we are thankful for this when the spring storms deposit unwelcome snow. It tends to leave as quickly as it came, thank goodness. We are anxious.

I spoke with a neighbor who said that he would rather we had not experienced the warming period of two weeks ago, for it has made the return to the arctic temperatures that much more difficult to bear. I asked if this was rather like having not ever loved at all, versus having loved and then lost. We both decided that this was too deep for comparison and simply wished that winter would depart without fanfare.

No sooner was the grass exposed then did a dozen robins descend to the yard and begin to forage. In short order they spaced themselves equally and went to work searching for food, running ahead in short bursts and then stopping to cock their heads to the side, giving the appearance that they were listening to some earthly noise or feeling some signaling vibration. Some would continue on, and others would peck violently at the ground, dislodging some early worm or insect, free from the blanket of covering snow yet exposed to the dangers from above.

These are the robins of spring, congregating now in search of food, calling to one another at the coming of the dawn to signal their intent for the feeding grounds for the day. There is rain forecast for tomorrow – a soaking rain that will assuredly bring the larger worms to the surface, where they will spill onto the driveway to escape the drowning in the saturated soil. These robins will no doubt appreciate the boon.

April 7

The Holden Road out of Paxton descends appreciably as it approaches Kendall Reservoir, changing in elevation nearly six hundred feet within the two miles from the Grove cross street to the bridge that spans the water. This change is enough that the microclimate at the bottom is nearly two weeks ahead of those of us who dwell in the rarified air of Paxton. Grandiose claims aside, in truth it's fair to observe that the grass "is greener" near the reservoir, and the trees are simply farther along. Forsythia is almost blooming near the woods that border the southerly exposed hill on the north side of the reservoir, and if you look closely there are dandelions poking up amid the grasses of the slopes.

April 8

The tomato seeds I planted a month ago had grown to nearly two inches high, each making the most of the small styrofoam wedge into which it had been developing. I've kept them in a plastic greenhouse inside, safe from the poking curiosity of the cat and exposed to the daylight that comes through the sunroom window. Seeds had given way to germination and then in time to the emergent true leaves that to me signify the adolescence of these young plants. It's silly really to think in these terms, but we treasure our tomato plants as children, celebrating their transitions as they make their way from one small pot to another before eventually going outside sometime in May.

Today the chore was the first transplanting, as the seedlings had become root bound within the small wedges. I filled three-inch plastic pots with soil, pushed my finger down into each, and gently pulled each seedling free from the styrofoam, before gently dropping it into the waiting pot. The transition was evidently stressful, as each succumbed to the drooping effect of being forcibly removed. The whole lot of forty eight plastic pots are now secure within the greenhouse, each plant looking pathetically limp the comfort of its new environment, with room enough for the roots to push outward and stems to elongate further.

If the weather holds and does not get too cold at night, we'll move them all to the cold frames near the side of the house, where they will enjoy the warming sun through the angled glass and harden enough through the cooler nights. All this until the threat of some vengeful frost is well past. Perhaps early May. Then off to their final home in the raised beds, where spring and summer can do their work and we will mark their daily progress with anticipation and longing.

April 9

The sky was mostly overcast at dawn, save for a clearing patch over the eastern horizon, and the combination gave a striking orange hue to the sunrise. Initially it shone upon the upper portions of the trees of the lower woods, making them seem alive as if lit by an atmospheric fire, their color contrasted against the grey clouds in the background.

We walked the dogs down the access road in the building light, letting them trot well ahead as we stopped briefly to watch the change in the tree tops from deep orange to the muted yellow of daybreak. There wasn't a whisper of wind, and it seemed as though we could hear the forest awakening to the coming of the day.

Up ahead, Kipper stopped momentarily in the path at the point where the outlet of the vernal pool cuts across the trail, making a small drainage cut that empties into the lower woods. The stream is only a foot across and barely three inches deep. It is full now, with the melting of the snow having passed and the vernal pool fully charged from the recent rains. It will drain away slowly across this cut for the next several months, until the drought of late summer into autumn does its work. It is here where the chorus of frogs is the strongest in the morning and evening, though they become silent when passersby come along.

Kipper paused briefly to consider the stream, leaned back on his haunches, and launched somewhat awkwardly onto the far side. He trotted onward for a few steps then turned to look back to check that we were following. It is bittersweet to see him so, for it was only a year or two ago that he would leap across the stream without pause, bounding ahead without a care. Now the years have begun to show. He is slower as he moves and more careful, still wanting to walk the paths he has known well these past twelve years.

April 10

Though it was chilly today, there were clear skies and nearly no breeze, making it pleasant enough to sit on the back porch in the afternoon sunshine. It is noticeably higher in the sky now, so much so that the shadows of the still bare branches of the big maple in the side yard no longer reach the porch.

From somewhere down in the lower woods came the strident laughter of the pileated woodpecker. It is a secretive bird, and though we often hear them throughout the day, it is still a rare treat when one comes flapping by with its distinctive swooping pattern.

There is a very old tree at the side of the road past the bend at Robinson's, where the pavement descends gradually toward Pond. The warming temperatures of spring have surely hastened the flow of sap in this giant maple, and given that it bears deep scars from years of live, the emergent beetles and ants must too be traversing within its cavities. I suspect this, as beneath the tree on the dark pavement is a noticeable pile of small wood chips, most the size of a typical pinky finger. These are the extracts of some pileated woodpecker, which has decided to hammer this tree in search of a ready meal.

On a still day, the rapport is loud – "thwok, thwok" in striking succession the bird will strike, throwing chips outward and to the ground one after another. In no time it excavates a cavity large enough to permit a person's fist.

April 11

A flock of grackles descended upon the bird feeders this afternoon, and within the span of twenty minutes both tubes were emptied. While they are striking to behold, with their iridescent feathers and golden eyes, they are largely a nuisance to the other birds that inhabit the dooryard. The same can be said of the starlings – pretty in their own way and somewhat musical in their call, but annoying.

Sarah saw a female and male cowbird – the first pair of the season, which means that if the weather warms a little more we might see the first oriole or rose-breasted grosbeak within a week or two. Our spring tenants seem to be returning on schedule, which is comforting after the unusually warm winter.

April 12

There are small shoots everywhere now among the tan grasses from last autumn. The field edges across the road and the bare hump that runs between the two tracks are starting to look tinged with green, where new grasses push their way to the surface. It is still muted at this point, and the predominant colors are yet shades of brown and greys – the lifeless products of last year hanging on to be replaced by the bursting of new growth.

The pulse is beginning to hasten now, and shortly we will scarcely be able to keep up with the changes all around us. Grasses will lengthen, buds will fatten to reveal the new leaves within, early wildflowers will make their appearance in the lawns and roadsides. The new greens of spring will arrive, lighter at the outset of May, as if the alchemy of new growth is concocted with a universal shade of tender green. It will deepen as the spring progresses, slowly building to the varied hues of greens we associate with summer in its full splendor. This is a magical time.

April 13

It's amazing what two warm days strung together can do in this stretch of early spring. In the small border plot near the front walkway, the perennial chive has grown six inches seemingly overnight, making a bunched group of slender deep-green shoots that rise upward among the brown of the leftover mulch. Not three feet away in between the space made by two bricks that form part of the walkway, a Johnny Jump Up now sits in display, its yellow and purple face turned toward the south in search of the passing sunshine.

The dogs and I sat for a while in the afternoon warmth, all of us simply content to rest in the full sun with our eyes closed (though they had taken the added measure of flopping over on their sides on the heat of the driveway pavement). Somewhere in the berm a red-winged blackbird called insistently in the strange metallic way – not the trilling we normally hear this time of year but rather the raised whistle that must mean something unique. Just then I heard a truck pass slowly by out front, and within several seconds the slight acrid smell of fertilizer came wafting past. This made me think of the verdant odors yet to come – the turned loam across the field, the pungent smell of alder, beech and elm pollen, the mixture of oil and dirt made volatile by an afternoon spring shower. All things returning to our senses now.

For fun I grabbed a small sprig of the chive and pulled it free, crushing and rolling it between my fingers. This is another wonderful smell of spring and summer.

April 14

I pulled the garden hoses out of the barn this afternoon and went to the basement to turn the valves so that the water would divert to the outside faucets. This is a small accomplishment in the scheme of things, but it is certainly more pleasurable to be preparing for the garden in contrast to closing things down as we did in November. The faucet out front comes out through the baseboard of the frame, emerging in a spot next to the Viburnum we planted several years ago. This bush has fattening leaf and flower buds, the latter will erupt in another month or so in a profusion of small white blossoms that have the most beautiful odor.

Around the Viburnum is a border of Vinca minor, which my Grandmother always called "the myrtle" when I was younger. Among its deep green leaves are now splashes of purple flowers. These will multiply as spring continues, forming a pretty patchwork of color set against the barn red of the house.

As I was coiling the hose next to the faucet, I caught sight of a flash of purple down near the ground, thinking it was one of the Vinca flowers until it surprised me by flitting away. And there it was! The first butterfly of the season. A spring azure made its debut, showing its delicate sky-purple wings as they unfolded to fly about near the ground. I watched it move about the garden, which is still largely bare apart from the remnants of the crocuses and snowdrops, both of which have no flowers left to sample. Daffodils are still sparse, and the hyacinths are a week or two away.

April 15

I stand corrected. There is a grape hyacinth blooming in the sunny portion of the knot garden. Its purple clusters must have sprung up nearly overnight and now sit in rather lonely display, surrounded by the majority of those which don't look very far along yet. Who knows why this particular bulb decided to burst forth, while the others remain decidedly juvenile.

Also, within the front yard there are violets now in bloom as tiny splashes of purple hidden within the grass that has been slowly greening and growing for a couple of weeks. Soon, they will be everywhere and will combine with the arriving dandelions to make a patchwork of brilliant yellow and purple which will be resignedly pretty for a time. Admittedly, I both love and loath them, for they continue to invade the lawn, as do the cinquefoil and strawberry, creating color among the front. This comes at the expense of the grass, which seems to be fighting a losing battle of late, giving way to the transition our lawn has evolved toward more pasture than cultivate.

April 16

It was inevitable. The warmer days of spring we've enjoyed this past week have hastened the development of the mosquito. Yesterday, we saw our first one buzzing lazily in the evening around the screen that covers the front glass of the kitchen window. No doubt there will be more as things progress, which means too that the greater nemesis of the black gnat will make its appearance any day.

We have been spoiled by the calm of the past several days, being able to work outside tidying the yard or the garden space without being accosted by the pestilence of gnats. I truly hate to complain, and I am thankful for the arrival of spring, but of all the creatures that reemerge in this wondrous period of renewal, I am not thankful for the black gnats.

We can only hope for a steady breeze now, at least for a few weeks until their lifecycle runs its course. Sigh.

April 17

Our tomatoes needed transplanting today, as they had outgrown the 3 x 3 inch plastic pots I had used several weeks ago. They are now nearly eight inches tall and starting to get top heavy and in risk of falling over within the pots. This afternoon we walked across the street to ask Fred about borrowing some larger containers. Lord knows their back barn has a room filled with extras from the years of doing such work – seeding, transplanting, and etc. In short order we returned home with enough to do the job and set about putting soil in the bottom of each.

The seedlings were certainly root bound, and getting them transferred to the new pots was easy enough. As we sat there in the shaded area within the nook by the front door, two visitors made their first seasonal appearance. First came the bumblebee, buzzing lazily about near the holly bushes and likely in search of their tiny flowers that won't appear for another few weeks. This must be one of the recently emerged queens, awake from her winter hibernation and working in the spring warmth to gather what resources she can.

The second also came flying by – a cabbage white butterfly all flittering about, before lifting gently higher into the air in a haphazard flight, barely clearing the roof line and catching the slight breeze. Cabbage whites have three periods of emergence – one in the spring, one in the summer, and the final one in the fall. We'll see them soon in greater numbers about the garden, often as two lone individuals who meet from afar, closing the distance in their loopy flight then uniting nearly as one, flapping together for a time in some greeting.

April 18

These are the mornings we dream of in winter, when the building daylight chases out the grey veil of dawn, and there is a steady call of tree frogs and peepers from down in the lower woods. It is warm enough now to sit outside on the back porch, with a blanket to ward off the chill and a cup of coffee that shows tendrils of steam rising upward before dissipating. Every moment seems to bring something else awake – the call of a Canada goose high overhead, flying northeast across the fields and beyond, the red-bellied woodpecker squawking in greeting as he descends from the upper branches of the old pine that borders the berm, and the gregarious chickadees who come to call one by one.

There are almost too many awakenings now, in the birds and animals that come to visit and in the earth itself, which seems to be increasing its pace in an effort to put forth new growth. Even our own pulse quickens at the coming of spring, and it's impossible not to get swept up by the renewal that is all around us.

April 19

The first of our Towhees arrived today, seen first beneath the scrubby spruce that borders the access road near the berm. They hopped out furtively to the open space of yard where we keep the shepherd's poles that hang the feeders and proceeded to do their distinctive jitterbug step to dislodge the cast-off seed that littered the ground. They are amusing to watch, jumping backwards quickly twice and once forward then scanning the ground quickly to locate a possible prize. Jump, jump, look, repeat, and we like to imagine that the other birds who have alighted on the tube also look down in amusement.

April 20
In Tucson

The sun crested the eastern Rincon Mountains at 6:10 this morning. I was standing on a hill in just a position to see the Tucson Mountains far to the west, the Rincons to the east, and the Catalina Range dominating the north.

The sunrise first shown on the tips of the Tucson range and slowly descended down the slopes, giving the impression of the mountains rising slowly as one to meet the new day. Then, the halo of gold brightened enough on the eastern Rincon in anticipation of the sun's rays cresting the summit and striking where I stood in greeting.

The only sounds that accompanied were the periodic calls of mourning doves traveling among the saguaro forest and the occasional cardinal expressing itself from the top of a mesquite tree.

Quickly did the sun's warmth awaken the desert, and a gentle breeze stirred from the north as if the land were sighing awake.

April 21
In Tucson

Throughout the day a flicker comes to visit, seeking out the red candle blossoms of the ocotillo cactus. It perches near the top and inspects each tiny red flower, bell shaped and in clusters, placed just so that the flicker can put its beak in a dozen flowers within several seconds.

It has the same markings as those that frequent our lawns in Paxton, though its personality is decidedly less shy. Ours will fly low to the ground, stopping almost furtively to search for grubs and insects in the lawn, taking flight at the slightest disturbance. This desert relative pays no mind to my presence below it, seeking its fare and calling below in the way of flickers, a cross between the jay's squawk and the grackle's two-tone alarm.

April 22
In Tucson

The Jasmine is blooming on the vines that cover the adobe house where we are staying. When the sun's rays crest the mountains on the eastern horizon in the morning, they strike a wall resplendent with the vines, and the perfume that is released makes me think of the Egyptian scents that I've only read about.

Small breezes pick up the scent and combine with the smells of mesquite and blooming Palo Verde, and the smell of the desert in the morning is like no other.

April 23
In Tucson

The desert wildflowers are so beautiful, in part because of the harshness in which the flourish. This year I'm told is a good year on account of the rains that came in February and March, encouraging even the most reluctant foliage to display color.

Here are my favorites: The ocotillo are all in bloom and leaf, strange looking stalks with tiny leaves and small fiery red candle clusters on each long arm, looking similar to the flowers of our sumac trees, but more orange in flower than red. The prickly pear pads seem to be in competition among one another to produce the perfect shade of yellow and orange, with some as pink. The flowers on the tops of the pads open quickly at midmorning, when the sun's rays warm the plant. They remain displayed throughout the day, and close again at dusk. Pentsimon reminds me of the Catchfly coloring, striking pink and tiny petals on a light colored and corded stalk. It seems to favor dry washes and trail sides.

The Palo Verde trees are covered in tiny yellow flowers, thousands tucked within its branches, giving the tree a constellation of green and yellow, delicate looking as it moves about in the breeze.

April 24

Just before the big snows of last December, I took down the wren house and put it away on one of the upper shelves in the garden shed. It's been sitting there waiting for spring, counting on us to watch for the signs of our vernal transition, when the juncos begin to disperse and the male finches show increasing shades of yellow in their plumage.

At some point during the winter, the box must have become dislodged by one of the red squirrels who makes its home in the small rafters above, knocking it off the shelf and onto the dirt floor, where the impact popped open the trap door and spilled part of the old nesting material about. This is how I found things as I opened the shed door – a pile of twigs, pieces of moss, and small clumps of drier lint all mixed together so carefully that the nest still lay mostly intact upon the ground beside the box. What a wonder that so diminutive a bird creates something so substantial, through such careful engineering each spring.

I shook the old nest from the box and closed the trap door, securing it with the wooden dowel that had become loose from the fall. Then I took the box to the small oak tree that sits adjacent to the berm, placing it so that the hole in the rear fit securely over the rusty mason nail protruding from the bark.

Sarah said yesterday she thought she saw the return of the wren, and this should be just about on schedule, though it will be several weeks before we hear the trilling call of mating season.

April 25

The grey veil of building light comes now at 5:00 in the morning, and there is now a scattering of birdsong to accompany the din of calling frogs from the woods below. Why the birds have now decided to begin their nesting tunes is a mystery, when only a week ago they were silent until nearly the sun had crested the eastern horizon. Over the next month others will join, and the predawn period will be alive with the return of spring fever. It is such a departure from a month ago, when we were greeted only by the sounds of shifting winds through the pine boughs. Now it is as if all things are announcing their vernal celebration.

The small blades of the Canada Mayflower have returned to the front yard and across the road in the buffer between the asphalt and the spruce line. Each plant is merely a singular wide green leaf, resting upright from the ground and awaiting the small stalk that will soon lift the tiny white flowers overhead. There are hundreds of them now, giving the yard a green design of mayflower amid the building shades of the varied grasses that have come out of dormancy.

April 26

There are several Pussy Toe flowers showing themselves in the sparse grass of the fields that front the college. It's difficult not to smile at these diminutive looking things, strewn about amid the greening of the strawberry and dandelions that predominate the poor soils that each prefers. The scientific name is *Antennaria neglecta*, which seems particularly appropriate, as the flowers protrude upward as small white cat's paws on rising stalks, looking like clusters of fluffy antennae. I'm to understand that the genus name actually derives from the appearance of the seedpods, which resemble the antennae of butterflies. The species *neglecta* must come from the fact that they seem to prefer open areas, which lack richness of organic matter or nutrients, thriving in the harshness of the open sun as do many of the wildflowers that grow in such places.

The basal leaves of the wild strawberry are greening here, and within the month we should see their small flowers strewn about, visited by the cabbage whites and clouded sulphurs, which rely on the bounty of the early spring wildflowers to gather their nectar. On warm days, in the afternoon sunshine, the field expanse comes alive with the flitting of these butterflies as partners meet through some pheromone signal to dance briefly in courtship. They rise together above the field, until one or the other breaks away to flitter toward some destination beyond.

April 27

Two male Rose Breasted Grosbeaks have returned, seemingly content to resume foraging below the feeders in the side yard. This afternoon they were sharing time with three Eastern Towhees, five Yellow Finches, 2 Blue jays, 2 House Finches, 4 Chickadees, and one lone Flycatcher. The latter only congregates nearby, using the handrail post of the porch as a perching place to watch for any emergent insects. Not once today did a Junco make an appearance, and the Red-winged Blackbirds might be mating down in the wet areas near Asnebumskit Pond.

In the afternoon sunshine, a Chipmunk sat resting on a
small cairn of rocks we placed decoratively in the border
garden next to the porch. It seemed unconcerned of the
squirrels below, which chased one another about the yard
and up the tree trunks in spiraling patterns, before
returning to the ground beneath the tubes. The Chipmunk
stayed motionless for many minutes, until something set it
off to chirp loudly, staccato bursts that were shrill enough
to disrupt the relative peace of the windless day.

The nights have been warm enough these past few days to
hasten the germination of the grass seed I placed in the
thin spots of the yard a few weeks ago. Now, where
before there were patches of tilled soil and winnowed
seeds of fescue and perennial rye, small shoots of delicate
green seedlings have risen upward, giving the bare ground
just a hint of greenish tinge when it is viewed obliquely
from close to the earth. If this warmth holds, the grass will
fill nicely in no time, though it will look strangely out of
place with its uniform color and devoid of weeds among
the rest of the lawn that is decidedly neither.

April 28

Where the spillway descends from the Kettlebrook
Reservoirs on route 56, in the broadened plain just before
the water crosses underneath, there are Trout Lilies
blooming profusely off the roadside. The morning sunrise
backlights the speckled yellow of their leaves, and the
effect is somewhat dreamy against the muted green of the
grasses that are growing throughout. At the base of their
stalks, each has two large primary leaves, mottled with
spots, as are the flowers, rising upward from a small bulb
that is buried quite deeply underground. These are known
also as Spotted Adder's Tongue, because of the shape of
their stamens. The leaves do resemble the speckled sides of
a brook trout. Go look for yourself. These flowers last a
couple of weeks at most, so don't delay. They are worth
seeing.

In the afternoon sunshine, a young boy stood silently at
the edge of the Grove Street with his father, both looking
across the road and toward the field on the other side,
where Fred was pulling the large plow in preparation of
the ground. The boy's expression was endearing, standing
there holding hands and pointing excitedly at the "big"
tractor and the farmer working laboriously back and forth,
trailing clouds of dust behind that billowed upward and
away. How we all would benefit from watching the
rhythms of farm life more often. There are such pleasant
experiences to observe throughout the cycle of the seasons.

The turned fields look uniformly brown now, as the sere
stubble from last autumn's crop and the emergent early
weeds have been turned under, exposing the moist soil to
the surface. It is beautiful in its own way like this - acres of
rich soil that looks more like chocolate. This is how we like
to imagine it.

April 29

The circle around Highland has Bluets growing in the grassy margins. I simply love these spring flowers and look forward to their return. This means that soon the college field will start showing them, as they prefer the open spaces of nutrient-poor land, much as the wild Strawberry, Cinquefoil and Pussytoes. The Bluets range from nearly white to a tender pale blue, with a striking yellow center that defines the diminutive pistil. They grow in clusters close to the ground and are relatively easy to transplant, provided that they are done so with some of the accompanying soil.

I am reminded that our tomatoes will need transplanting soon. They're presently in the cold frame outside, and are nearing the limit of tolerance for the 3x3" pots. The weather was so warm last week that they became leggy, and I dare not put them in the ground just yet for fear of a spring frost. But, I simply can't leave them in the cold frame much longer, else they get too tall.

April 30

As April comes to an end, the acceleration of spring seems to be hastening into May. The pace of growth is almost intoxicating, and we are near the point where the muted browns from last autumn are being eclipsed by the verdant greens of this rebirth.

Where the land makes a parallel swale to South Road, roughly a hundred yards past the intersection of the Holden Road, there is a striking patch of Marsh Marigolds. They look almost synthetic nestled alone among the deadfall leaves from months ago. They are a strikingly deep green color, with brilliant yellow flowers sitting conspicuously atop the mass.

Further on, where the canopy thins slightly and the midday sunshine has greater purchase to the roadside below, the invasive Garlic Mustard weeds are now beginning to flower, displaying the first hints of their white flowers. Soon they will be everywhere. Nearby are the purple flowers of the season's first Henbit, growing closely to the ground. On the opposite side, where there is more shade in the lower land, the Fiddleheads of the emergent ferns reach upward almost 8 inches. They too will slowly overtake the darker domains of the lower woodlands, making a verdant expanse of green.

May

May 1

Who remembers when on this very day people used to
secretly deliver May Day baskets to neighbors? These were
meant as tokens of affection or measures of thanks, placed
on the doorstep of the intended as an unexpected
pleasantry to begin this month. Now, I suspect there are
very few who still recall this rather provincial tradition.

May has always been my favorite month, and even now I
smiled this morning on my walk up Grove Street in the
fine mist of what would develop later into a rather steady
rain. May saw the return of the warm weather to stay. No
ebb and flow from early spring. Even the rains were finally
warm, soaking into the grassy greens of fields and lawns
that simply called for us to explore. May meant that school
would soon let out, and in short order we'd be unfettered
as spoiled children to pursue our adventures outside.

I still feel this way when this month begins. The pulse of
renewal has been quickening for several weeks, ready to
explode in life around us. It's impossible not to get caught
up in the sights and sounds that have returned, where
each day brings something new to experience. There is
such energy about us now. Where summer brings the
lassitude of maturity, and autumn reveals itself in
satisfaction of a season that has begun to wind down,
spring awakens us with youthful vigor from the restful
winter. Everything is alive, unblemished and new.

A week ago, Sarah cut several oranges in half and placed
them on large nails that protruded from the big maple in
the side yard. Sure enough, this morning we heard the
insistent chirp from high up in the canopy of the lower
woods, moving closer to the maple over the course of
several minutes. We watched silently from within the
sunroom, waiting for him to feel confortable enough to

43

return. Then, a flash of brilliant orange! Our oriole alighted gently to the tree and begun poking at the fruit.

May 2

It's been cool and rainy for the past two days, and the forecast is for several more of the same, according to the weatherman. The term he used is a stalled low, and evidently there isn't much to push away the unsettled air mass that presently sits southeast of the coast of Nantucket. There's no denying that it has been a little dismal. We already miss the spring sunshine.

The upshot is that the yard has exploded in emerald green with the cool, damp weather. Even the bare patches where I seeded a few weeks ago have started to germinate, pushing forth delicate new blades that easily gather the dewy rain, making them seem fuzzy among the surrounding mature grasses.

In the berm, the blades of the Irises rise upward like long knives, perhaps eight inches high and yet to separate. It will be nearly a month before the flower buds make an appearance. So too have the Lilly of the Valley shoots grown by the side of the house. Only yesterday they lifted upward like little green straws. Now I see that they've begun to unfurl slightly, still narrow at the base but spreading into a broader leaf near the top where the small bells of the white flowers will soon arrive.

May 3

This morning I heard the unmistakable mewing of the Catbird out front near the barn. All day it called from within the woods, waiting to make an appearance until later in the afternoon when it tentatively flew in to inspect the cake of suet that hangs in the cage by the big maple. It is presently sitting on the edge of the cement birdbath by the berm, watching intently the activity of the big Red-bellied Woodpecker as he forcefully pecks the cake.

The Catbird's tail is as expressive as its voice, as he fans it upward in display then closes it abruptly before flicking it downward in some show. He hops gingerly around the circumference of the bath, cocking his head upward and regarding the now vacant suet cage with his dark eye.

Below, two Red-winged Blackbirds share space on the ground beneath the feeder with two Towhees and one Mourning Dove. All seem content to scour intently through the wet cast offs, while one rather large and likely pregnant Grey Squirrel does the same. Her tail flicks restlessly as she moves purposefully through the emerald grass.

May 4

Small puddles have formed in the cupped depressions along the cedar boards of the back deck. Several weeks ago, such water would slowly soak into the wood and eventually drip to the ground beneath, but I applied a topcoat of stain during a dry period in April. Now the water beads up when it begins to rain until enough collects and coheres to create the puddles. The boards must be scalloped badly, for nearly all have enough water on top of the dark surface that it looks like a curious pond has formed just outside the door.

There on the deck I see reflections of the trees above. Some, like the small ash that sits on the edge of the berm and sheltered by the large windward spruce, show their newly emerged leaves in the image on the water. A gentle sprinkle overhead creates drops, making the reflection of the trees shimmer as if a small breeze pushes through the leaves, casting them about here and there.

Our pale Red Squirrel pauses beneath the tubes and walks to the edge of the porch, hops up, and flicks its tail in its skittish way, then dips its head briefly to the boards to gather a drink.

May 5

The rains set free the catkins from the birch, and now they lay beneath like confetti on the lengthening grass. In their place, the new leaves are emerging, still small and lime green, waiting for the return of sunshine to stimulate the production of chlorophyll and growth. Everything now shows the promise of what spring will bring.

All about, the woods are beginning to soften as the elms, birch and maples start to put forth the hint of spring foliage. Where before the horizon was punctuated with the distinct lines of crisscrossing bare branches in patterns of greys and browns, the woods have taken on a slight haze, almost dreamy. Soon, our vistas to the hillsides we see through the forest will be gone, as the comfort of the verdant woods returns again.

May 6

Good heavens to be a Robin right now, after nearly six days of drizzle. There are two rather fat ones in the front yard, who need nothing more than a square foot apiece in which to turn, cock their head, and pierce downward to gather yet another meal. Typically we see them running in short bursts to locate food, but these rains have brought enough to the surface that there is obviously no sense in having to work too hard for the worm.

The tomatoes I transplanted outside five days ago are bent over touching the earth. Though we've dodged the fear of nightly frost, the gloomy stretch hasn't helped them adjust to their new surroundings. Without the sun, they continue to get leggy, which will require something drastic soon, if the warmth doesn't make a hasty return.

May 7

The *Lunaria* has begun to bloom, showing its deep purple flowers atop a tall spike of richly green. There are two areas in town that seem to have them year after year. First is on South Road, at the bend in street before it begins the descent downward toward the reservoirs below. Look to the border of the rock wall that juts off into the woods beyond. There at the base is typically a grouping of the purple blossoms. Second is in the vicinity of the red barn that houses the antique store out on Route 31, a mile or so past Moore State Park on the way to Spencer. There, tucked behind the barn on the side road that descends to the mill falls, are usually several groupings of Lunaria.

Lunaria annua, or "Annual Moon," refers to the seedpod that develops in late June, beginning first as a small flat disk, then growing through July into one that is deeply green, thin and the size of a half dollar. Each disk contains either two or sometimes three seeds, seen through the membrane of the disk when backlit by the sunshine. As July gives way to August, the disks dry and turn light tan, and with the onset of autumn they almost glow in the light, like silvery moons hanging from the sere pendant of the fading plant.

May 8

The sun returned this morning, after what has been nearly a week of cold, dreary weather. We normally know May as the month of our relaxation; a celebration of the ending of what has been the ebb and flow of spring's arrival. Rather, this year has been the fourth coldest beginning of May on record, nearly seven degrees below average. This is enough to warrant our complaints; even silent ones where we grumble to ourselves how cold the daytime highs feel in the upper forties and low fifties.

This is all behind us now, we hope. The sun has climbed high enough this morning to warm the moisture on the roof, making it steam as tendrils of vapor, which lift skyward and away. So too go the puddles on the porch, vanishing slowly in the building heat. It is a morning that reminds us how May should begin.

May 9

A large flatbed truck arrived across the road this afternoon, carrying the defining green of a new John Deere tractor. We caught a glimpse of its coming through the spruce line, seeing the flash of color move slowly up the farm driveway. This warranted an excuse to go and be nosy, so we took a stroll up the road to investigate.

Fred waited eagerly near the store front, watching in anticipation as both tractor and another large machine were slowly pushed backward onto the skids and then the driveway. We came as the flatbed was pulling away, leaving the three of us to admire the new toys, which looked ironically pristine for where they were destined to serve.

The tractor was self explanatory, but Fred needed to educate us on the other new machine. It was, we were told, a "no till" planter for cover crops, something he had wanted to integrate into the farm operations for several years. Apparently this planter would gently harrow and prepare only a few inches of the upper soil, before inserting any desired seed into newly furrowed ground just beneath. The idea is to avoid the traditional deep plowing of the land, so as to spare the soil pan from breakup, thus sparing the diverse ecosystem of existing bacteria, fungi and organic matter from potentially destructive activity. All this to maintain healthier soil, necessitating potentially less synthetic fertilizer and such as the microorganisms augment what is in the soil.

May 10

The blossoms of our viburnum opened overnight, giving it the appearance of a collection of white poms when seen from a distance. The warming sunshine must have activated the nectaries within somehow, for in the gentle breeze of the afternoon the air was scented beautifully with its sweet smell. This is the first real perfume of spring for me, joined soon by the lilacs, which should open within a day or so. The viburnum reminds me of something from my youth that I can't exactly place, perhaps some memory of our home in the Midwest from which there is nothing precise apart from this sweet smelling recollection. I have the same feeling about the honeysuckle, which will blossom at the beginning of next month and gently waft its powerful scent throughout the day.

There are starflowers blooming now, particularly in the shaded roadsides where they frequent. There are also Trillium in bloom along Marshall Road, as it ascends from Route 56 and on the right side within the border forest. So too are the garlic mustards in flower; these invasive plants show their fecundity all along the roadsides.

May 11

The musical trilling of the female Wren came insistently this afternoon from somewhere within the older forest on the north side of the house. Over the course of fifteen minutes, she moved slowly closer to the edge, finally landing in the upper boughs of a small ash that sits on the border of the lawn. From here, I suspect she was surveying the location and in particular the Wren box I built several years ago and recently cleaned in anticipation of her arrival.

Soon enough, she descended to the box, resting for a moment on the small perch outside the entry hole, her head bobbing in out of the opening to inspect the home within. Though she flew away in what seemed resignation, she returned an hour later with a stick held crosswise in her beak, landed precariously on the perch, and tilted her head in such a way that she was able to insert one end of the stick through the opening and into the interior.

For several hours we watched her come and go to the woods, each return carrying some small stick or piece of moss with which she would engineer her nest within the box. And at the end of the day, she was evidently settled.

Note: Ruby-throated Hummingbird returned today

May 12

Look closely at the branch ends of the spruce trees, where yesterday the brown casing of the buds held tightly to the dormant growth within. They survived the cold stretch of winter, against the assault of the bitter chill that came with the Alberta Clippers and Nor'easters of December and remained protective until only several weeks ago.

The buds have swollen with the coming of spring, pushing against the casing and working them outward, splitting them loose so that they tumble to the ground. Now revealed are the emergent soft needles of new growth, small and lime green, slowly moving outward as this year's branch takes form. For several weeks they will be delicate and strangely soft, waiting as the continued progress of spring produces the protective wax on each of the needles, and chlorophyll condenses within, making each darker green and stiff, adapted to the conditions of the summer that will be.

There are candles on the white pines, sitting upward a half an inch and lifting a few millimeters each day. In another week they will rise up and begin to slowly spread.

May 13

The front lawn needs its first mowing, as there are patches of uneven grasses that rise upward, nearly at seed head, while the younger shoots still linger behind. Spread throughout are the flower heads of hundreds of purple violets and yellow cinquefoil.

Kipper lay on his side in the afternoon sunshine, his tongue lolling out and white belly rising and falling quickly as he rested blissfully in the lawn. These are days we dream about in the deficit of midwinter, and I took the liberty of joining him silently in the grass, resting my head among the blades and looking with unfocused vision across the expanse of new growth.

How intoxicating are the sights and smells of early spring, seen here from this vantage point where the lawn resembles some impressionist expression of green with indistinct splotches of yellow and purple mixed within. There are not yet the pests of late spring and summer to bother this reverie, and I lay contentedly alongside him, two of us older dogs simply happy to rest peacefully in the sunshine.

May 14

The Starflower leaves have been dotting the shaded roadside for the past two weeks. I know of a spot not fifty feet up from our driveway, near the Cournoyer's entrance, among the growing weeds and leafing poison ivy, where the white petals seem to show themselves before most others. It's been this way each year that we've lived here, fourteen of them now, and I suspect that it will continue once we're gone. I hope it will continue this way. There is something comforting about the successional regularity of even the most insignificant things. That this small patch of shaded roadside encourages the flower to blossom, often days before the others that are only yards away, is an affirmation that the seasons continue one after another with an orderly pattern. Right here, there is just the proper light and warmth and nutrients that each spring it returns on schedule, this diminutive plant with the delicate blossoms of spring.

I desperately want to believe it will continue like this.

In the afternoon, a squall blew in from the west, rapidly changing the sky from what had been a cerulean blue to an ominous grey of a building storm. The wind picked up rather quickly, coming across the field and assaulting the tall spruce line next to the road, sending tired needles raining down onto the pavement below, before moving in an instant toward the house. As it crossed the yard, the wind tousled the large apple tree near the roadside, shaking it so that the white blossoms caught hold, releasing themselves into the tempest and cascading like falling snow spread out on the green grass below.

May 15

The Lilacs by the front corner of the house are now in bloom; the sweet perfume mixes with that of the nearby Viburnum, making the air about us delightful and intoxicating. How quickly we are able to cast off the odorless and seemingly colorless coat of winter in exchange for the vernal assault on our sensations. There are too many changes taking place now to keep track, and we must simply content ourselves in being caught up in the rush of new growth.

Across the road this morning they put down thirty rows of clear plastic, and then in the afternoon the tractor slowly retraced the paths to plant early corn into the soil underneath. This means for us the summer clock has been wound, as seed will give way to germination and then to small blade, pushing upward over the course of the next two months as mature stalks begin to take shape. With luck, there will be early ears ready by the end of July, and this is something wonderful indeed.

May 16

This evening marks the first time this year that the sun will set after 8:00 pm. April saw the greatest rate of gain for total daylight since the beginning of January, and the pace has been slackening since, though we will gather more light until the summer solstice arrives in a month hence. The days feel decadently long now, starting with the veil of predawn at 4:50 and continuing throughout till late evening, when the gloaming of twilight seems to linger longer than it did only a few weeks ago.

Thought we stand firmly within the bounds of spring, the slowing of the daylight gain reflects a larger change that is soon to come. The pace of new life and growth will too diminish, to be replaced by the more stately maturity of summer. The leaves will be in full splendor, in varied shades of deeper greens, free yet from blight or blemish that will come soon enough as June gives way to July.

May 17

One of the male Ruby-throated Hummingbirds is perched on guard within the still leafless interior of the Rose of Sharon at the corner of the house. Nearby, perhaps three feet away, hangs the glass feeder, half filled with the diluted nectar these tiny birds so enjoy. He watches for a rival, who has been buzzing in repeatedly for the past half hour, rounding the other corner of the house and descending quickly to the feeder, only to be chased off by the sentinel male.

Then the newcomer returns, flying quickly by and landing on the other Rose of Sharon, and fixing his gaze upon his rival who guards the prize with honor. They chatter at one another in their high-pitched manner, and the hopeful male lifts gently into the air and hovers strangely, quickly back and forth like a rapidly ticking pendulum. He makes more threatening noises, carrying on in this oscillating manner until the aggressor decides he has had enough.

Both lift quickly into the air, one chasing the other out of sight and into the woods beyond, gone in the blink of an eye. Seconds later, the aggressor returns, buzzing once around the feeder before returning to his post, his

54

diminutive head set back and beak raised upward, moving quickly to and fro like a conductor's baton in staccato.

The newcomer returns, and the process begins anew. For fifteen minutes this continues, until both fly away to the forest.

Notes: Robin's Plantain in fields as are the first Buttercups

March 18

A tenth of a mile east, into the thick of the woods that encompasses the low land where the creek from Asnebumskit meanders downhill toward Streeter Pond, there is a small clearing. I came upon it this afternoon while out hiking to see the stream. The space is only twenty feet or so across, and is really more an opening in the canopy above from the demise and fall of a deadfall oak than it is an opening in the sense of cleared land. The tree lay nearby and looked to be only a few years gone, which aligns with the absence of any new undergrowth shrubbery having yet become established in the space.

I saw it from a distance, the place where the light from above penetrated through the opening and down nearly unobstructed to the floor below. What caught my eye was the splash of brilliant red near the middle, and it wasn't until I was close enough to recognize it as a flowering Bleeding Heart, somehow having taken hold in this small space and evidently flourishing. So there it rested, arching gracefully over in the manner of these plants, bright pendants of red flowers dangling beneath, on display for no one in particular.

How it got here is a mystery. Surely a bird must have unwittingly deposited a seed last year, or perhaps the prior. The conditions must have been just right, for there it was in full bloom, lit from above as if on stage, with the dark contrasting forest just beyond.

May 19

A Great Blue Heron flew high overhead from the west, likely heading toward the waters of Asnebumskit or perhaps further to Kettlebrook. As it descended across Grove, it gave a single guttural squawk and flapped its wings gracefully, then changed direction slightly to the south before vanishing over the trees.

In the stillness of the afternoon, a male Towhee perched in the lower branches of a sapling red maple by the berm. For five minutes the little bird joyously trilled in a musical call, tilting his head backward at the point in the song when the notes became tremulous. The sunshine from above filtered through the translucent greens of the new growth, softening the light in the understory where he sat, casting him in earthy shades that highlighted the dewy humidity of the spring afternoon.

May 20

Kipper, Tag and I went to the fields of Anna Maria this afternoon, stopping on the knoll where the cross sits overlooking the entrance at the bottom of the gentle slope. We three sat in the silently in the grass, content to enjoy the warm sunshine.

Seen from ground level, the fields are a patchwork of grasses and wildflowers; a mosaic of Robin's Plantain, Wood Sorrel, Strawberry, Pussytoes and Buttercups, amid the green grasses of varied types. Cabbage whites dot the land, flitting from place to place as they traverse the field.

It is beautiful here now, so distinct from the harsh lines of winter's snowdrifts which existed not so long ago. In the pleasant reverie of our short stay, winter's austerity seemed distant, and we look ahead to the months of growth and life.

May 21

At 5:30 the throaty chugging of the old International Harvester mixed with the building calls of the birdsong. Across the road the peas are roughly three inches high, and between the rows are the first signs of the annual weeds, which if left unchecked would overrun everything. Hence the tractor making passes up and down, pulling an antique cultivator with arched tines spaced so that they turn the soil in the troughs between the rows of peas. The forecast is for warm and dry conditions today, ideal for this job where the goal is to dislodge the root structure of the weeds enough so that the plants die from dehydration.

I stood silently in the driveway watching Fred drive the rows, and with each pass as the tractor receded toward the distant field in the west, there was a point not too far past the tree line of Grove where the rising sunshine caught the antique red in full view, highlighting both driver and machine in the warm tones of another morning.

May 22

The Honeysuckle is starting to bloom, showing its early white flowers where soon the entire shrub will be covered. The nectaries within have yet to put forth their distinctive perfume, though I suspect in the warming week there will be the sweet smell of early summer as the afternoon sunshine heats the landscape.

Up on Nanigian Road there are also early Wild Geraniums or Cranesbill. Look to the roadside before the intersection with Rockland Street, there on the right where the wild grasses mix with emerged ferns. Things warm nicely here in the afternoon light, enough so that the Geraniums are among the first to arrive in town.

A few years ago we put a small section of log upright in the knot garden to serve as a stand for a decorative armillary. This spring we noticed the Chickadees were using a small hole in the side as an entry for something. Likely the log had begun to decompose, perhaps by the action of ants within, and the Chickadees were going after something for food. Concerned that the armillary would topple, we moved it to another location and replaced it with an old birdhouse.

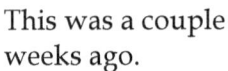

This was a couple weeks ago.

Since, we've seen the Wrens using the box, bringing small sticks from the woods and putting them carefully into the hole. This is surprising for two reasons. First, the box is as dilapidated as can be – a shanty of rotted wood and drafty interior, where the roof is nothing more than a worn shingle of cedar that is split so that it is a wonder it stays on in a breeze. Second, this same pair of Wrens also use another box not a hundred feet away near the berm. This box I built a few years ago specifically for Wrens, with careful attention to design. By comparison, this box is upscale.

We can't explain why the birds seem content on two homes, but indeed they bide their time during the day between them.

May 23

We hadn't seen our wild rabbit Porch for several weeks, and fearing that some predator had sadly taken it, we stopped looking for its visits to the dooryard.

This afternoon, in the enclosed space before the front entry to the houses, where the Vinca grows thickly near the foundation, we discovered a nest of young rabbits. There were five little ones, each roughly the size of a large potato, sitting haphazardly within the cool shade offered by the ivy and the bordering Coreopsis. They must have been several weeks old at this point, for their eyes were open wide, and they seemed quite aware of our presence. Mother was nowhere to be found, though we took comfort that each baby bore a distinctive white spot on its forehead – a spot nearly identical to the one Porch displayed. Perhaps, just maybe, mother and Porch are one and the same.

It was this time last year when we discovered Porch and four siblings in the base of the Coreopsis of the knot garden. The siblings vanished one by one as spring gave way to summer. Come fall, only Porch remained, having grown large and wary enough to fend for itself, taking residence under the back porch, and taking its namesake from that place.

May 24

It remained warm overnight, causing a heavy dew to form by morning on the new leaves and green grass, all glistening as the sunrise topped the trees of the lower woods. I sat quietly on the back porch and simply listened to the calls of the spring birds, most of who cared nothing for my presence so close to the feeders by the side yard.

My cup of coffee rested on the arm of the Adirondack chair, wisps of steam rising several inches before dissipating in the gentle breeze which carried the warming perfume of Lilac mixed with the earthy smell of turned loam from across the road.

The only thing that seemed to mind was the chipmunk that lives in the stone wall. It sat upright on one of the lichen-covered rocks, chirping incessantly in alarm at my intrusion into its domain.

May 25

A few years ago, Sarah planted thyme in a small section of one of the raised beds near the back of the house. It seemed to thrive, and as memory recalls we enjoyed it well enough, along with the other herbs that she planted here and there for our kitchen use.

Since, we've discovered that thyme is quite prolific, through extensive runners and seed it has escaped well beyond the raised bed and has now encompassed a notable portion of the back yard. It has formed small islands of deep green among the cut field grasses, and when it takes a new spot by spreading, its extensive roots quickly crowd out anything that was growing there before.

At first I tried to pull out the escapees, hoping to contain the herb to the intended bed. This quickly proved to be hopeless, as small root sections remained in the soil and quickly reestablished themselves. At its present rate, the yard will be overrun within a few more years.

I read somewhere that the British consider a Thyme expanse to be a luxury, and they even take great care to establish a yard of their own fashioned as such. I can only chuckle. Our yard, through neglect and disdain, has achieved something evidently enviable.

It could be worse.

May 26

The roadside grasses have now gone to seed, and they bend over in the night as the dew collects, weighing them down so they arch toward the ground. As the morning sun hastens evaporation, they rise slowly upward toward the sky, moving gently in the breezes that develop with the warming earth.

Up the road there are several stalks still bent as morning wanes. They are held fast by the anchors of a web spider, who must have worked through the night to construct this intricate design. Its beautiful web is covered in the glistening dew, backlit from the road and making tiny rainbows of refracted light in each little drop.

These seed heads remind me that transitions are around the corner. No spring lasts forever, and we feel the change even now as the explosive growth of May tempers to a more sedate pace, where the early flowers have started producing seed. There is no need to mourn this transition or prolong the coming of maturity. One day simply leads into the next, as does the season that begins to wane give way to the coming of something new. It goes on like this, month after month and then year after year. We so enjoy these cycles of the seasons.

May 27

This afternoon on the old railroad bed that runs from Barre to Rutland, we saw three notable red things among the green background that is everywhere. First came a Scarlet Tanager flying across the path and into the bordering woods, stopping to rest on an outstretched branch of a sugar maple and showing itself brilliantly against the backdrop. We too stopped in wonder, watching this bird with near disbelief that something could be so decidedly crimson and black, so much so that it seemed artificial in comparison to the surrounding woods.

The second came as we ascended the trail after it crosses Whitehall Road. On the left side at the point when the trail began to level and not five feet within the woods hung perfectly a group of Lady slipper pendants in the diffuse light that spilled from above to the forest floor. There was a similar bunch at this very spot last year, and it is comforting to see them again. Left unmolested, they should return.

A little further and there was a small bunch of brilliant Wild Columbines on display in a sunny patch where the canopy had thinned from some disturbance. On the ground about them were yellow splashes of Buttercups and the white stars of field Strawberries.

In the building heat of the afternoon, the wind blew across the water of the pond that skirts along the path, making the air fragrant not with the perfumes of spring but with the promise of summer's languid pace. June will be here soon enough, and there were signs that May is losing its grip on the season. The air smelled of Lilly Pads, nearly flowering with yellow blossoms, and of Cat Tails and the carried scent of freshwater, which only a large lake in summer can produce. There were the first dragonflies near the shore, where the puffy white Dandelions of last week have taken flight, leaving the bare stalk standing resolute in the breezes that come swiftly across the expanse of water. Some still hold their seeds, those tiny parachutes that release into the air toward distant places. It is only a matter of time before they too let go.

May 28

I took a walk down the access road this afternoon for no particular reason. It didn't last too long, for the mosquitoes were unbearable. I'm sure I must have looked like a man possessed, waving my hands in the air and slapping my head and neck repeatedly.

As the road turns toward Asnebumskit Pond, there in a sunny patch between the two track, was a small patch of Blue-eyed Grass, each tall teal blade having a single periwinkle flower atop. Admittedly, this is one of my favorites, and it was a treat to come upon it serendipitously, despite the surrounding frenzy of buzzing marauders.

May 29

Over the past two days the oaks have released their sere catkins, and they now lay evenly strewn about the yard, transforming it from a spring green to what from a distance looks like a late summer lawn that has seen drought. Those that gather in the driveway somehow cluster together in the breeze, forming clumps like balls of dust in the corners of the house. It is easy enough to broom them together as one large pile, and then put them across the road where they will soon erode and decompose as the season continues.

So many may mean something, and it is tempting to forecast that the trees know about the winter that will be. If the yard is any indication, there will be acorns in plenty come September.

The fields have King Devils nearly ready to open. Their stalks stand high above the surrounding grass, with calyx holding loosely to the yellow petals that will likely burst open today or tomorrow. King Devils in bloom mean that their cousins the Orange Hawkweed can't be too far behind. They tend to lag by a week or more, before showing their flowers. Theirs is one of the few truly orange blossoms, apart from the Day Lilies that will arrive near the end of June.

May 30

In the still air, the Chokecherry trees released their tiny blossoms, falling gently like small bits of ash from some far away eruption and landing delicately on the ground below. They mixed with the yellow tinge of pollen from the pines, which decided a week ago to cloud the air with their potential, coating everything in their wake and collecting in the low spots of the driveway after the puddle from a small shower has evaporated.

The tall grasses on the periphery of the mowed fields have a few early Yarrows in bloom, and the green shoots of

Goldenrod are everywhere, silently marking time toward later summer when they will explode in profuse yellow.

On the window screen a Crane Fly beats insistently to enter the house, and out front in the knot garden a large toad rests stoically underneath the shade of the Coreopsis.

These things whisper the June is close at hand, when the heat of the day extends well into the twilight, which lingers late enough now so that we must steal from our sleep to sit on the driveway to watch the brown bats emerge from the attic.

May 31

As May comes to a close, we see all around us the transition to summer. It has been happening slowly for several weeks but is now moving in earnest as life seems content to settle in toward the maturity that will come next month. We have also heard changes in the air. The songbirds are less frenetic in the morning, as some have surely gone to nest. The trilling call of the wren all day has lessened to sporadic notes from the woods. A few crickets now chirp in the evening and through the night, going silent only when the first bird of the morning makes a note at 4:15 am.

Across the road, the noise of plowing, harrowing and bed preparation have given way to the more leisurely pace of the tractor as they move up the rows transplanting vegetables. Yesterday, there was the slow chugging sound of the old International, making its way through the peas to cultivate the emerged weeds before they get too deep a foothold.

I celebrate May's arrival each year – the explosive growth of new life and sights and sounds that simply fills my spirit with the promise of beginnings. It is easy to feel awakened this month, as we so desperately want to be outside, emerged in the world that is full of rejuvenation.

May's ending is the passing of youth, and though the changes will bring maturity and richness of their own, there is something innocent that is left behind.

June

June 1

The tomatoes have their first yellow flowers, and I am
frankly relieved. There was a stretch last month when we
had such cold that I feared they wouldn't survive. Now,
they've grown so in the heat of the past two weeks that
they are in need of staking.

Several years ago, a friend gave us seeds from an heirloom
variety of cherry tomatillos called Galapagos. We planted
them in the lower garden and watched them grow well
enough, finally resulting in dozens of small, lantern-
covered tomatoes that were pale yellow and tasted
remarkably like pineapples. After collecting and giving
away over a hundred of them, we saved a few to ferment
the tiny seeds for the following year.

We are on the fourth generation of these unusual
tomatillos, though their survival looked doubtful at the
beginning of May. Now there are three richly green plants
spaced near enough to one another, in the raised beds near
the house and growing healthily in the full sunshine.

If luck holds, we should begin to see the paper lanterns by
the end of July.

June 2

There is a seldom-traveled road that connects from the old
Nazarus School on Mulberry Street in Leicester northeast
toward Marshall. Where it notably ascends and then
emerges into an arching stretch then passes by the airport
end, the view north takes in a hidden valley now deep in
green shades that are cast in sharp relief against the deep
blue of this clear day.

Here, the roadside grasses are tall, and there are many groupings of yellow Birdsfoot Tresfoil and clumps of white Daisies. There too must be water nearby, for a painted turtle walked leisurely across toward the south side.

The road pitches slightly further on, entering at once into the thick woods, and it is disorienting to adjust to the filtered light through the canopy above. There must be many pines nearby, for the air is scented with the earthy smell of fallen needles that have been warmed by the day's heat.

This is a beautiful stretch to see now, without the sultry humidity that will come soon. No. Today is clear and vibrant as only early June can be.

Note: There are false Solomon Seal flowers nearly everywhere in the roadsides.

June 3

Ecologists speak of carrying capacity when referring to the maximum number of a living organism that is sustainable in a particular habitat. This could be a plant or a worm, bird or butterfly, coyote or frog. In short, anything that lives and reproduces, gathers resources and establishes itself is restricted in numbers by various forces. These might be things like competition with members of the same species for food or space or mates. Or, there could be competition with other species for certain resources. And, other forces like predation or herbivory exert culling pressure on population numbers.

Our side yard may be one location to which the models of carrying capacity do not evidently apply.

We are presently overrun with Eastern Grey Squirrels. There are eight individuals carrying on near the bird feeders as I write this. They do not appear overly disturbed by each other's presence, though it is likely that this dray (or scurry, if you prefer) share familiar relations and are more tolerant of one another. This latter point seems reasonable, as several are smaller than the others, though they bear similar coat colors and markings – my guess is that they come from a recent litter of the remaining adults.

Regardless, eight squirrels must surely violate some universal law in ecology? The dogs are beside themselves watching the dray from the sunroom window. They groan and whine in protest that so many vermin have invaded their domain. It is unnatural to a terrier to have even one squirrel or chipmunk survive, let alone a peck (sorry, a dray or scurry).

June 4

Last fall, we used some leftover cement to make a rudimentary birdbath by pouring it over a small mound of packed soil. We put it in the barn and forgot about it until yesterday, when Sarah went looking for a small garden fork and discovered it sitting near the back.

We put it on an old section of cut log in the front, near the viburnum and among the Phlox, which are tall enough now to reach the edge of the cement and almost hide it within the garden.

By the afternoon there was a queue of birds waiting to take a bath. We sat silently nearby on the brick walkway, tucked within the horseshoe enclosure of the house. In the span of twenty minutes, a dozen different birds alighted on the edge of the basin and made use of the water; some like the Chickadee seemed to rejoice in splashing about, tucking their head quickly below then bobbing up to shake the water on its back and away. They'd flit quickly to the shelter of the viburnum nearby, preen for a minute, and then return to the basin to repeat, all the while chattering away in what seemed like bliss.

Others, like the robins, were more secretive. They would land shyly on the edge and chirp softly, regarding us carefully with their white-ringed eyes, cocking their head just so as they would dip slowly to the surface to take a quick drink.

June 5

The early season crickets are becoming more strident, especially in the mornings like today when the temperature is above sixty degrees. These aren't the masses that we will hear in a couple of months, when the noise is a near constant din of hundreds of grasshoppers and field crickets mixed with the fading sounds of the emerged cicada. What we hear now are the early arrivals, and their calls are more notable because they break the relative silence of the morning, as they chirp just before the songbirds begin to usher in the daybreak.

June 6

Note: Mountain Laurel is starting to bloom.

The morning warmth strengthens the already humid air, and small breezes begin early in the day. They are seen in the tops of the boughs of trees that surround the house; the large oak that overhangs the barn in back is fully in leaf and moves gracefully as the wind pushes through its branches. Moments later the cherry and maple in the lower woods bend in the following wind, and their leaves are caught in the backlit glow of the morning light so that they appear to shimmer as flashes of light and dark green as they move.

The breeze is softened through the hundreds of leaves, sounding like a wave on the shore as it recedes across the pebbled beach. How different from only a couple months ago, when the spring winds called stridently unseen through the bare branches, where now even the most gentle drift makes patterns of softly calling green above.

The color has deepened since early May; the chlorophyll has gathered strength, and the leaves are in full measure. Even the Arbor Vitae has rebounded, when only last week they looked blighted as they shed their spring needles.

Everything about speaks of maturity now. There is a slackening of the pace as life seems content to settle into a rhythm of comfort and production.

June 7

The Orange Hawkweed is beginning to flower in the open fields of Anna Maria, and there should be blossoms along the roadside in the next day or so. I've been looking for them for the past several days, as they tend to follow their sibling King Devils by a week or so. Soon, both will be in display, dotting the meadows with patches of yellow and orange.

The Hawkweed seems to advertise the coming of summer; its face displays a composite of petals with those in the middle having a more yellow color then fading to the deeper orange toward the periphery of the flower. Like the King Devils, the blossoms cluster near the end of a hairy stem, which rises nearly six inches above the basal leaves. Hawkweed is one of the few truly orange wildflowers around New England, save for the Jewel Weed that will arrive early in August.

Our knot garden is in transition now. The pinks and whites of last month have given way to shades of purple, with the blooming of the Mints, Lavender, Irises, Johnny Jump-ups, and the Wild Geranium. Somehow a migrant Bladder Campion became established, and it provides the sole white flower until the Daisies come to bloom. They are late in opening this year.

Across the driveway near the fence, the Beach Rose has begun to open, and the air is perfumed sweetly with its scent. Presently the Honeybees are enjoying a bounty they could only wish for three weeks ago, though I fear the Japanese Beetles will soon discover the Rose when they make their first appearance.

June 8

Notes: Tall Meadow Rue now blooming along Route 56
near the reservoir.

Clouds developed in the afternoon heat as large
thunderheads, rising upward high overhead, becoming
flat on top as they reached the limits of the troposphere.
These collected, turning dense and grey and making the
sky dark by early evening. Somewhere south the lightning
flashed indistinct, and the wind picked up quickly in the
trees overhead, turning the leaves over so that their lighter
undersides were exposed.

The air smelled of something electric as only a summer
storm can do.

Across the road, we watched a sheet of rain approach from
the far side of the planted fields. It moved as a curtain,
hiding everything behind it in the veil of falling water. It
reached the spruce line and swallowed them quickly; the
last of the blowing branches dissolved into the wall of
water and wind that came up the driveway and reached
the house.

In an instant the rain deluged, striking with such force that
we could just see the barn shingles bouncing water
upward in a spray; the rebounding rain made a mist three
feet above the roofline like the plume below a waterfall.
Rain streamed off the shingles, hitting the porch below and
draining into the small garden near the back. In thirty
seconds it was flooded three inches deep.

The noise then changed, becoming strident in its rapport.
Sharp, staccato pings came too rapid to distinguish, as the
rain changed to pea-sized hail, falling forcefully to the
earth as a layer of icy white. It was over in a minute; the
ground left covered in a skin of white that melted quickly

in the sunshine that reemerged as if nothing had happened.

June 9

Yesterday's tempest blew in a change of air, leaving today windy and cool and feeling more like mid September than early June. Come late July, a day such as this will be a welcome change from the summer heat. Now it is simply premature – too much a reminder of the chilly spring that was rather than the relief of autumn's reprieve.

Only the dogs seem content, as the driveway heats nicely in the sunshine, and they are perfectly happy to lie idly on their sides to soak up the warmth.

The yard is full of tiny strawberries now, where only a short time ago it was replete with the small white flowers amid the lengthening grass. Strange that nothing seems to come sample them. Perhaps there is food enough for the browsers in the woods and surrounding fields that our yard need not be visited. Regardless I filled a small glass with several dozen and washed them thoroughly. They were sweet enough, these miniature versions of our store bought varieties, and they are free to boot.

They mowed the fields of Anna Maria sometime this morning, transforming what had been the promise of a beautiful meadow into nothing more than short weedy grass. Gone are the King Devils, Hawkweeds, Daisies, and left over Pussy Toes. How pointless it seems to mow here so close to the ground, when no one walks among the grasses apart from us. I suspect even the dogs would rather the taller grasses to navigate; they seem more energetic when bounding through the fields in contrast to the open cultivated lawn.

On the periphery, the Cournoyer's field has been fallow with planted cover crops for the past two months. Here there are tall King Devils and yellow Mustards along with occasional tiny white Chickweed.

June 10

We are near midway through this cycle of the seasons. It is nearly impossible not to fall in love with June with its clear skies and warm winds, deep green leaves that have yet to blight, and puffy clouds that drift overhead with no fear of something sinister in store. These are the days we dream of in winter, when we wish for just a moment that we might be transported to experience these days of light and heat and life. Soon enough we will feel the sizzle in all its measure, and the lassitude of July will become the sultry fatigue of August. We will then look ahead to the cool relief that September will bring, only to turn our attention to the first frost or snow.

How tempting it is to anticipate the changes of tomorrow. We do so at the expense of missing the beauty in this day, in this season. Perhaps it is because we measure our lives in terms of the changes in seasons that we have the luxury of looking ahead, to think in terms of next season or next year. We live believing that there will be another spring or summer. Knowing this affords us a gift of anticipation, but perhaps it detracts from our appreciation of this moment.

June 11

Several swallows spent the better part of midday flying a low circuitous path around and across the cover crop field next to Anna Maria. We sat in the grass at the edge and watched them for a while as they lifted upward and away, arcing back in a long curve and diving close to the reaching rye grass. They searched for butterflies and moths, of which several frequent this open field. There has been the second metamorphosis of the cabbage white, and they flitter briefly in pairs upward to the sky, plainly visible for the predatory swallows that hunt like circling sharks, unaffected by our presence nearby.

June 12

Hiking the road to the summit of Mount Wachusett is like going back in time to mid spring. Here the Mountain Laurel has yet to emerge, and Bluets dot the roadsides. Many of the maples still have red tinges to their early leaves, waiting yet for the building chlorophyll to concentrate to the summer green. So too the Dogwood and Apple are still in bloom, where down below their blossoms have long since fallen to the ground.

Where the road ascends before the final turn to the summit, there is an open spot that affords a spectacular view to the south, and in the clear air we were able to see perhaps fifty miles. Here the winds lift upslope and cool, shifting breezes that sound themselves in the moving leaves of the canopy. We stop to listen to the wind as it blows across the road, starting first like a crashing wave in the downslope woods. Its rapport fades as the wave recedes but moves onward to the higher trees. They too bend in response, building their own white noise that ebbs and flows in the shifting pattern.

Here, near the roadside

where a culvert drains to a man-made ditch, moisture from the summit run off is collected and diverted downslope. The sun's rays do not reach here throughout the day, affording the grasses and flowers near continual moisture. In a spot several feed upslope from the drain grows a unique wildflower, called Ragged Robin, its pink petals set wildly atop a thin stalk among the surrounding deep green grasses and ferns.

June 13

In the early evening, the sunlight comes angled low over the planted fields across the road, filtered by the spruce trunks and low hanging boughs of the pines, maples and leaves of the bittersweet vines. What passes through is a golden green sheen that reaches the yard, making long shadows of the grass we've failed to mow for too many days. The spruces are backlit in hues only possible this time of year, and a gentle breeze catches the maple leaves, turning them over lazily back and forth and reflecting shades of deep warm green in the golden light.

Beyond, the tractor moves slowly in the remaining fallow field, pulling a plow that turns the soil, each blade lifting the weeded earth and rolling it over onto itself like an ocean wave progressing down the beach. Both tractor and plow are in shadow from our viewpoint as darkened cutouts that move across the fields. Only the dust cloud that trails behind is lit in brilliant light, reflecting the setting sun as a white haze which catches the breeze and moves southerly toward the forest edge.

The adjacent rows have corn in them, and their stalks are roughly a foot tall. Over further are the sugar snaps, which should be ready for harvest in a couple weeks.

The wind shifts just so, and we smell the diesel from the exhaust and hear the labored noise of the engine soften as Fred lifts the plow to turn for another pass.

June 14

The air is laced with the smell of sweet hay on Whittemore Street about a half mile up from where it meets 56. There is an old white farmhouse at the crest in the road, and the hay is intended for the large barn that sits adjacent to the fields on the same side. Across the street, the baler has already been out, and there now sits the rectangles of bound grass, dotting the landscape in roughly sequential patterns. On the near side to the barn the hay is cut and drying in rows, waiting to be bailed and transported to the mow.

The grass Is infused with bound clover and vetch, and each bale gives off the scent of early summer and sparks a memory of those summers long ago when I worked the fields up north baling hay. It's pleasant to see that they still use the antiquated rectangles here.

We'd stand atop the flatbed, us kids, as the Oliver Tractor pulled along, jostling across the uneven fields along loosely defined rows of waiting bales. The elevator connected to the side, and every few seconds it would receive another bale, scooping it into chute and lifting it upward along the belt, higher and higher until it dropped downward onto the rising bed. We'd take turns catching them as they fell, waiting for just the right moment to swing the bale hook and spike the middle of the prize, pulling it away and positioning it like a puzzle; with each new tier made orthogonal to the last, we'd rise upward higher above the bed.

June 15

Note: Nightshade had been in bloom for several days.

The past several evenings have remained warm throughout the night, with morning temperatures still in the low sixties. This has hastened the germination of the summer crab grass, as now there are small lime green blades emerging in the thin spots of the yard. Soon enough they will fill, making the lawn appear thick and vibrant for a while, albeit a mosaic of greens that will last only so long as the temperatures remain warm – at least until September.

Near the lower woods, the Butter and Eggs are nearly two feet high, though they have yet to show any buds of the flowers that will eventually develop. These have spread nicely from the single plant of several years ago, and now fifty square feet are filled with dozens of them.

According to the guide, Butter and Eggs thrive in waste lots and poor soil, and so evidently the periphery of our yard is of dubious character, or perhaps these particular plants are sufficiently high brow to take residence here.

June 16

The coming of the crabgrass yesterday is merely an indication of the continual succession that is a part of our yearly seasons. Though we neatly divide into winter, spring, summer and fall, in truth there is no ending and no beginning as such. There are signs now that spring is fading and summer is close at hand, though the change is more evolutionary than succinct.

The maple leaves are showing signs of fading, so different now than a few weeks ago when each was newly green and perfectly formed. Now, with the coming of the heat and drought, many have given way to age and stress. How strange that this should be, when only a month ago they were first emerged into the light. The pace of production can only be sustained for so long, and what remains must carry for several months yet.

Were we to measure that pace, would we discover the frenzy of May production? The rush to grow must be overwhelming and give way to the steadiness and consistency of what continues through autumn.

June 17

He clings upside down to the large maple in the side yard and chatters incessantly at the slightest disturbance. This has upset the relatively harmony among the other residents, including us within the calm of the sunroom where we enjoy watching and listening to our familiar visitors.

The newcomer is a young red squirrel, who is likely one of the upstart offspring of the mother that comes and goes throughout the week. He (or she, it is difficult to tell at this point), typifies Beatrix Potter's characterization. He has become territorial of the feeders, and is intent on chasing away any chipmunks or grey squirrels that have the audacity to come within ten feet of his domain. This includes us, and he isn't shy about yammering and stamping and carrying on, retreating quickly from the trunk upward to one of the higher branches when we step outside to the porch.

June 18

There is a small length of the Rutland Rail Trail where the canopy opens into a sunny field, and the old cinder bed cuts across, skirting a small gully that at one time shows evidence that it may have been used for sand or fill. On the opposing side, tall grasses grow amid the tailings of whatever was left from the removal, and though this space is nothing more than a series of large excavation pits, it has softened through the years to give it a more natural look in which primary succession of small shrubs has taken hold.

Where the trail emerges from the trees, heading south along the track toward Barre, it abruptly switches from the cool enclosure of the thick woods to the bright heat of the open field. Here, alongside the edge of the trail, in the short span of only a few feet where the sunlight is permitted to reach the ground, tall daisies grow densely, thriving in the full sun. Here too the odor changes from the fecundity of the shaded wood to the dusty smell of sweet grass and clover, mixed with the scent of sere white pine needles.

Further along, the trail descends into the trees again before taking an angle slightly on the edge of a large pond, now covered with lily pads that each bear a rising yellow flower. Scattered throughout are the poking shafts of Pickerelweed (*Pontederia cordata*), each ending in a single green leaf that points upward, awaiting the purple flowers which will develop in a couple weeks.

June 19

The dawn is ushered in softly for nearly forty-five minutes before the actual sunrise, filled with the awakening of the various birds as the morning veil of building light comes slowly. Across the road is the staccato pounding of a hammer against wooden stakes, as someone is out before daybreak putting in supports for the growing tomato plants. The rapport comes sharply in the still morning and sounds much like the hammer of our downy or hoary when they strike repeatedly into a hardwood tree.

On cue at 5:10, as the first rays came filtering through the lower trees, a tiny wren sang jubilantly from the top of the roof, as if she were singing in the morning. She may know that the longest day approaches, and we should all celebrate the pleasure of so much warmth and light. Tomorrow, the sunrise is again at 5:10, and then it will retard from that point, 5:11 on the 21st and so on, as the days begin slowly to shorten.

By 7:00, the sun is high enough to crest the tops of the trees down below, casting the back porch in first light and warming the collected dew on the plastic chairs. Within a few minutes, small streams of vapor rise from the heated surfaces, combining with the steam from my coffee cup that sits on the arm of the Adirondack chair. The air is seemingly alive with motion; the steam swirls about in the gentle draft, visible in the backlit sunlight as are the currents of pollen that drift about in the breeze.

June 20

Our son stayed up late last evening, playing football on the darkened field at Anna Maria until after 10:00 pm. We were fast asleep by the time he returned, though in the morning he relayed that the border woods became full of fireflies as the dusk had settled into evening. This seems about right, perhaps a tad early, though we have had a warm stretch for several weeks, and likely this has hastened the arrival of many things.

We are so lucky to have the fireflies here. Their coming signals the transition to warm evenings – the kind where it is comfortable to remain outside without a jacket and listen to the background din of the crickets from the lower woods. As the light fades, we search the tree line for the familiar flash of the Photinus, whose mating pattern is unique to its species. Like the use of Morris Code, the males and females call to one another in a rush to locate and unite. So too the competitor firefly, Photuris calls, and the backyard may at once contain both species, and as the darkness descends they emerge one by one, until there are dozens upon dozens of flashing points, yellow bioluminescents against the inky black of the near moonless night.

In a twist, there is danger in the air. The females of one of the species (I can't remember which, and so let's pick Photuris), mimics the mating response of the competitive female. Photuris then responds to the Photinus male call by replying in the pattern of the Photinus female! This is very amazing. She mimics the competitive female in order to lure the Photuris male to her, and then she kills him as he nears. In this way, she seeks to promote the supremacy of her species.

All this takes place within the serenity of the backyard, as we watch the flashes come and go. "There's one!" we shout, and I remember my childhood as we'd run to the point where we last saw the flash, hands cupped quickly trying to catch the firefly to be put in a waiting jar. "There's another!"

Summer

Maturity

June 21

The full moon rose from the southeastern horizon at 8:30
this evening, first visible through the far trees of the town
fields as an orange glow that illuminated a low band of
clouds. As it gained height above the upper branches of
the forest, it shone alone against the deepening indigo of
the building evening. This is the strawberry moon, and it
uniquely coincides with this day as the summer solstice.

The Earth is in apogee in its orbit around the sun, meaning
that its position is furthest away in its gravitational tether.
For us folks here in the north, it ironically coincides with
our summer, and this confounds the misconception that
our seasons are caused by earthly distance.

Tomorrow, we will enjoy ever so slightly less daylight, as
we accelerate in our orbital path. Around we go, slightly
closer tomorrow to the sun, moving hour-by-hour in our
yearly progression.

June 22

Toadflax is blooming along the roadsides. There is a pretty
patch that grows in the sandy shoulder of the valley next
to the cemetery on route 56. This morning, the air was cool
here for early summer, and a thin layer of mist hung above
the pond before the entrance, obscuring the far side apart
from the sedge reeds that seem to vanish in the distance. In
the near shore, a lone blue heron stood stoically in his
search for breakfast, wading slowly among the aquatic
plants that have spread well the past few weeks. Here too
a family of Canada Geese shares space with the heron,
though they keep a cautious eye on his movements, and
they protest my passage by squawking in a low murmur

and moving from the grass on the edge to the littoral waters.

The air is laced with the scents of early summer. The pond smells of warming freshwater and aquatic plants, of moist shoreline and dewy grass. Mixed within are the fragrant perfumes of the *Rosa multiflora*, an invasive shrub that grows profusely in the periphery of nearly every yard or field. They have been in blossom for nearly two weeks, showing their pretty white flowers amid their tangled mass of thorny green. Only within the past few days have their nectaries produced the sweet smell, signaling their readiness. Though they seem destined to overrun the open woods, as are the bittersweet, bindweed and honeysuckle, at least we have the benefit of their lovely appearance and odor for a while.

The Toadflax is a curious little thing. It grows ramrod straight as nearly a single stalk, roughly a foot tall and ending in a blunted cap that contains one or more small blue snapdragon-like flowers. It's easy to miss them altogether unless you happen to walk by and notice. In a few weeks, the flower shell will have long wilted away, leaving a small cup that will be filled with tiny charcoal black seeds, no bigger than the smallest poppy seeds.

June 23

We've enjoyed the yellow swallowtail for several weeks, and the cabbage whites and spring azures have been flitting about the garden since early May.

The Monarch Butterfly made an appearance this afternoon, coming around the side of the house and flying haphazardly into the lower canopy of the cherry trees at the wood's edge. It lifted high into the air and disappeared in the boughs of the old white pine that sits deeper in the middle of the forest.

This timing coincides nicely with the bloom of the Milkweed, whose sweet perfume has just begun to distribute in the summer air. We have several of them among the tomatoes in the raised beds, and they've only recently begun to open their blossoms that have been dangling from pendants for the past week. With luck, one of the plants will serve as an egg site for the butterfly, and we'll enjoy seeing a chrysalis develop as the summer unfolds.

The Milkweed scent carries memories of summers past, of two-track northern roads in Michigan where the air is perfumed with the mixture of pine needles, dusty sand, sweet grass and milkweed nectar.

June 24

In the afternoon heat, the young Cotton Tail seeks shelter within the tall groupings of mints in the knot garden. At the base, where the plants group together beneath the purple flowers that rise upward in two-foot high spikes, there is shade and camouflage enough to hide this little one from the wandering eyes of the dogs, who know from experience that the rabbit prefers the tender plants nearby.

Even if they were about, I doubt they'd give much chase in this heat, which resembles late July rather than June. Nearly everything looks a little tired and dusty, and we could use a gentle shower from a cold front.

Across the road, cars have been steadily going to the store since it opened this morning at 9:00, and in the still air we can hear the muted conversations of patrons who greet the Cournoyers and celebrate the opening of the farm. It's been nearly six months since the last of the squash and potatoes were sold to the community or made ready for the food pantries in the big town. After the long winter, we've anticipated the sugar snaps and strawberries, lettuce and asparagus that come with the renewal of the farm.

June 25

Both the Rose Breasted Grosbeak and the Eastern Towhee have stayed longer than usual. The Grosbeak pair is strangely bold this year, apparently undisturbed by our presence in the side yard. He alights on the feeder and cocks his head slowly to the side, regarding us carefully in a distinctive manner compared to the other birds whose movements are more jerky. His tilt looks thoughtful and measured, as if he intends to comment about something in a dignified way. His coloring is brilliant now; the cardinal red splash of feathers that descends down his front are set distinctly apart from the contrasting white and black. He is only bothered when the Red Bellied Woodpecker (our "big red") comes quickly in to the feeder.

Big red has been busy with his brood. Somewhere high in the maple are the tinny whistles of the fledglings, and they grow insistent at the moment he leaves the feeder with a seed and returns to them within the tree cover.

In the background is rustling of the sere leaves from last fall. It is loud enough that we think for a moment that something large is approaching, a turkey perhaps. But no, it is only the Towhee, who looks earnestly through the litter, using his legs to scratch violently backward and making the noise too large for his diminutive frame.

June 26

The town has yet to mow the road sides, which has allowed the early summer weeds and grasses to grow sufficiently tall and softening the edges of the road. Several of the taller grasses have been in seed head for a couple weeks, and they sway gently next to one another when cars pass by. Tucked within are the white heads of yarrow and the green stalks of the Wild Carrot, which will begin to produce blossoms within a few weeks.

Bindweed is marching ever onward in the absence of a mow. It now outpaces even the tallest grass head, reaching upward with its sinewy vine toward whatever height it can obtain. Where two grow close together, it is wondrous to see how they cooperate, twisting around one another to create a strengthened braid that allows both to ascend. Should they reach a lower branch of some nearby tree, they will grab hold and twist, working steadily upward.

Poison Ivy too seems to thrive now, more so than only a few years ago. Perhaps the warming trends seem to favor its growth, for so many of the maple and oak trunks are covered with it, as are the stone walls that line the fields.

June 27

The tree pollen seems to have abated finally after several weeks of what seemed like a constant yellow dust settling on every surface. When the pines were releasing in full measure earlier in the month, it was pointless to wash the house or cars. Within minutes after cleaning any surface would begin to show a film of pollen. In the late afternoon, as the sun came angled across the fields and illuminated the house, we could see the air infused with a hazy mass, particularly when the wind shook the spruce line across the road. It was a wonder we could breathe at all.

Now, the air is laced with the dust of topsoil, made loose by the tractor that is cultivating the peas in the long rows. We've had so little rain that the soil is nearly bone dry – not so much that the weeds haven't taken hold, which explains the cultivating. There is a small cloud of dusty air that trails the tractor. It hovers briefly behind as a backlit thing, before a breeze lifts it and carries it through the trees and toward the house, where it will find its way in the screen and settle on the counter.

It's a curious thing – to see a tiny layer of soil on the windowsill and think that it is one and the same that we occasionally walk.

June 28

There are splashes of cerulean blue in the Chicory blossom that have begun to dot the roadsides and waste areas, and soon the heat and humidity will build toward the summer days of July.

The Chicory color matches the deep blue of a crystal clear summer day; its blossoms open with the dawn and seem to track the sunshine, giving the dusty shoulders of the road a brilliant contrast.

So too the Sundrops and Evening Primrose have arrived; they resemble one another with deep yellow petals, though the former opens throughout the day, and the Primrose favors the cool of the evening.

June 29

Early dragonflies crisscross the backyard in the afternoon heat, searching for mosquitoes and insects that have come into their own. They skirt the edge of the side wood and then jerk suddenly ninety degrees across the expanse of lawn, flying straight for a dozen yards before altering course once again. Why they fly so linearly is a mystery. What possible advantage can there be in searching for prey in straight lines? A dozen or so roam about the yard in this way, occasionally becoming agitated with one another when two paths fly too near.

A mystery too that the mosquitoes have emerged so prolifically. It's been dry for several weeks, giving little standing water for the larva to develop. Likely they have come from the vernal pool down slope, where enough bog remains to sustain the amphibious creatures and the like through the early summer stretch.

June 30

June is at an end. It has been a month of green growth and vibrant song, of field flowers on display amid the grass grown tall in the full day sun. It's seen new birds taken to wing from nests built in trees and shrubs we've come to expect. It has perfumed us with the fecundity of pollen in the air, of still nights where the scents of honeysuckle waft slowly by. It has seen our longest day come to pass, and June knows that we will pay for this leisure in six months hence.

It ends with the first hints of change. Look closely now. The oaks and maples have leaves that show blight, curled and yellowed. The vegetables are growing yet, to be sure, but there is also fruit on the vine, expanding each day as maturity nears. Crab grass is taking hold in the yard, thriving in the hotter days and warm nights that will mark July.

The rush of May and June is over, and things seem to be waiting for July to arrive. The pace will continue to slow as the heat builds all the while the days slowly begin to soften.

July

July 1
Northern Michigan

In the border field along the hardscrabble road near the
farm, the uncut tall grasses have long gone to seed head. In
the midst of several weeks of drought, they have turned
from green to tan, and in the morning breeze they sway
gently, making soft swishing sounds as they chafe
together. From the roadside, the field undulates like waves
across the ocean, and wind shifts show themselves as
moving things across the expanse.

The light is soft here, made so by the humidity that rises
from the fields, coalescing as a thin layer of cloud that
hovers no more than a few feet from the top of the grasses
and is backlit from the sunrise that crests the pine woods
beyond.

There is movement within the blades. Something disturbs
the patterns of the grass, going against the bend. Two Sand
Hill Cranes walk silently across the fields, their auburn
heads just below the top of the weighted grass and
revealed only when the breeze bends the seed heads
around them enough that their crests show momentarily
above the burdened waves. They call out in their distinct
cry, a throaty and deep call with a cadence like the wild
turkey but more prehistoric and raw. It is both beautiful
and strangely frightening to hear them so.

July 2
Northern Michigan

The two-lane roads here run straight across the landscape
that undulates as open fields and thick woods, stretching
for miles in either direction east or west. The latter leads
toward the coast, rising in the distance as gradual hills, so
that the ribbon of old asphalt can be seen for several miles

95

where the section runs within the cleared land. Seen from the lower valley, the pavement gives off heat shimmers in the distance, making oncoming cars look ghostly from so far away.

Up and over the ridge line the road ascends from the small town of Bliss and into the older forest that borders the tracks of land that descend gently from here to the shore. These hills were formed thousands of years ago, when the ebb and flow of retreating glacial ice pushed the ridge upward and receded slowly, ultimately to melt away as the mass of Lake Michigan which lies below.

The road begins to turn sharply left and right then heads straight for a short stretch, curving back again as it starts the descent to the sandy dunes that mark the transitional zones.

July 3
Northern Michigan

Queen Anne's Lace is starting to go to flower, with its broad nest-like cluster of miniature white atop a singular stalk. Seeing this invariably reminds me of my mother describing to me its namesake. As a child, I believe Queen Anne's Lace was the first wildflower to which I became familiar, no doubt on account of the story.

The common version is that the queen was embroidering lace when she accidentally pricked herself, drawing a single drop of blood. This is represented as the small cluster of deep red petals in the center of the field of white. Look closely over the next month, for the red develops as the white unfolds.

St. John's Wort is also proliferating now. There's a nice grouping in the undeveloped fields at the top of Highland

Street, and I've also seen it growing along the roadside at the lower end of Grove, just before it meets Pond Street.

St. John's has tight clusters of yellow flowers, sitting on stalks that have small leaflets coming out from each axial node, giving the green an almost feathery look. The petals are a brilliant yellow, nearly an inch across, with dozens of stamens protruding from the center point.

Its distinguishing feature almost requires a strong lens or loupe. I use a 30x loupe, which is easy to carry and hold just above the petals. On the outer petal edge is a remarkable line of small black dots, nearly invisible to the naked eye (and surely indistinguishable to the middle-aged eye), and they remind me of the small blue eyes of the scallop, which are visible in the margins between its shell halves.

July 4
Northern Michigan

At noon we gathered at the Mercke House that sits high on the bluff, where the open front porch and yard overlook the expanse of the lake. Generations of families assembled loosely outside, young and old reacquainting with friends and reminiscing of days and years past.

The sunshine glistened on the lake, and from this height it was easy to spot the shifting winds, patterns of darkened water which moved across the surface along with shaded areas of cloud cover that made a patchwork of light and dark.

We are celebrating here, as we have done for over forty years; family and friends present and many only in memory, sharing our lives and our commitment to this

97

place and this time, yet paying our deepest respect to the liberties that we enjoy.

Shortly, Nat reads a portion of the Declaration, and the faces of the crowd register a mixture; the adults are somewhat reverent, while the children fidget and giggle at the reading, some resorting to playing tag or spying upon one another.

I have witnessed this same scene for over forty years, and my own giggles of long ago have been replaced with a profound sense of appreciation. As Nat reads, it is easy to become distracted from the words, and I scan the faces of people I have known my entire life – friends who have grown older with the years, and children who are yet the next generation. The reverence I feel at this moment is enhanced by an overwhelming sense of belonging, to these people, to this place, and to these rituals.

July 5
Northern Michigan

In the stillness of the oncoming dark, after the wind has calmed, and we sat enjoying a few quiet moments before turning in, two loons began calling to one another in their mournful way. They must have been fairly far apart on the lake, for the first call came from off near the eastern shore, closer to where we sat than did the answering cry, which came a half a minute or so from the opposite direction and more distant.

Their daylight call is the trilling familiar laughter, and we see them occasionally out on the lake, usually alone and away from shore. They will dive and swim if encroached upon, and it is remarkable the distance they can travel underwater, head reemerging on the surface hundreds of feet away.

July 6
Northern Michigan

White birch and willows spread their branches outward
over the shoreline, dipping low so that they gently touch
the water when the wind blows across the lake. Their
trunks emerge from the berm of sandy soil that has been
pushed upward by successive years of winter ice, and
within a few years hence they will give way to their own
weight and fall slowly into the water.

Here the sandy shore is narrow and mixed with puzzle
grass, sedge and wild mint, and tiny toads hide within,
their bodies no larger than a half an inch. They jump away
in inch-long hops when danger nears, heading for the
thicker mats of grassy shore where the tree roots hold as
best as possible.

The smell of crushed mint, no matter where I am in the world, reminds me of here, where as a child I explored these shores and walked through the sandy grasses, my footfalls releasing the odors of warm water and summer mint, infused by the July sunshine of many years.

July 7
Northern Michigan

Somewhere from deep within the woods came the building call of a single Cicada this afternoon. It began as a quiet rasp but rose quickly to the staccato buzz that all but silenced the other sounds of the afternoon. The call lasted nearly twenty seconds and faded in the same way it began, slowly becoming quieter until it could be heard no more. There was no repeat.

The Cicada call is the clarion of midsummer, of long days where the sticky heat builds and lasts well into evening, and the night is sometimes filled with the shimmering sights of heat lightning in the distant clouds.

There will be more soon, and their calls will fill the days one after another. As the ending volume of one diminishes into the background din, the call of another from close by will rise and take its place.

July 8
Northern Michigan

White clover is blooming in the roadsides, as are thistles. The white clover resembles tiny loosestrife, and the leaves smell vaguely like vanilla when crushed.

The second cut of hay was made yesterday at the farm and now sits in rows in the field drying in the summer sunshine until the baler can be put to service. Midsummer sees round bales nearly everywhere these days, but we worked the fields thirty years ago with square bales (which were rectangular really). In the sunshine we'd ride on the unsteady flatbed, pulled behind the Oliver tractor, two of us with hay picks in hand to catch and position the bales thrown up to us from below. When the tiers became too high, an elevator was hitched to the flatbed, lifting the bales up six to seven tiers and dropping them over for placement.

This second cut seems early, but perhaps the rainy June has hastened its growth. There is clover and vetch cut within, and the cows enjoy the additive all the more.

Notes:
Wild Bergamot and Bee balm in bloom

July 9
Northern Michigan

A warm and gentle rain fell today, a truly summer rain without the windborne front or violent storm. With a slicker and mud boots, it was perfectly pleasant to walk the two-track road and admire the effects of water everywhere.

The rain must have begun overnight, for the puddles in the low spots of gravel in the road were already full this morning, making the depressions look like miniature brown colored kettle ponds seen from high overhead; the sparse grassy ridge of the two track was the imaginary forest that divides them.

The surrounding trees were bent lower to the road, burdened by the moisture, and in several places the effect was a canopy where the boughs of one tree on one side met those from the other. Every leaf and needle had miniature droplets, and when any breeze stirred they collected and fell through the boughs making a sound like a rain chime.

Where the road departs from the cottage fronts, it makes a bend upon itself in a place where the canopy opens, permitting more sunlight. Here, just at the ditch edge where the gravel meets the mixture of wild grasses, heal all, Queen Anne's Lace, and Creeping Dogbane, I noticed plump red raspberries within. They are full this year on account of all the moisture, and I stopped to sample several, picking them off the rain-soaked bushes and putting them in my mouth one-by-one. This very spot I've known and enjoyed berries for over forty years, and I recall walking to this bend as a child in summer with pale white bucket in hand to pull berries and place within for eating.

Notes:
Purple Coneflower in Bloom.

July 10
Northern Michigan

The tall grasses between the dirt two-track on Ingleside are nearly foot tall, kept in check only by the infrequent passing of some car that is brave enough to hazard this stretch of the backwoods. Here in the afternoon sunshine, summer is on full display. On one side of the road an open field stretches away for a half mile, rising slowly to a hill upon which sits an abandoned house from decades ago. The field is littered with daisies that peek in and out of the field grasses that sway gently in the breeze warmed by the heat of the afternoon.

As we walk the side rut of the two-track closest to the field, grasshoppers jump away quickly from our approach, their brief aerial flight adding to the numbers of dragonflies and damselflies that hover over the grasses. Chicory grows thickly here, as do late blooming buttercups. So too the white clover and milkweed, whose combined scents perfume the dusty road in way that only summer here can produce.

The other side is bordered closely by the deep forest, where red cedar, birch and balsam fir populate the moist lowland, making the air tinged with the humid odor of earthy woods. Here the light barely penetrates to the forest floor, and the juxtaposition from the two-track enlivens our senses; the bright sunshine and dusty growth on one side contrasts with the dark and verdant woods on the other.

This is a seldom-used road, and we may be the only to pass here today, making this scene our own private keepsake of summer's offering.

July 11
Northern Michigan

Last week's green nests of Queen Anne's Lace have now opened fully on the roadsides and sunny fields, displaying their beautiful array of tiny white blossoms. Several already show the distinctive single deep-red floral cluster that sits in the center of the lace, marking the place where the eponymous Anne may have pricked her finger while working to sew the intricate patterns. Surely there is some selective reason for the spot? Perhaps it serves to attract would-be pollinators, like bees and wasps.

Nearby, the Chicory continues to flourish in the summer heat. At sunrise on the shady side of the two track, its flowers were bundled tightly closed, concentrating the deep periwinkle color to clusters of nearly indigo buds. As I passed by a particular spot, the sunlight was just beginning to rise high enough over the tree line to cast its rays directly on the closed blossoms. I walked along a looping circle of dusty road and returned to this sunny place after a half hour had passed. Within this time, the flowers had opened fully to face the warming rays, their color lessened with the expanse to the more familiar cerulean blue and no less wondrous.

July 12
Northern Michigan

There are trails here that wind from one cottage to the next, sometimes down to the shore. The woodland paths have been trod for generations, traversing small brooks that outlet from the lake and navigating over tree roots and mossy stretches, where the coolness of the canopy affords a pleasant walk when the summer warmth has set in.

These are the trails of my childhood, where freedom and exploration began out the doorstep, as I sought out my friends down the shore to share in my summer adventures.

There were secret paths that we created, made by forays into some hidden fort within the trees or to access the beach, shell strewn and in the company of emergent frogs.

Many of these paths have vanished with the years, and even some of the main trails have gone fallow with the passing of generations. It seems that children explore less outdoors, and the highways of my own use are returning to the wild slowly, most only a memory now.

July 13
Northern Michigan

The open meadows are slowly changing color and beginning to show signs of summer fatigue among the late growing grasses and wildflowers. Across the expanse, the warm breeze moves the brown tinged blades of the tall grass, which undulates and makes a drier sound against one another than it did only a month ago. Seen from a distance, the meadow has evolved from the deep greens of June's growth to the changing maturity that comes with this milestone of heat and light.

Mixed within are Spotted Knapweed, and their sinewy teal and branching stems have grown tall enough that we notice them. They give the undergrowth beneath the grasses a softening look of aquamarine, so that the meadow is infused with something vaguely green beneath the moving blades of sweet grass, Fox and Timothy.

Here and there the flowers have appeared, the Knapweed's poms of fluffy purple, almost like those of Burdock or even Thistle, but softer somehow and spread helter skelter among the low growth of the meadow and the border ditches.

July 14
Northern Michigan

In the wet areas, whether along the roadside or near a pond, look now for teasel heads. They are a finicky thing and prefer fairly wet and yet sunny locations, which is why they frequent the in-between ditch of some divided highways in the state or the accompaniment of cattail and reed grass at shore's edge of the lesser ponds.

Teasels must be close cousin to the thistles, for they too are beginning to bloom in the fields and waste lots.

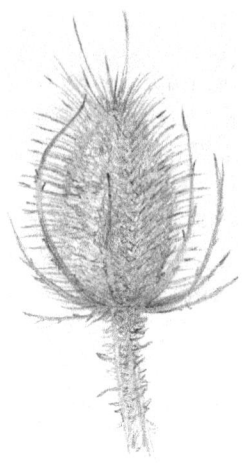

Often, the easiest method of locating teasels is to simply seek out the brown heads from last year, dark brown with the distinct teasel leaves and prickly comb. When driving on potential roadways for teasels and thistles, it is the sere cluster from last year that advertises the spot. This year's growth is light green, with small purple flowers that grow in a curious ring in the teasel head, lifting ever upward toward the tip with each passing day.

I'm told the dried heads were used as wool combs long ago, and I believe it. They are prickly things.

July 15
Northern Michigan

Small tendrils of vapor rise from the surface of the brook where it widens in an elbow that meets the two-track road. Here a break in the tree line to the east allows the morning sun to strike directly, providing enough early warmth to this place that the Chicory has opened well before its shaded neighbors only a dozen yards away.

Sometimes in the morning a lone Blue Heron stands patiently on the far bank, scanning the shallow, tanned-colored water for its meal. Today is too cold, almost autumnal with temperatures in the mid forties, tempering the usual enthusiasm of the summer insects whose calls make a near constant din of chirps and buzzing.

This is a strange glimpse of what will arrive soon enough, when the first frost of September quickly ends what we've grown accustomed to hear since May. This cool morning in July is an ephemeral thing; the heat will return in due course, as will the varied life that is dependent on the warmth of summer's gift.

Look closely now. There are signs that summer is beginning to wane. The first Goldenrod flowers are beginning to appear in the sunny spots along the road. Here by the brook is a small cluster, where yesterday the buds rose from the branching stalk in small green bunches that were barely noticeable. Today they have a yellow tinge, and even a few have opened slightly to reveal the tiny petals within.

July 16
Northern Michigan

A gentle mist hung over the lake this morning, obscuring the far side and highlighting the shoreline leaves and pine needles in a dewy sheen. Shortly, the mist turned to a steady rain, which lasted well into the afternoon, giving the land an inch or so of desperately needed moisture. It's been over a month since we've last had rain, which may account for the early yellow tinge to the tall grasses along the roadside and the notable July abscission from the maples and oaks.

By afternoon, in the places along the two track where time and traffic have created pot hole depressions, the rain had collected and made small kettle ponds of mocha-colored water. The remainder soaked well into the sandy roadbed, apart from those several spots where the earth had become so desiccated that no amount of adhesive forces could overcome the tenacity of the beads to simply roll about on the surface like water poured into a bowl of flour.

Low hanging limbs now burdened with the extra weight arch across the road, creating verdant tunnels of darkened shades of green. They let loose fattened drops of water that splash below onto the sand or into one of the watery depressions or cascade from one bough to another, creating a natural percussion that complements the few birds that brave the conditions to sing.

July 17 – Northern Michigan

We walked the deep woods last night, after the full moon rose high enough to bathe the forest in a soft light just bright enough that we could barely discern the rooted single track that meandered in and out of the shoreline. From somewhere within came the high whistle of the flying squirrels, calling to one another in wakened alarm as we passed by underneath. Theirs is the evening world of activity, this dark woods where large moths flit by in search of one another and small creatures make rustling noises from just beyond.

We brought a flashlight and pointed the beam in an arching band into the trees, revealing forest eyes of all sorts, luminous points that regarded us carefully, silent watchers of our intrusion into their world.

Lights off and the woods were made momentarily black, as our eyes needed time to readjust to the filtered moon from above. On one side of the path, the trees thickened into old growth, reaching well overhead and blocking the sky with a canopy of leaves. On the other, the shoreline lay not fifteen feet away with the smooth surface of the evening lake stretching beyond.

July 18 – Northern Michigan

Since the first of the month, the Yellow Goat's Beard has made the transition from its yellowy expanse of composite flower to the oversized puff of light grey seed wings. They now dot the field expanses, rising above the tops of the tallest wild grasses so that the heads catch the passing breeze, releasing the tiny parachutes into the wind when the timing is just so.

These aren't the Dandelions of June, despite their resemblance in form and lifecycle. They thrive among the Milkweed and Knapweed, Chicory and Thistle, all of which are in maturity and displaying that July is beginning to wane. Their time is marked with the sweet air of Milkweed pollen, combined with the pleasant odor of the dusty road, laced with hints of wild Raspberries that thrive where the sun strikes the ground.

July 19 – Northern Michigan

Low hanging boughs of the Red Cedars reach outward from the shore toward the open water of the lake, providing shade to the small stretch of sandy beach where the puzzle grass is mixed within wave strewn rocks. In the calm, the water laps gently against the rising sand, and there is a line of yesterday's detritus that begins where the wave action reaches its apex. Within are small bits of decaying wood and tiny shells of lake snails and casings of various larva. Beyond, the sand reaches to the stony shore, and here small toads, no bigger than a quarter inch, hop frantically about in search of tiny food.

Overhead the strident call of the Kingfisher sounds its staccato alarm. It takes flight from one Cedar bough and glides downward across the shoreline then lifts gently to alight on another. Its movement sets others to call, which in the still of the morning makes a rolling series of laughing cries down the beach, as one bird sets off another for a quarter of a mile or more.

July 20 – Northern Michigan

A narrow single track trail emerges from the deep pines that border MacArthur Farm to the south. At once there is a transition from the humid twilight of the old woods into a open clearing where the path cuts up and over a small hill that is covered mostly with the mature stalks of tall grass embedded within the sandy soil. Here and there are the yellow heads of Rudbeckia and the white splashes of Ox eye Daiseys and Bouncing Bet, all which thrive in the full exposure of the July heat.

Here too the grasshoppers seem to congregate, and they jump frantically away at our passing, dozens of them leaping ahead of our footsteps like a curling wave of divided water from the prow of some passing boat. Some merely jump to the safety of the border grasses, avoiding our footfalls by leaping quickly aside to take hold of the arching blades. Others take to flight, springing ahead and spreading blurry wings of dark grey, some whose wingtips are highlighted with bands of yellow.

In the stillness here the Cicadas call the sounds of waning summer, and the dry sand gives off a dusty shimmer in the midday heat, mixing with the sweet smells of those Milkweed blossoms that still remain.

July 21

We've ignored it for a couple of weeks, but now there is no denying the setting sun has shifted notably on the horizon since our summer solstice of a month ago. Though we still

110

bask in the leisure of what seems like endless days, make no mistake the celestial forces conspire to see that our accounts will balance in merely a few months hence.

The heat too has settled in, as we move closer to the "Dog Days" of early August, marked by the return of Canniculus, or Sirius, the bright star which will again be visible in the dog constellation of Canis Minor as twilight gives way to evening. See now how the sun sets slightly more south of yesterday? It sinks slowly, made hazy and orange with the July humidity that lasts well into the night, scattering the rays of light so that the blues and violets disperse more than the oranges and reds. So too the twilight seems to last forever, marked by the dark lines of the forest horizon and the deep indigo veil of the lingering light above, where the first stars twinkle in one by one.

It's warm enough now to enjoy this beauty with no excuse.

July 22

In marshaling evidence in support of natural selection, Darwin writes of the prolific degree to which organisms of all kinds produce offspring. The argument claims that the world would soon be overrun should all the progeny and subsequent generations survive from a single parentage. Thus nature is daily scrutinizing and on balance selecting only those progeny, all things being equal, who have some advantage be it small or great.

Take the wild columbine as an example. The dried seed pods are brown now and pointed upright so that if you grasp the sere stalk and gently shake it, the sound of a rattle is made. I placed my hand underneath a single pod and bent it with the other so that the seeds fell into my palm in a neat pile. I counted nine coal-black seeds the size of small peppercorns. A little arithmetic assists the example. There were 18 total pods (in clusters of 3 or 4) from the entire plant. 18 times 9 equals 162 total seeds from this single columbine. If all the seeds were to successfully overwinter and germinate next spring, the knot garden would be overrun. Let's assume that last year's columbine also similarly produced 160 or so seeds. One evidently survived, making the likelihood of survival a meager 1 in 162.

Dandelions must assuredly be less, with their silken blowies everywhere in late May. I wonder about the maple keys or acorns, particularly in those mast years when production seems to be in the thousands.

It is a wonder we have columbines or dandelions or oaks at all.

Notes:
Bouncing Bet (Soapwort) on South Road in bloom.

July 23

Yesterday, I said to Sarah, "Have you seen any hummingbird moths yet?" for we normally have a few by now flittering above the knot garden. She hadn't, and I was beginning to think we'd miss a year.

Today, I caught the movement of one out of the corner of my eye, flying quickly among our many pink phlox blossoms. The other appeared, and they shared time sampling phlox and white loosestrife, seemingly unconcerned with each other.

Rarely do they land, and the time spent at any one flower is ephemeral – a quick placement of proboscis and removal, as if merely having a brief taste of what nectar dwells within. The calyx of the phlox is rather disproportionately long (approximately 1 to 1.5″), and the moth must have quite a lengthy tongue itself to compensate.

The real wonders are the wings, for in one species they are transparent across a large portion, and for what purpose I can only guess. I photographed one sampling the phlox, and the image captured its wing in still, revealing the beauty of its patterned design.

Notes:
Yellow Tansy in Bloom

July 24

I opened the sunroom door this morning to discover that both bird feeder poles were bent straight over to the ground, and one feeder itself had gone missing entirely. The dogs padded out in my wake and immediately became curious of some foreign scent in the vicinity, both noses to the ground weaving about. Tag paused just once to look up with what appeared to be a quizzical .expression, as if he were to exclaim "what in the world is that?"

I suspect there's been a black bear come up from the lower woods, intent on easy pickings from the black sunflower seed and suet cakes, which we keep well stocked. There have been several sightings of bear in Paxton over the past couple of years, which isn't too surprising given how the town sees fit to allow more woodland acreage to be cut over to development.

The same city folks who then move this way, desirous of life in the country, will undoubtedly complain about the intrusion of wildlife in their yards. Such is the hypocrisy of things.

We have town members who serve on committees charged with preserving the open space and agricultural heritage while at the same time they advocate for the destruction of such land to accommodate unnecessary senior housing complexes. Were it not so irreversible, it might be pathetically comical.

I put on tall muck boots and a mesh shirt designed to confuse the deer flies and headed down the access road toward the lower woods, intent on finding the feeder. No such luck, though the suet holder did turn up a hundred yards from the house.

How the bear managed to ferry that feeder across the berm, through the tall brush, and to Lord knows where I will never know.

Notes:
Pokeweed in bloom

July 25

Two months ago, we noticed a small clump of green shoots coming up in the small border garden by the back side of the house. It was in this spot last year that I had planted a few seeds from the teaseled heads of wild grasses I collected while hiking in the desert near Tucson some time before, and these had grown well into the same ornamental grass through the autumn. These had long

114

since been cut prior the onset of winter, and the sere base was accidentally covered by some mulch I spread around this spring when the snow finally relinquished its grip. Given that I couldn't remember the appearance of the shoots from the ornamental grass, I simply assumed that the green shoots last May had been its renewal.

Now the growth is nearly six feet high, with deep green leaves that branch in an alternating pattern and flower heads that extend upward in slender candles, each bearing small deep purple blossoms that open only for a day, before others take their turn higher up on the stalk. Their bloom is similar to that of the Common Mullein, where yellow flowers open not in unison but in succession, lifting upward through the days until the tip of the rising stalk is adorned with its deep yellow petals.

Our vibrant clump was no ornamental but rather the chance deposit of the Blue Vervain, whose tiny seeds may have been carried in the mulch somehow or carried by some bird or creature to this location. Now it is stands beautifully erect, with dozens of candle stalks, each containing a few deep purple blossoms.

In the morning, when the sun strikes it fully and before the heat builds toward midday, the stalks are covered with all manner of bees, who somehow gain enough through sampling the wares of such tiny blossoms.

July 26

The drought continues, and we are desperate for something more than a passing heat shower. Nearly everything looks tired and droopy – more like a late August stretch than the mature feel of what should be July at its high mark.

Across the road there was activity this morning of a new sort. Fred and several helpers had resurrected from the storage barns dozens of large pipes for irrigation, and they were busy staging to ready them for use. In fifteen years we've not seen these employed, so desperate are they for want of water to save the crops.

Next to the lower fields that abut the College's woods, there is an open stretch of a half acre that sits atop an underlying shelf of some unseen bedrock beneath where the water table rises upward close to the surface, made evident by the perpetual wetness of the land in even the most dry conditions. So too the topography reveals how the surface falls away gently to the woods beyond, slightly downhill until the underground flow emerges thirty yards within the trees as a artesian spring. Its discharge continues as a small creek that meanders for a hundred yards until it empties into a natural pond concealed nicely in the lower woods.

It is here where they submerge a pump and connect the tractor as its source of power, running the large metal pipes upward and across the fields for nearly a quarter mile to the rows of peppers near Grove Street. When it is made to work, the water shoots upward and across the many rows, arching through the air and creating thousands of iridescent rainbows, its rapport a steady "chh" "chh" "chh" of water to the fields below.

July 27

The air has been laced with the sweet smell of corn pollen, and even the early harvest has begun, made evident by the uptick in customer traffic to the store. Once word gets out there will be a steady stream of eager patrons like us, who have dreamt of the arrival of the sweet corn since mid winter.

These early ears will be small and somewhat lacking in the concentrated sugars of what will mature throughout the next two months. Soon we will see the farm truck making multiple trips back and forth to the lower fields as the workers do all they can to keep up with demand. Though they could pick an excess of bushels in the late evening and simply draw from such reserves throughout the following day, they steadfastly hold to the practice of freshly picked, which certainly contributes to the reputation the farm deserves.

We'll walk up the driveway later in the afternoon and purchase several ears of the butter-n-sugar variety, visit for a moment with whomever is behind the counter (though not linger too long this time of year, as undoubtedly they are both busy and tired). Sometimes we will go behind the store to the workroom beyond, where the freshly picked bushels will be unloaded from the bed of the truck and placed on the cement floor, as Louise sits upon an old stool waiting to begin grading the new arrivals.

She works in rhythm, with practiced hands that gently slice and peal each tip and critical glance that looks for anything unworthy. The ears come one after another, from bushel to grading and from grading to the store, where they sit not long until purchase.

July 28

Though the knot garden looks tired from so little water, there are still flowers enough to tempt several butterflies that flit in and out throughout the day. The Purple Coneflower is frequented by one of the first Monarchs we've seen, and a Great Spangled Fritillary drifts between the small yellow blossoms of the Coreopsis and the few

Phlox plants that remain from the devastation done by the resident rabbit.

Near the south edge of the yard where the tall trees provide enough shade throughout the day, Jewelweed has begun to show its orange blossoms. There are yellow versions in this portion of New England, though they are far more rare. Look for Jewelweed now in the shaded hollows where moisture collects.

We took a leisurely bike ride on the rail trail in Rutland in the afternoon, beginning as we do near the access in Barre and riding upgrade for a half dozen miles or so until the trail ends. The landscape has evolved since we were here a month ago, as summer's maturity is evident in full measure.

There is plenty of Jewelweed here, particularly in the valley cut that follows the tunnel, where the old trail was made by blasting the bedrock. It is cool here, even in the most warm of summer's days, making the passage through refreshing for a minute or two until the trail rises enough to meet the waiting wetlands beyond. Look now for the Cardinal flower here, where the standing water collects to the north side of the trail in the boggy swamp. In the sandy berm it thrives, shooting its stalks upward to reveal the brilliant red of its blossoms. You'll find few other examples of such color in nature, apart from the Scarlet Tanager. Go look for yourself.

July 29

Past the Kettlebrook Reservoirs, where 56 ascends to the high pass that bisects the view of the airport runway on one side and the open field that is dotted with Holstein cows on the other, the roadsides appear lined with miniature hedges. Here the Rabbit's Foot Clover thrives in

118

a narrow line that follows the road, reaching upward nearly ten inches or so and giving the byway the appearance of an English country road if you use a little imagination.

Here too Purple Loosestrife seems to do well, with its purple flower stalks reaching upward now and contrasting nicely with the deep greens of the lower shrubs and poison ivy that predominate the berm. With each passing year the Loosestrife gains more ground, and though we shouldn't celebrate this invasive species I admit to admiring its vibrant color. Why it does so well here is curious; it prefers the moist ditches and shorelines where cattail and sedge are the norm, spreading its copious seeds through any traversing water.

Another invasive is now beginning to show its white blossoms. The Chinese Knotweed has been growing steadily since late May, seeming intent to take over the sides of the roads that haven't yet been cut back. It's flowers will open in clusters of white, much like the Choke Cherries of late May, though the Knotweed blossoms produce an odor which is similar to Honeysuckle though slightly more acrid.

July 30

In early May, I cleaned the Wren house that hangs on a nail in the side of a small oak tree by the side berm. This is the same house I built according to plans several years ago, and it had up to this year been occupied by at least one family of Wrens throughout the summer. The location is peaceful enough, with protection from the sun and from human traffic given by the overhanging boughs of the oaks and maples that form the major trees within the berm.

We had no takers this year. Rather, the Wrens chose an old, broken down house that I plopped on a stump in the middle of the front garden as a piece of rustic decoration. This house had barely a roof, was exposed to the elements from sunup to sundown, and most certainly was in the line of traffic by both people and dogs throughout the day.

This morning Sarah heard the insistent cries of the second brood of babies. A tiny pair was born in early June and has since left the nest. Now there are more, with mom and dad flying frantically back and forth to the forest of the side yard for insects and such to feed the new arrivals. They pass right by the empty house on their way, and there is no accounting for taste.

July 31

The end of July brought a cold front late last evening, ushering in a gentle rain that began after midnight and continued well into the morning hours. It's been so long since we've had appreciable moisture that the sound of gentle drops hitting the trees and falling to the ground is an unfamiliar white noise that mixes strangely with the few songbirds that call to one another in the background.

Small puddles gathered in the low spots of the driveway, and several yellow finches stood at the edge of one particularly large and shallow depression. They drank and bathed with what seemed like reckless abandon. They too have suffered through the unusual heat and dryness of this past month.

The rain continued, and the small puddles coalesced, creating little rivers of water that flowed down the driveway and into the roadside, blending with the passing stream of runoff that gathered speed as it moved downhill. It is hopeful to think of the passing of July in this way.

Perhaps the pattern of stagnant heat and drought has been swept aside with the coming of August.

By midday the rain had stopped, and the sun poked through enough to cause steamy clouds of vapor above the driveway and yard, mixing with the earthy smell of moistened growth. Where July ends, August begins.

August

August 1

The month began as expected, with temperatures
remaining in the low seventies overnight. Combined with
the needed moisture of yesterday, the lawn is now
peppered with the seedlings of emergent crabgrass. These
typically arrive in mid July with the summer heat, but
there's simply been no water to spark their germination.

The Kentucky grass and Fescue so vibrantly green in early
June have long given way to dormancy, leaving the yard
weed strewn and tired – more like a motley field than a
decent lawn. Only the spreading Thyme has remained
deep green and thriving, slowly reaching out across the
expanse of hillside in the back with new clones of new
growth.

Today, in the thin spots where only the Chickweed and
Purslane seem able to survive, there is a new covering of
lime green as the crab shoots upward. Soon, the lawn will
appear healthy again, as a patchwork of colors of summer
growth that will continue until the coming chill of
September.

August 2

The Wren babies are insistent in the box out front, as the
parents spend the day continually flying to and from the
nearby woods and garden in search of food for them. In
the afternoon we sat on the large granite stone that hearths
the front door and watched as mother flew to clump of
Phlox in the knot garden. She flits among the stems and
disappeared briefly into the deep recess of the Coreopsis,
before emerging with a large lime green Katydid between
her beaks. From here she flew upward to a hanging branch

of one of the oaks out front, perching on a small twig to regard our presence.

As we remained still, she descended directly to the old box and alighted on the dilapidated roof. This set off the musical calls of the babies within, which became more frantic as she hopped from the peak to the small hole in front. A moment later there was silence, as mother emerged from the box with empty beak and flew directly to the inner branches of the Viburnum nearby. She rhythmically scraped the sides of her beak on a small twig, paused to regard her surroundings, then took flight to the woods beyond, likely in search of something more.

In her absence we walked quietly to the silent box. I reached down and gently scratched the roof, setting off the young ones within, though they silenced quickly when our shadow passed before the open hole of the front.

August 3

Darkness lingers in the early morning now, more like an April dawn than the luxury we enjoyed only two months ago. Wasn't it just yesterday that the bird call began at 4:30 in the morning to usher in the grey veil of the summer dawn? Somehow the summer days have passed us by too quickly, and in no time we will feel the first chill of the change that is coming soon enough.

For now the morning remains August warm, and the sultry heat of last evening collected as a heavy dew on every surface in the building light of today. Even the roof moistened through the night so much that the break of sunlight above the lower woods caused vapors of steam to rise as the shingles began to dry. Seen from the driveway, the evaporation above the peak sent tendrils of clouds into the air, backlit from the daylight in shimmery patterns that looked like smoke.

So too the steam lifted from my coffee cup as it rested on the arm of the Adirondack chair on the porch, while I sat blissfully enjoying the passing of another summer morning of warmth and light.

August 4

The roadside has been full of the grasses, weeds and wildflowers of the season since the first shoots emerged last April. We've witnessed the slow succession from the lime greens of the Canada Mayflower blades and the colored mosaic of Orange Hawkweed and yellow Buttercup to the tall heads of the Fox grass and deep greens of the Poison Ivy that predominate in early August. So too the Ragweed has come into its own, now sending up the small candles that will soon enough release their pollen and plague the allergy sufferers anew.

In the afternoon we heard the sound of a large machine coming down the road, moving slowly and making a racket. Before it came into view, the breeze carried the distinctive scent of plants that had been thrashed; their volatiles released to the wind as acrid indicators of injury.

The tractor followed slowly, bearing a single outrigger arm that arched up and over to position the rolling thrasher close to the ground, its spinning drum mostly hidden by the protective shield that served to keep flying debris from the operator and beyond. What a destructive thing to witness, albeit efficient in its razing of the summer's growth, leaving the roadside raped of aesthetic life.

How different this from what was done years ago, when workers would walk down the road, each on a side of the street and sweeping large scythes to cut the foliage and clear the edge. How gentle it must have been to watch the rhythmic movement and see the newly cut grass, folding over upon itself and sparing the growth underneath to continue unmolested.

August 5

Coming up Maple Street from the center of town, the road crests the hill and begins to descend a quarter mile until it ends at Grove, which travels loosely either north or south depending where you need to go. North leads past the old Van Dyke house on the corner (though few remain who know it as such) then downhill toward lower Grove and the old mills far below. South skirts the fallow fields to the east. At the intersection here sits a large old farm house, painted white with black shutters and a commanding porch that wraps around to afford beautiful views of the small valley that descends beyond and rises again in the distance as Asnebumskit summit.

Approaching from Maple, the sun crested the far hills at roughly 5:40 as a golden ball of late summer heat, perfectly in line with the straight path of the road like some celestial clock to mark this very day. The farmhouse below was back lit, casting reaching shadows of the chimneys far onto the pavement.

August 6

Almost any field or roadside in town still shows healthy clusters of Queen Anne's Lace. They seem to thrive in the drought this summer has provided, opening new mosaics with each day, even as the early blossoms of mid July have long dropped their tiny white petals. Theirs will be the first to close as the autumn chill arrives, making the small bird's nest of clustered seed heads that will dot the fields when the light snows appear and stay sere well into the depths of winter's hold.

It is impossible not to marvel at their design and be in awe of the potential that resides within each cluster. Here by the road there is a group of eight different laces. Examining one, I count 30 stems arising from the central core, each bearing a small composite of white flowers that total approximately 50. At 30 times 50, there are nearly 1500 blossoms on each Queen Anne's Lace.

There are eight different composites here by the road, which means 12,000 small flowers in this rather typical group. Across the open field, there are hundreds if not thousands of such groups, each carrying the legacy of last year's success and bearing the promise of tomorrow's succession if conditions favor.

August 7

Sometimes in the early evening, when the air is still, we hear the distant call of the loons down on Pine Hill reservoir. There is an old two-track road that begins where Pond Street makes an elbow away from the lily-covered surface of the waters of Streeter. The road climbs up and over the higher ground and descends roughly to the valley where the waters of Pine Hill reservoir come out through the old sluice. Next to the sluice is a long neglected asphalt road that follows the valley upward for a mile, climbing through old pine woods that see little human traffic, despite the impressive structures of the long sluice and granite gate houses that peek in and out of the ascending view.

The climb culminates at a sharp turn, exiting the woods abruptly and revealing the expanse of the Pine Hill dam stretching several hundred feet across and nearly eighty feet tall, holding back the waters of the reservoir that are hidden on the other side of the massive concrete. It is a stunning piece of engineering, constructed nearly 100 years ago and though its presence is artificial in the midst of this verdant valley, there is an abandoned feel to this place that seems to accept the blending of the fertile growth and the human design.

The road ends at the near summit of the dam but continues across as a path, affording a spectacular view of the expanse of Pine Hill on one side and the deep valley below on the other. Here sometimes the loons congregate in the still waters held in check, in the solace of this place where few people come to visit.

August 8

This morning, after nearly two weeks of constant goings and comings to the box by the parents, one of the young Wrens fledged to the nearby knot garden. It flew rather tentatively the short distance across the driveway and descended awkwardly to the small copse of Echinacea that edge the near corner. It rested there for several minutes and made harsh chirping sounds that plainly revealed both its presence and alarm. The parents were nowhere to be found, which was such a change from their frequent monitoring of the box.

We suspect the parents have simply given up. They've done their job to Herculean degrees, flying to and from the woods day and night in search of food and cleaning the brood's wastes several times each day. As the days progressed, they faced the insistent cries of the babies, who would quiet gently as the parents departed and cry in anticipation upon their return. No two parents were so devoted.

Now at least one is loose upon the world, making guttural chirps from the security of the garden. I walked slowly to its hiding place and pressed my face only a few inches away. The diminutive thing regarded me stoically with tiny coal-black eyes that blinked quickly and beak that opened slightly in response. Its tail feathers looked still undeveloped and its legs wobbled slightly when the breeze lifted to catch the upright stalks of the flowers in which it tentatively perched.

A moment more and it flew away in a sharp burst, flapping its wings unsteadily across the yard and to the base of the burning bush, where it sat beneath and chirped.

August 9

Our two old red oaks near the road have been slowly dropping acorns for the past week. It's a bit early for this to happen, though the summer drought has hastened the fading of all sorts of things around the landscape.

It's a curious thing why they are released. What advantage must there be in letting go of so small a thing before its proper time; the acorns that fall are yet green and small beneath the braided cap which itself is still developing. They are too new even to tempt the grey squirrels who spend the majority of their time beneath the bird feeders.

So too the maples are releasing pairs of keys, as the road is littered in places where the brisk winds of the afternoon pull them one by one downward. They fall with no design nor grace, prematurely before their readiness, which will be marked in several weeks by the whirling descent of hundreds of them, singly in small clusters spurred on by the timely urge.

Most everything bears the effect of late summer's fatigue, made more so by a season unusually warm and dry. The deep greens of early June have slowly shifted. Some remain, though there are tired shades of yellow within and not the lime blend of new growth that is waiting to develop.

August 10

The skies are now still dark at 4:30 in the morning, and it's hard to believe only two months ago at the same time the sun was preparing to rise on the eastern horizon. The birdsong that greeted us in early June has been replaced by the background din of crickets, which is nevertheless a pleasant sound to experience through the night.

The constellation Perseus takes prominence among the backdrop of other stars in the northeast skies this month, as the annual Perseid meteor shower has begun today. They should last several days, with the apex of activity to occur tomorrow evening, and this year is predicted to be especially magnificent. Evidently, Jupiter's celestial location in the solar system is nicely aligned with the passage of the comet Swift-Tuttle so that its massive gravitational pull is deflecting the comet's tail slightly more in Earth's path. Hence the more spectacular show, we are told.

I went out on the back porch at 4:30 and stood in the darkness, surrounded by the white noise of August insects and the occasional strange crunching from somewhere deep in the lower woods. A thin cover of clouds blanketed the skies, blotting the stars entirely and obscuring any view of the wonder above.

August 11

Resting in sharp contrast against the dark brown garage door was a brilliant green walking stick. Though I suspect they are more frequent this time of year, we rarely see them, and this singular specimen seemed intent on displaying itself. It must have been five inches long from indiscriminate head to the tips of (what I could discern) were its back legs.

Curious where they reside? Or how they find one another and reproduce? With moths and butterflies there are pheromone signals. Various insects like beetles, crickets, grasshoppers and the like employ clicks, rasps and other such calls. How does a walking stick attract a mate, and where does it lay eggs? What does it eat? What preys upon it? (What could possibly find a walking stick worth the effort?).

August 12

In the ditch valleys along Marshall Road, up along the higher stretch past Hemlock and on the east side of the street, where the canopy is thick enough through the day that there is mostly shade and moisture, the Jewelweed is thriving here. So too the first signs of the Thin, White-toothed Asters mixed within, giving the dark green surrounding foliage splashes of white and orange.

Aster derives from "star," and it's coincidence this year that these white-toothed versions are appearing at the same time the "falling stars" of the Perseids are at their apex. (The sky was clear enough at 4:30 this morning, and there were nearly a dozen meteor streaks across the northeastern sky). The drought continues to reveal its effect; so many things like the coming of the asters are progressing sooner than normal.

White-toothed asters are one thing. They do typically arrive before the coming of the autumn asters, and soon enough they will pepper the roadsides just like the garlic mustard of early June. However, we had a surprise this afternoon while walking the dogs up Grove past the open field of the college. There, by the side of the road where there is an access point for the tractor to enter the nearby field, a single purple flash of color sat atop a slender stalk. A New England Aster has opened, revealing its light lavender petals and yellow center.

Too soon I thought, and this is true. These flowers shouldn't be here until early September, as they usher in the changing seasons. It is unsettling to see this purple

132

here now, when August heat reigns and the chill of autumn is by no means around the corner.

August 13

The tomatoes we seeded last March are the most productive we've had in years, despite what has been a summer of little moisture. It seems long ago when we transplanted the small seedlings into the newly turned soil of the boxes and placed plastic cups over them in the late April evenings when the threat of frost remained very real. Our early planting must have paid well, for the roots evidently went deep enough to access some water throughout arid June and July.

Now we are overrun with the bounty, delighting daily in varieties that ripen for eating (or giving away, as we have too many to use ourselves). In the far corner grow the cherries on an indeterminate plant, their branches spreading well across the stonewall and draping around the base of the other plants that have been tied to posts. Only the cherry plant shows signs of yellowing and blight, even while its fruit is in the apex of maturity. We pick dozens every day.

The Yellow Toms are fat and sweet, as if each has captured both the color and flavor of the summer sunshine. They are best sliced thin and placed over a layer of cheese on toast, topped with a leaf of fresh basil taken from the clay pot that rests on the near porch. The smaller Reds concentrate the flavor, giving color and texture and taste to the summer salads.

Finally, the Galapagos have matured to the point of readiness. Our neighbor Sandy gave us seeds from this curious heirloom several years ago, and we've kept the line going since by growing and eating the majority and selecting a few samples to ferment the seeds when autumn arrives. Galapagos is a tomatillo and produces hundreds of small pendants of paper lanterns that turn from lime green to light brown when they are ready for harvest. Within resides the dark yellow fruit that tastes curiously of pineapple and tomato mixed as one.

August 14

The humidity climbed through the afternoon, making the air so thick that the distant vista of Wachusett Mountain all but vanished in a haze. Without any breeze to provide relief, the atmosphere became oppressive, and we contented ourselves to the shade of the side yard and sat listlessly waiting for the sun to arch lower below the spruce line across the road.

By evening storm clouds had blossomed, first as isolated aggregates of darkly shaded patterns that moved slowly, then growing into towering things that gathered strength. The idle wind of earlier picked up suddenly, coming across the fields and the road, picking up the early-fallen leaves and setting them in a dervish whirl toward the house.

Then the distant rows of corn vanished one by one as the line of rain moved steadily toward us, preceded by a white noise of falling deluge and wind until the tempest was upon us. Rain! Violent rain that hit the house and spilled quickly off the roof as torrents of water that formed puddles and then small ponds that had nowhere to go.

A crash of lightning split the dark sky, arching sideways across the horizon to the north and brightening the yard for a split second so that the oak trunks out front stood in sharp relief. The thunder rolled as the wind gathered speed, ushering in the change of air so desperately needed.

August 15

No sooner had I passed by the side of the house and descended the small hill to the backyard did the lawnmower begin sputtering and hesitating. We made it to the middle of the lawn (which is really a glorified field of weeds, thyme and occasional patches of grasses) before the mower gave out, evidently running out of gas. I proceeded to walk around the other side of the house toward the side where the bird feeders flank the porch and sunroom and noticed immediately that the feeder poles were bent over nearly to the ground. They were perfectly fine not five minutes ago when I took the mower out of the barn.

As I passed by, movement caught my eye from within the former access road that borders the property, separated from the side yard by a little berm of sapling trees and the large maple that shades the house. The road has been fallow for many years, having since been taken over by the slow succession of small bushes and briars, with the thin remnant of a "trail" where the high spot of the two-track descends toward Asnebumskit pond below.

Here a dark shape moved slowly, rusted among the briars and paused to regard my passage. The bear was young and healthy looking and completely unafraid of my surprised expression. It regarded me stoically with coal black eyes, sat on its haunches to scratch some bothersome pest, and waited patiently for me to move onward.

August 16

A pop-up shower passed by this afternoon, the kind where the puffy white clouds aggregate in the midday heat and form towering thunderheads that flatten somewhere way above in the troposphere. Only summer can make such wonders of contrast – the brilliant white edges of far away clouds against the cerulean blue of the sky. They tower above, billowing outward and ever higher until they reach some limit where nothing more can ascend.

The rain came briefly yet with force, like a simple squeeze of some cloud to release its pent up moisture, putting down a tenth of an inch quickly before giving way once again to the sunshine.

Rivulets of water made their way to the low spots in the driveway, while the remainder steamed away with the return of the sun. Within minutes, several yellow finches descended to the nearest pool, arranging themselves along the edges and taking turns drinking and bathing in temporary relief.

August 17

Rain came hard last night, followed by clearing that made the sunrise reflect off the water that still glistened on every surface. The humidity of the ground steamed in the building daylight, making a strange fog-like layer that ended about 6 feet high.

The water over the spillway at Moore State Park was flowing quickly on account of the deluge, and there was a fair roar of it as the volume made its way down the cascades past the old mill site.

The mill pond is particularly pretty now, with lily pads thriving and Joe Pye Weed and goldenrod thrust up on the near shore line. I suspect the pool was more stagnant yesterday owing to the drought, but the overnight rain took care of that.

The sandy path from the mill into the woods was still damp, and a few low spots had small puddles waiting to soak into the ground. Where the trail descended into the pine woods, as it formed a single track, the fallen pine needles were arranged in horizontal bands roughly 3 feet apart, evidence of an effluvial flow down the path making eddies of floating debris.

August 18

As the sunlight angles low in the afternoon and comes through the open spaces between the dark trunks of the spruce line across the road, it now casts the berm grasses and flowers directly for several minutes before dropping lower on the horizon. Only now, as we move slowly toward the coming of autumn and we notice the shifting arc of the sun further each day to the south do certain patches of ground earn their share of the light.

On the berm the Lunaria pods have dried and turned light brown. Each is composed of three layers; an outer skin covers each side of the translucent seed membrane within. Most still cling to all three, and they look slightly soiled in the direct light. Some have begun to lose their outer shells, leaving only the thin membrane where the flattened seeds used to be and flashing brilliantly when the wind catches their evanescent form.

August 19

According to the weatherman, the new version of the Farmer's Almanac has been released today. We'll get around to picking up a copy in due time, looking forward to the flotsam and jetsam of useful information it contains. The early prediction for New England's upcoming winter is dire, or as the Almanac supposedly indicates a "return to an old-fashioned New England winter."

Given that the Almanac tends to be accurate fifty percent of the time, we'd be wise to pay attention to its forecasting, not that there's much to be done at this point. Frankly, at this juncture of the hot summer, the thought of a little cold ushering in from out Alberta way sounds fairly good. We could use some relief.

Last spring we had a crew come to cut down a rather large maple that arched up an over toward the north side of the house. This was a big tree and certainly something more suited to a professional. They shinnied up the trunk with ropes and spikes and slowly sectioned it; we watched as long sections would tumble downward and hit the ground with an alarming thud. When complete, they cut each portion of trunk into lengths of roughly twenty inches, and we spent a couple hours rolling these from the former site of the tree down to the barn near the lower woods. Here we loosely arranged them on long boards, putting the larger sections of trunk on the bottom and working our way upward in pyramid fashion with the small portions on the top. In all there must have been a hundred pieces of trunk and somewhere in the neighborhood of several tons of hardwood.

A month ago we started hand splitting the portions, using one of the large sections as a base and placing each log to be split upon it. This was honest work. The wood was still fairly wet, and the summer heat didn't aid in fracturing the pieces. Still, we worked our way through most during the course of a few weeks, and there is now a couple cords of good maple drying by the side of the barn, waiting for the winter that will be here soon enough.

August 20

High overhead two young red tailed hawks trace looping
circles in the blue sky. Their wings catch rising thermals
from the fields below, allowing them to remain suspended
as they pirouette around one another, calling occasionally
in a high pitched scream.

Once or twice a crow will take flight from the upper
reaches of the spruce trees and give chase, rising upward
quickly to join the hawks. They arch downward easily,
gaining speed and turning tightly where the crow can't
maneuver. It gives up and returns to the spruce as the
hawks ascend gently on the rising air.

They likely hunt for mice in the fields, and it is remarkable
they can spot furtive movements from so far away.
Perhaps the task is easier this year; Fred reports a boon of
mice in the fields on account of the mild winter and the
relative lack of water this summer. They seek the shelter of
the plastic, where any moisture from the recent rains
remains trapped beneath, and there is cover from the
direct sun above.

August 21

An adult cicada lay dead at the end of the driveway,
having no evidence of injury. It is if it simply tired and lay
down to die peacefully. I am surprised we don't see more
of them as such, for their afternoon calls are strident,
surely requiring exhaustion to produce. We hear them
now in earnest, beginning loudly enough as a buzzing call,
then rising in both volume and pitch, often being joined in
concert by a neighboring cicada. This lasts as long as a
minute, until abruptly the calls cease, leaving a stillness
that gives the impression that the insects are recharging.

This adult was large, perhaps the size of my thumb, with a whitish underbelly and dorsal surface that was a mottled green and brown. This camouflage explains so well that we often hear them if ever see them perched on the trees.

Its wings were striking, simply beautiful, folded backward to rest against its body, with deep venous lines that divided the cellulose-looking material of the wing proper. It reminded me of a stained glass window, absent of color yet no less intricate, as if by some design.

Notes:
Indian Pipe in bloom.

August 22

The old farm truck turned slowly from the driveway up the road and headed up Grove toward Streeter, likely making way to the fields over at Echo. Several boys were in the bed as Fred drove cautiously away; two stood upright and held on to the top of the cab for balance while two others sat idly on the lowered tailgate, letting their dust-covered pant legs dangle beneath.

The corn is in full measure now after coming late from the July drought. It is all that they can do across the road to keep up with demand, and hence we see the truck making several trips each day to the fields and back. They'll be gone an hour or so, then return with a dozen bushels or so of freshly picked corn.

Fred was one of those boys over twenty years ago, as was his father well before. Now he is the mentor of the younger hands, and he seems content to work alongside them in the summer heat. How many boys and girls through the years have worked the harvest in this farm? Hundreds surely. They profit from the role model of strong work ethos and honest labor that this family provides, sharing in the camaraderie of long days and tiring work.

August 23

The morning glory continues to thrive, twining around the split rail fence that forms the border of the front dooryard where we sometimes sit among the holly bushes and the phlox. It began as a fragile thing, just two small leaves that Sarah surrounded with a ring of wire mesh to keep the chipmunks at bay. Now it stands nearly four feet tall and covered with brilliant leaves and arching stems that reach outward for something on which to purchase new growth.

Within are a dozen deep purple blossoms, fluting outward richly as the morning glories do. They open fully with daybreak to reveal their deep interior and last through the late afternoon, though by noon they show slight signs of wilt. Some have dribbles of yellow pollen on the lower protruding petal, where some visitor withdrew in haste and left the accidental discard.

Years ago we owned an old Edison Cylinder Machine, made sometime around 1905. With it were two horns, the standard black one that was relatively small and easy to maneuver, and the large deep blue bell that had hand painted copies of lightly colored morning glory flowers inside the flute. This horn was called the Morning Glory, and it required a metal stand to support it from a small ring that was attached at its neck. When connected, the tinny music would play loudly across the room.

Our living version in the garden is a patient thing. It sends tendrils of new stems in all directions, and some gain a tenuous hold on another growing plant or new part of the rail, and in two days time it has wrapped itself around for support and put forth new leaves in full display.

141

August 24

The wind shifted last evening and ushered in cool air from the northwest. For so long we've become used to the sultry feel of night and the difficulty in falling asleep on top of the covers with only the box fan in the window to provide any measure of relief. The breeze picked up after nine o'clock and almost instantly the air within the house was cleansed by the inrush of its cool deliverance. Even the dogs seemed to rejoice, putting their noses in the air and sniffing what seemed to be the first signs of an approaching autumn.

By morning it was in the low fifties outside and with heavy dew on every surface, making a slight fog above the grass in the back yard that was backlit by the now later rising sunshine. After the lethargy of summer's maturity, this felt refreshing in both body and spirit, and we took the simple pleasure of merely sitting on the porch in the warming sun of the cool morning.

Changes are ahead. The succession of the seasons is not and ebb and flow but rather a slow progression from one to the next, sometimes delayed and sometimes not, but assuredly so. The transitions have been happening since summer's apex, though they were small things. Now they are too numerous to overlook, and we rejoice in the passing from one phase to the next.

Overhead the first Canada Geese flew from out of the north, thirteen of them in a near perfect "V" arcing across the tops of the trees of the lower woods and toward the open fields across the road. They are another harbinger that speaks of change ahead, perhaps tomorrow or the next day.

August 25

There in the middle of the road lay a single sugar maple leaf having fallen overnight from an overhanging branch. It stood out, because its color was a mixture of deep reds, blazing yellows and still dark greens, as if this single specimen contained the transition from one season to the next all in itself. The branch belonged to a large tree, set back from the road but old enough that several long arms reached outward across Grove, making a slight canopy by joining with neighbor spruce and oak limbs from the west side. Curiously, only the leaves on one particular branch showed this early sign of change; the rest of the tree remained content within the bounds of late summer production.

We've grown used to the uniformity of the deep greens of summer, following our wonder of so many varied shades when spring witnessed the return of new life and production. Look now at the maples. Recall not too long ago how light green the new leaves appeared? So too the willows and oaks, ash and elm. The woods were a patchwork of differing hues of chlorophyll that slowly developed and concentrated as the months progressed. As growth gave way to maturity, and May give way to July, so did the canopy become more uniform in its transition to darker greens.

Now things are starting to change. Chlorophyll is beginning to degrade. Perhaps it was the cooler night or the shortened daylight. Or perhaps something else triggered this one branch to accept the change that is coming. Its leaves show reds and yellows above, much like this fallen sample below. No longer are these brilliant hues bound to serve in production but rather cast askew, to be absorbed or reflected by something else, enjoyed by our senses as we pass beneath.

August 26

The houses near the summit of Asnebumskit Road are set well back from the street, and the roadside buffer is large, so that driveways interrupt small fields of tall grasses and late summer (or early autumn) wildflowers. Here the Goldenrod grows tall and bends slightly to the earth with the weight of its yellowy blossoms on the end of the stalks. They mix well with the splashes of purple from thistles and spotted knapweed that hide among the tall grasses now gone from deep green to more yellow and brown.

Here and there tall Mulleins rise above the din, their candles now largely sere brown. They resemble saguaro cacti, particularly when straggler yellow blossoms still adorn the tips of one or more of their arms, and with some imagination the moths that occasionally flit about the stalk become Cactus Wrens intent on securing a home.

Jewelweed still thrives a little farther down the road where the woods comes closer to the street edge and there is more shade from the afternoon heat.

August 27

Cool air filtered in through the bedroom window last evening, making sleep far more comfortable then it's been in several weeks. For once we didn't need to use the fan, which was especially welcome since it blocks the ambient sounds of the outdoors.

The crickets and grasshoppers called through the night, making a background white noise more soothing than anything imaginable apart perhaps from the spring peepers and wood frogs that herald the return of spring

144

life in the woods below. The sounds now are of lassitude rather than emergence, which is preferable really for sleeping.

The reverie was interrupted by the paired calls of two barred owls from somewhere far off. They seemed intent on contesting with one another for some territorial prize. A closer one would gently cry out "who cooks for you," and several seconds would pass with only the background noise as response. Then, from further still, would come the reply. A back and forth ensued for over an hour, until one or both became satisfied that they were the winner of some undeclared event.

From deep within the trees, a twig snapped, and there was rustling of movement. Something stirred along the access road down in the border woods near the barn. Perhaps a deer come up from Asnebumskit, following the old trail up toward the front where the apple trees have released their bounty to the ground.

August 28

Several chickens were loose upon the road this morning at the intersection of Grove and Maple, escapees from the small pen located in the back yard of the older white house on the corner. Two (what looked like) Bantam hens and one Rhode Island Red wandered about the middle of the road while cars navigated the mayhem. The drivers were rubbernecking as much as were the poultry.

All the while, a lone rooster still in the yard crowed in protest, though its call was a pathetic whistle groan, something similar to the old Klaxon horns common in the prewar cars of the thirties.

We're used to seeing all manner of livestock running with abandon from the Cheney place down the road. Our favorite are the Guinea Hens, who tend to walk carefree across the street and stop to look at oncoming cars with indignant repose. Lean out the window to shoo them away, and they'll squawk incessantly at you in their manner. Sarah wants several of these for our yard to add character. My contribution to the household only allows so much.

Guinea Fowl are good for foraging ticks and other insects, which would be a boon under normal circumstances; this year the drought has thankfully kept the ticks at bay, though likely the nymphs will be plentiful enough come October. Maybe we should get a hen or two.

August 29

Pestiferous insects of all kinds have been relatively low this year on account of the prolonged moisture. I'm certain that there's been an imbalance in the ecological food web somehow, and though I have distal concern for the food supply of the bats and birds who typically prey upon the mosquitoes, deer flies and ticks, it's difficult not to be selfishly happy that their numbers have been low this summer.

The situation opens new possibilities for unmolested excursions. For example, it's simply a delight to hike the Asnebumskit trails without worry. Surprising moreover is that the trails are still relatively open, given that so few people know enough to venture onto these wonderful paths.

A new connecting trail was recently completed from midway on South Road, and it winds it way loosely westward upslope, across the ubiquitous rocks and roots so typical of New England trails, until it intersects one of the looping paths that ascends to the summit near the radio station.

Even during the most hot and humid days, the woods here are thick enough to provide welcome shade and relief; the predominant colors are muted greens and browns this month, made soft by the understory of small bushes such as mountain laurel which grows nearly everywhere. In another month, this forest will begin to come alive with the vibrancy of approaching autumn, as the deep greens give way to shades of filtered red, orange and yellow from above.

August 30

The shelves on the farm store are becoming filled with local apples; early word is that the crop is small on account of the drought, though the sugars are concentrated. Right now, there are bins of Macintosh, Pink Lady, xx, xx and of course the Granny Smith. These local versions are nowhere near the perfection of the grocery product down the road, where engineering and selection have produced large and nearly unblemished specimens that are covered in wax and appear ideal. They taste terrible by comparison and are bland and rather mealy.

Some will turn up their noses at the local crop. The apples are a mosaic of colors and shapes, and some have slight spots of early blight or bruising. But those who know better don't mind. Bite into one of these Pink Ladies and the flavor encapsulates early autumn, crisp and sweet.

It's too warm yet to be thinking about the next progression, which is cider, but soon enough the chill will settle. The local orchards surely are selecting crop for pressing, which means that we will start seeing the half gallon and gallon jugs of cider on the shelf next to the apples themselves. There is succession here as there has been in the fields. The jugs will sit in the very spot where not long ago the strawberries and blueberry cartons were placed. And near the cider and the apples, bins of yellow and acorn squash will arrive within a week or two. Then the pumpkins, and we are in full swing. Who remembers summer now, when autumn has as many things or more to offer?

August 31

A slight chill came last night on the heels of a shift in the wind that brought dry air down from the north. August is letting go to make way for a transitional month. Only two nights ago, with temperatures still well into the seventies, the crickets called rapidly to one another in their strident way. Last evening they became far more sluggish after the front had passed. From here onward their cadence will decrease as the slow chill of the coming autumn presses in.

In August we felt the lassitude of the dog days in full measure. We watched the late summer weeds creep ever closer to the edges of the yard and roadside, changing what was once the cultivated look of early summer into maturity (or tiredness) of the succession of the season. September will bring refreshing change on cool winds and brilliant colors, blowing the humidity that has so affected our energy to do much more than lethargically observe.

It seems fitting that the Phlox have begun to pop open today. In the area of the front dooryard and among the edges of the wooden gate next to the driveway, we've grown both pink and white phlox each year, allowing them simply to self seed and spread as the years have passed. This afternoon, while many of the plants still have vibrant blossoms and provide nectar enough for the bees

148

and hummingbirds that remain, there are also dozens of mature pods on each plant. Their petals fell away two weeks ago, and the ovaries inside have hardened and grown to small sized balls, no bigger than a couple millimeters. These turned light brown as they seasoned through August, and now they've begun to pop open in the heat of the afternoon sun. When the pressure within bursts to release the small black seeds, they make rather loud "snaps," throwing them asunder to the ground that one might by chance grow into next spring's plant.

September

September 1

It is still dark at 5:00 in the morning, and there is no
indication of the daybreak yet to arrive. At this time two
months ago, the sun was rising on the eastern horizon,
casting the fields in the golden light that comes with the
special mixture of July air that is laced with humidity and
particles from the fertile release of pollen. Now those days
of production and longevity are behind us, and the air
brings promise of the turning of the season. How can we
not look forward to what lies waiting with this new
month?

An old friend is back above the horizon in the eastern sky.
It never really left, of course, but our changing inclination
that now affords us the darkness in the morning also
reveals its magnificence in full measure. The constellation
Orion is brilliant against the inky black of the predawn,
visible through a gap in the forest where the margin of sky
above the horizon is in view. So too is the dog star Sirius,
twinkling incandescently in many colors just below and
close to the tree tops. It blazes with kaleidoscopic change,
as its light scatters through the low atmosphere to reach
our eyes just so.

They will climb ever higher each morning and become
crisper and less surreal as the autumn air dries while the
winter cold approaches.

September 2

By mid afternoon, the sun had warmed the large, table-
shaped stone that sits before the foundation of the house in
front of the old wooden door. We sat there for an hour and
watched the trickle of cars make their way past down the
hill toward Robinsons. The greenhouse is busy once again

151

now that the mums and asters are in season. It's been since early May that I paid a visit to see the growing plants. They were filled with pansies and geraniums, coleus and herbs, and we took pleasure in seeing the color of the spring plants well before our own garden had shown much signs of renewal. Now it is getting closer to the end of the season, and it is bittersweet to see the mums. The asters are another thing; there have been so many increasing along the roadsides and in the fields that we've been allowed to gradually see them as the coming of autumn.

A yellow school bus passed the house, and it slowed somewhere several houses down out of sight. Then followed the playful noise of the children as they rushed up the driveway toward waiting dooryards, filled with the excitement of school that has only been in session a few days. This too will wane as the things progress. We looked to one another wistfully as the sound of the bus continued onward; our own son has now grown, and we long a little for the afternoons when he would rush up to the house eager to share his day.

September 3

A thin crescent moon rested a little over a hand width above the western horizon this evening, trailing the sunset by a half hour or so and reflecting clearly against the deep purple sky. This seems like the first such moon we've seen in several months, as the air is free of the humidity of summer and the familiar objects in the sky take on a definition that comes with the change. Ending soon are the dreamy skies we knew through August, when the haze softened the atmosphere and enveloped us in the laziness of summer's comfort.

152

No longer do we ease into the evening as before but rather become revived by the building chill that arrives in partner with the change in the season and the setting of the sun that is earlier each night. This waxing crescent will bear witness to this change, growing larger through the next ten days until it reaches the apex of brilliance and shines in full upon the landscape that is beginning to wane.

September 4

Our catbirds returned several days ago from their summer retreat, and now they content themselves near the side yard among the arbor vitae. We are a transient home this time of year, and they will likely remain for a few weeks before continuing onward. For now, it's pleasant to hear them once again and watch their antics around the feeder and the bath. Of the pair, one (it is difficult to distinguish him from her) is more willing to visit the basin. It lands softly on the pebbled edge and splashes itself freely in the afternoon, while its mate waits patiently from within the woods edge.

Curiously the towhees have remained in residence since April, rather than taking to the upper elevation of the mountains to the north. Their signature "rustle rustle" reveals their foraging among the sere deadfall leaves in the berm that have yet to fully decompose from nearly a year ago.

September 5

The town has yet to mow the roadsides again, and we benefit in seeing the changes to the tall grasses that predominate among the asters that add splashes of color. Fox and Timothy grass have grown tall, and their laden heads bend over from the weight, adding added mass that accentuates their tendency to sway in even the most gentle breeze. Their stems have changed to golden brown, so altered from the deep greens of only a few weeks ago, though the transition was too gradual to notice.

Within thrive patches of Quake, whose tiny heads burst in fractured patterns like fireworks caught in mid explosion. Where the Timothy and Fox add contrasts of moving lines, groupings of Quake only appear to soften the roadside, making the lichen-covered rocks of the stone walls less contrasting amid the other foliage that has overgrown since mid July.

The change is slow to come, which is typical of September. How unlike the pace of May, when the landscape was infused with the rush of new life and explosive growth. Spring is exhaustive this way, though we don't mind the frenetic return of shoot and leaf, color and smell. Summer's maturity has given way to a more stately cadence, when the lassitude of last month has also released its grip but only to be replaced by a slow acceptance of the graceful decline before the quiet sets in again.

September 6

There were six field hands among the rows of peppers that border Anna Maria's hillside. Each was bent over in the hot sun of the afternoon and moving slowly from one plant to the next, searching within the deep green foliage for the prized fruit made ready from the maturity of summer. From the vantage of the road, there doesn't appear to be any rhyme for the pattern of colors that pendant beneath the canopy of leaves. There are deep reds, yellows, greens and mosaics, and of course there is variety in the sizes and shapes. Each worker pulls behind a worn bushel basket and dutifully places their collected prize within. When full, the bushel is carried to the end of the row where Fred has left the faded truck with the gate open, and the basket is deposited in the bed.

These are the same fields where not too long ago we helped transplant the small seedlings that were destined to offer what has been harvested today. How diminutive each plant appeared, and vulnerable too, plucked from the comfort of the plastic tray that housed its growing cell and displaying the twisted maze of its bound roots as we lifted each downward to the waiting hole in the plastic row. From one to the next, we progressed in succession, working the row until hundreds of small plants rested two by two, erect and vulnerable in the building heat of the late spring.

September 7

The front yard is littered with acorns from the two large red oaks, and our greys are more preoccupied with gathering now, in contrast to last week when they appeared intent on each other. It must have been a late mating period, or perhaps the desultory conditions simply prompted such activity versus the will to collect! The male suitor would chase the female from beneath the feeder toward the big maple, and she would ascend slowly in a twisting spiral around the trunk, keeping just far enough so the trailing male would stay playfully out of reach. Higher up, she'd emerge from behind onto one of the larger branches and quickly flick her tail, from which the light grey edges of fur among the mass of fluffy brown made reflective signals of who knows? Encouragement? Rejection? He'd trail behind, stopping furtively and bobbing his head slightly before walking slowly on approach.

Now there is no playful exchange. There is work to be done, initiated by some internal drive or celestial signal, and they make forays to the front yard from the woods to collect acorns for storage in granaries located where? Above likely, in the forest high where leafed nests remain hidden among the green foliage of this year's growth.

There are three out front now. They move among the fallen nuts, inspecting each, sometimes carrying one for a short distance before discarding it for another. They work alone, in bounding motion that looks playful enough.

September 8

They come slowly from the lower hollows, out of the wetlands from which they emerged, seeking the higher ground of forest cover and leaf bed in which to grow and mature before searching anew for another wetland to reproduce. These are the juveniles of the Eastern Newts, and early autumn is the pinnacle of their migration. Look closely along the roadways or the walking paths. You'll see them as small, bright orange things, almost too insignificant and artificial looking to consider as something alive. They are called the Red Eft, and they are wondrous to observe.

There must be hundreds that emerge, these iridescently orange little amphibians, with skin that is almost translucent apart from the darker spots that pepper its dorsal side. They walk slowly, almost imperceptibly and with a rather ungainly gate as they cross the road to some final destination. How they navigate and to what end are mysterious, much in the same way that any migratory animal which has never made such a trip before must somehow listen to the internal call of innate navigation. Across the road to where? "There is a parking lot where you are going," I sometimes whisper aloud to one that seems intent on heading the wrong way.

Inevitably so many will perish, destined as some Darwinian casualty of random chance, where sheer numbers of so many progeny serve to offset the loss of those who do not survive. This is the rule rather than the exception. The oak produces thousands of acorns as does the golden rod create as many or more seeds for the wind. So few survive to reproduce, their numbers cut back in the struggle. So too the Red Efts, whose tiny forms sadly perish at the fate of walkers, wheels or predators. Indeed some survive, of course, as we have Red Efts to begin, having emerged from the domain of their hatching, from parents who survived to continue the cycle.

September 9

The screeching began at precisely 3:30 this morning, waking us out of a deep sleep with such alacrity that we jumped upright in bed, just the way it is described in stories or shown in the movies. There was a high-pitched snarling and screaming from somewhere out in the back yard, punctuated with the noise of a tree branch thrashing about.

I grabbed a flashlight and made way to the sunroom door, admittedly a little nervous about the cacophony. It's difficult to behave rationally at that hour of the day, which is my way of justifying that my imagination conjured all manner of devil creatures plotting to descend up the house.

I opened the sliding door and stepped gingerly out onto the porch, as the racket continued only a couple dozen yards away and from twenty feet up inside the canopy of an oak tree next to the berm. Right there, just overhead, leaves were violently shaking as if some demonic tempest had taken hold of the branch and tossed it about. I pointed the flashlight directly on the spot. "Hey," I shouted in a whisper. (I intended to shout, but it occurred to me that it was 3:30 in the morning, and admittedly I lost my nerve to shout at the coming terror. So a whisper shout was the result.) Again. "Hey, cut it out!"

The noise died almost instantly as did the shaking. Then, two sets of luminous eyes, fiery yellow and closely set, peered out at me from within the darkness of the bough of which only the outer green leaves revealed themselves in the beam of light. "What's all this about?" I asked again in a more mature manner, hoping that my tone reflected less concern. (There were obviously two devils, and they didn't seem intent on rushing me outright, preferring to remain stationary as disembodied orbs).

Finally one of the pair turned slightly away and began to descend, moving from within the canopy downward along the trunk, and as I swept the beam in tandem the demon was revealed: a small raccoon. It continued downward in what I presume was contrition until it was only three feet from the ground, whereupon I whisper/yelled "shoo."

Does anyone yell "shoo" anymore?

This startled it enough that it fell the remaining distance and landed with an audible "thud" upon the bed of poison ivy below, after which it rather quickly scurried into the berm and toward the lower woods beyond.

Its partner (mate or adversary I'll never know) remained within the confines of the oak bough, content to watch me with glowing eyes. I hadn't the patience to stay and said simply "be quiet" as I went back into the house to bed, closing the door behind to the sounds of evening crickets.

September 10

No raccoons paid a visit last night, which made the evening blissfully quiet, apart from the pleasant background noise of crickets and katydids. How could anyone not enjoy these calls when the twilight gives way to evening? We lay in bed listening to the passing of another warm late summer night.

At some point we must have drifted off.

At 2:30 the acrid musk spray of some skunk came wafting through the window, made enhanced into the room by the fan we placed on the sill to help with the airflow during these warm evenings. Within moments we were awake, and the house became nearly unlivable. Even the dogs began to wine, and the cat retreated hastily from the room down the stairs toward the relatively cleanliness of the basement.

It was that bad. Our eyes stung, and we could even taste the odor. At that point, there was nothing to be done, apart from closing all the windows save for the one that contained the fan. This we reversed the flow, so that the air within the room was pushed outward, and we lay there helplessly assaulted for nearly an hour until we must have suffocated enough to pass out.

In the building light of the morning, I took a cursory walk around to see if the skunk had frankly sprayed directly on the house, for reasons that I could only fathom. There was no evidence of where it had discharged, nor was there anything to suggest a fight or quarrel. The odor, much attenuated, still lingered, and there were small spots all over the side yard where a skunk had dug with its paws to locate some morsel.

September 11

The coming front announced its intent in the tops of the tall trees, making them sway slowly while the air near the ground was still stagnant from the sultry morning. Out front, the two red oaks began to stir, causing their nuts to drop in rapid succession and contributing to what already had been a yard littered with hundreds of them. Some would hit the driveway and bounce in a random pattern. Nearly all the fallen acorns were without cap, which seems odd; hundreds of caps still remained in the leaf boughs, attached to the distal ends of the branches in clusters.

A more forceful breeze came across the field and through the spruce line, picking up the early fallen leaves in the yard and setting them about. It danced through the apple and maple, turning their leaves over to reveal the light colored underside, while the birch was content to wave its diminutive blades frantically to and fro.

The sky darkened as the horizon to the west revealed a line of deep grey. These clouds were not the heated leviathans of summer, infused with the building moisture of warmed earth and water wind. Rather, the clouds were uniform and dark, moving as one ever closer and pushing the rushing wind ahead with a force that increased with the passing minutes.

Rain came suddenly and hard, falling almost horizontal from west to east, and with it arrived cooler air. The thermometer dropped from 78 to 62 in a matter of moments, as the tempest front rushed by, leaving debris of small twigs and leaves strewn across the yard as the sun poked through the thinning clouds that remained with the coming of the cool air.

September 12

Kipper is content to lay on his side in the driveway, now that the angle of the sun is lower and the asphalt only gets warm and not hot. Though August technically contains the period of "dog days" when the heat and humidity typically reach their nadir, I wonder if mid September should more properly be conceived in those terms. After all, our dogs seem blissfully happy just to lie outside, with no real risk of overheating or being pestered by gnats or flies.

Kipper's chest rises and falls slowly, and his mouth is slightly ajar so that his tongue hangs loosely out – just enough to keep him cool. He seems unperturbed by the acorns that fall about the yard, and even those that hit driveway and bounce his way give no alarm. This again is evidence of earned happiness.

There are times when I join him in the yard and am too content to lie down in the grass and stare upward at the spreading oak and blue sky. How wonderful this season, with the soft sound of something mechanical moving in the distant field and the shifting breeze that catches the needles of the spruce and makes them sound like swells that break upon the shore. Shortly, we are joined by Tag, who has left the comfort of the shady *Vinca* and trots out to us in the soft grass. He sniffs my face briefly and wags his tail then moves to his brother and bites his ear. They tousle gently, rolling upon one another in the warmed yard of mid September.

September 13

Several Goldfinch fledglings appeared on the porch rail this afternoon, looking somewhat unsure of how to behave properly near the side yard feeder. There really isn't that much protocol we discern, apart from what seems like a general pecking order at the tubes. The Goldfinches predominated in late July, often with a dozen females and as many males surrounding the two feeders and driving away the few Chickadees and Titmice that had the temerity to want a few morsels. Goldfinches mate in August, which accounts for the drop in visits to the side yard as the month progressed and nesting took place.

Now we are witness to the new offspring who are tentative of their place in the scheme of things. Below, the two Towhees continue to scratch backward to dislodge cast off seed. I wonder if the newcomers think it normal to forage in this way? Surely not for a Goldfinch, but how do they instinctively know? They watch stoically from the porch rail as the Chickadees alight upon the tube, only to be chased away by the arrival of Big Red (our Red-bellied Woodpecker), whose approach is enough to frighten most of the small birds for a minute or two. Not so the fledglings, who seem unsure of this intruder.

The squirrels come and go, up the pole and into the baffle, then slide down in frustration to the ground. Again they try to no avail, and the fledglings look on in silent observation. The cardinal comes as daylight wanes, tentatively from the lower boughs of the scraggly spruce within the berm he flies cautiously to the ground. His mate remains within the security of the berm. And still, the fledglings look on, not risking upsetting the order of things.

September 14

Go outside in the darkness of the morning, if it is cool and dry, and find a place where there are no streetlights or house lights. We forget through the veil of summer's atmosphere how beautiful the night sky reigns, and now the changes of the coming autumn begin to reveal this beauty of the heavens with such clarity that it is simply breathtaking in every sense.

We are relatively fortunate here that the light pollution is still low enough to permit us the resplendency of the stars and planets. They are as pinpoints now, seen against the black velvet of the still dark sky, provided that the moon cooperates near its newness. Now is the season to enjoy it all the more, as the morning temperatures are warm enough to be comfortable, and the sky is often wrung free of the compounding moisture that is a normal part of the maturity of summer.

What a wondrous thing it is to sit in the field before dawn with the dewy grass beneath and the indistinct forms of horizon trees not far off. They reveal as darkened things, not foreboding but rather softened and familiar, yet seen now only as silhouette on the deep indigo horizon that forms the backdrop. Overhead the color deepens to black and as is filled with crystal points that luminesce in twinkling array. There is such beauty here, to scan from horizon to apex, to go from the comfort of life and growth to the austerity of beyond.

September 15

This morning, from somewhere deep within the lower woods came the lilting trumpet of the Guinea Fowl, which is a noise so incongruent with the usual menagerie of crickets, birds and occasional farm implement that it makes us both take notice and chuckle. Several minutes later the hen emerged through a clone of Goldenrod on the forest edge and proceeded cautiously into the yard, stopping a few feet inside to let out another warning call in her distinctive way.

Of course the dogs had a fit, as they tend to view all manner of smallish creatures as illegal aliens that should be chased down and driven out, particularly the various squirrels, chipmunks and rabbits. They are frankly more deserving of the side yard than we considering their near continual presence throughout most of the year. The dogs think otherwise, and though they've aged to the point of

164

having established a cessation in hostilities with the residents, they will on occasion give frantic chase to no avail. The Guinea Fowl is another matter; its presence is unique enough that the dogs simply can't abide.

It must have come down through the border woods from the Cheney place a half mile up Grove, where Bruce has kept a dozen or so Guineas for the past ten years as itinerant curiosities. The residents of our area have grown accustomed to the trumpeting of these birds and their tendency to wander arrogantly or stupidly into the road. Guinea Fowl are either overconfident or incompetent in the scheme of things. Regardless, we like them enough, as they add a little color and flavor to what has increasingly evolved to be a neighborhood divorced from such husbandry.

Our visitor must be a runaway, having likely decided that greener pastures lie in our direction, through the big woods that skirts Asnebumskit Pond and up the two-track access road that borders our back field that pretends to be a lawn. It continued its slow approach toward the house, all the while loudly calling "cop, cop, cop" as it bobbed and twisted its cardinal red head in declaration.

September 16

The angled sun catches the fading leaves of the False Solomon's Seal and reveals the undeniable truth, that summer is slowly being eclipsed by the arrival of autumn. The edges have turned from the deep green still present in the center to a mixture of sere brown and pale yellow. The flowers have long since passed, but now they show crimson fruit that hangs in pendant clusters beneath the outer tip, and where the Seal was all but insignificant among the other deep green weeds and grasses of a month ago, the splashes of cardinal color give it a proper place in

165

the transition to the faded earth tones that are developing ever more.

Color too still shows among the peppers, where unpicked fruit continues to thrive and show their mosaic of reds and yellows amid the still deep green foliage that seems unperturbed by the newly chilled nights. In the rows between the long beds there is abundant field mustard, and from the recessed vantage of the road looking down the length there are dozens of newly emerged cabbage whites flittering about. This marks their final hatch before the long dormancy till next spring.

September 17

Water spills gently over the small dam that holds Kettlebrook and travels down the concrete sluice which meanders for a quarter mile in the valley toward Leicester. The dam is visible from Route 56 as it passes by, though the sluice disappears behind a thick spruce stand that is choked beneath in its lower branches with bindweed and bittersweet, the latter which has yet to display the brilliant red fruit and yellow casing. Further below, the flow angles back, and the trees thin to reveal the small valley in full, while the water continues down toward Leicester beneath the road at Marshall and into the waiting reservoir beyond.

In early spring the Trout Lilly thrives here as does Red Trillium, which favors the shady moisture of the far bank where the tall trees of the rising hillside end close to the edge of the concrete sluice. Now, it is nearly impossible to see the water, for the ferns and Phragmites grass reach high and densely along the banks. Here too grow thousands of New England Asters and Golden Rod, both following the curve of the valley where the water below snakes its way through the descent.

When the sun is low and comes across the reservoir, it bathes this small valley in a golden light that catches these flowers in full, and the color is a wonder of autumn; a patchwork of gold and purple that shines among the still green foliage in this verdant place. Soon the evening chill will hasten the change in color, seen first in the emerald and cinnamon ferns as they fade from deep green to pale yellow and finally to sere brown when the frosts arrive in earnest.

Above the dam the reservoir glistens, reflecting the light of small waves that build upon the breeze from the northeast that travels down the length of the expanse. The water breaks upon a shore that is unusually low from the summer drought, which has created a ten foot buffer zone of exposed rocks that begin from the normal forest shoreline and extend downward until they meet the waves. Above, there are white pines and arbor vitae that follow the shoreline far into the distance, made distinct by the browse line five feet above the ground where the deer reach to earn their reward. The reservoir horizon looks as if someone had taken a pair of giant clippers and tended the lower portions of the evergreens so that the space beneath the lower boughs is cast in shadow from the dark woods within.

September 18

The six cherry trees on the small hillside that fronts Anna Maria are starting to change. A few leaves here and there have turned a beautiful mosaic of dark colors, and each year we remark how special these particular leaves become as September wanes. What makes them unusual is their mottled pattern of summer deep green spots that are surrounded by various shades of dark purple and red, with each color blending into the next so that the splotches, which are no more than the size of an eraser head, appear continuous. It is unique and beautiful each year.

The majority of the leaves on each tree are still uniformly green. Only a few have begun to change, though this recent chill will surely hasten their progression. Within the boughs hang leftover pendant fruit of small dark cherries, most of which are atypically small this year because of the drought. Soon, the birds will descend in gluttony to devour them whole; I once watched a small flock of Cedar Waxwings of perhaps ten birds land within one of these trees and nearly strip it clean of the fruit within the span of fifteen minutes.

September 19

How wondrous this cycle of familiar patterns which repeat year after year, and how we are fortunate to experience the continuity of succession through the seasons. Who can predict how any individual leaf will begin the change, when nearly all still hold the deep greens of summer's production. A few have begun to let go as the alchemy of daylight and temperature takes effect.

There is consistency in this change. Individual leaves appear randomly destined to let go of their summer color, though they are surely guided by their association with many factors, the majority of which are nearly imperceptible to us, who may regard the changing of the colors as something without order. Who is to say why a particular leaf in the midst of the cherry has turned brilliant yellow when its neighbors seem indifferent to the passing of September? And why does the arching bough of the sugar maple, the one that stretches over the road, has the majority of its leaves in beautiful shades of orange and red, while the rest of the tree remains still contently in summer?

September 20

For the past two weeks one of the large red oaks in front has been dropping acorns at a consistent rate. At first, we simply accepted it as a normal part of the shift to autumn, however when the acorns began to cover the yard it turned into something else. Of course, we've had mast years when one or the other oaks has produced an overabundance of nuts. This is normal, and it comes in loosely predictable cycles that coincide with the ebb and flow of the seasons.

This September has been unusual, to the point that we recently began to fear some sort of looming apocalypse. The nuts kept coming and coming, dropping from the tree like an arboreal Chinese water torture. "Plop," one would fall and hit the ground or driveway (after which it would bounce with an audible "tink"). A minute later another would fall, and then another, minute after minute and hour upon hour, and now the yard is littered with acorns. There must be thousands from this one tree, and this is no exaggeration.

What this means in the scheme of things is anyone's guess. Of course, we tend to prognosticate greatly this time of year, with winter's promise not too far off. (It is depressing to worry about a season after the one we have even yet to begin). Soon the Wooly Bear Caterpillars will be out, and this will lead to all sorts of speculation. Will it be cold? Snowy? Nor-easters? Warm? All bets are welcome, however acorns to this degree are something new.

Even the squirrels seem confused by so many. One would think that they'd be dancing in the front year, gleeful in collecting what will be the bounty of provender for the

169

upcoming months. But no. They yet remain in the side yard, content to sit beneath the tube feeders and gather the cast off sunflower seeds that are discarded by the gluttonous finches.

September 21

Our neighbor Jim drove slowly past the house as I was out beneath the two oaks in the front yard, using the snow shovel to push the deluge of acorns to the edge. I admittedly winced a little as I saw him approach, thinking myself a little silly looking, but Jim confirmed that he too felt obliged to such measures in his own yard. Evidently, our unusual bounty is shared by others who similarly have red oaks fully in mast. It's still remarkable. I've never seen such profligate production of seeds, the vast majority of which will never come close to possible germination. Such is the Darwinian mandate, I suppose.

Jim had roughly a dozen rough-sawn boards inside his car, and he was covered in sawdust. For a moment, I considered that he might have become so overwhelmed with the acorn invasion that he hastily decided to cut down the tree (not to mention plane a few boards). He said he was on his way to his son's place to help put new rough siding on the barn that they've been restoring, but he did show me a pail full of acorns in the foot well of the passenger's side. "These are for the pigs," he said simply, and I nodded and looked encouragingly at the notable piles of nuts I'd been shoveling for an hour or so.

We chatted briefly about the coming weather changes and the state of things these past few months on account of the prolonged drought, then he drove away and left me standing there leaning on the snow shovel (now acorn shovel) on the side of the yard next to the street. "Plunk," another acorn fell not too far from where I stood.

170

Autumn

Harvest

September 22

It is tempting to view the world in segments that have discreet beginnings and endings. Spring gives way to summer, which in turn departs as autumn arrives. By the celestial calendar, today is the autumnal equinox, which means that in its stately orbit around the sun, the earth is now positioned such that the amount of daylight received at most latitudes is approximately equal to the amount of darkness. This isn't exactly the case, of course, as the curvature of our little home confounds this generality, but this is a technicality.

The truth is that summer didn't just give way to autumn today, as if one season ended abruptly and the next began. There are few such discreet events in the scheme of things, after all. Rather, the cycle of the seasons is one of slow transitions, just as the movement of our globe around the sun is slow yet steady. Yesterday, there was slightly more daylight in the diurnal balance of things, and tomorrow there will be slightly less. This will continue, slowly, assuredly, until such time that we pass through the solstice and toward the new year that will be.

We've born witness to all the changes these past several months and years. The seedlings slowly turned into mature plants. These put to flower and then to fruit, which will in turn take to seed to continue the cycle, all happening as one day has given way to the next. So too the hand that writes gathers more wrinkles and lines, where yesterday there were fewer. And it reaches up to brush away tendrils of hair that have gone from brown to gray, as the writer himself passes slowly from the maturity of summer to the understanding that comes with the arrival of autumn.

September 23

The bees are beginning to become desperate as their
wildflower supply dwindles with the coming of October.
Yellow jackets seem particularly off kilter now, for they
will approach quizzically at any splash of bright color on
my clothing, though they seem to favor the shades that
bear their name. This afternoon while I was seated in the
shade beneath the maple tree in the side yard, one such
insect kept slowly buzzing about the yellow shirt I had on.
It wasn't threatening me or warning in the manner they do
when you get too close to a nest sight. (It's a little scary to
come unsuspectingly close to a ground nest of bees and
have several of them fly quickly by and bump into you in
warming).

This bee was searching back and forth across the shirt,
testing various spots for something to eat. I decided that as
long as I resisted the temptation to make any swatting
motions, it was safe enough to let my visitor have its way,
and so after a few minutes of foraging it departed across
the open yard toward the knot garden in front.

Not that there's much fare here either. The coreopsis is
past flowering. The mints have all but exhausted their tiny
purple blossoms. The lavender is fading, and the menarda
only show the sere tufted heads where once the pale
tubular petals provided nectar enough. Only the marigolds
seem content to thrive, but the bees pay them no mind.

September 24

Just like that the ferns have given way to faded yellow or
sere brown, where only last week they remained yet deep
green in the production of summer. We noticed them
altered a couple of days ago in the wooded hollow past
Robinson's Greenhouse, having begun to turn with the

approach of autumn. The change was evidently rapid and interesting, because while the calendar may now affirm that autumn has indeed arrived, both the day and night temperatures remain stubbornly set within late summer norms.

The ending of the ferns must, like most plants, be governed by a unique alchemy of ambient temperature and available daylight. With temperatures so warm, it follows that the ferns this year are particularly attuned to the ratio of day and night, and we've begun to accelerate our daily loss of sunshine for the past few weeks, as the equinox approached and autumn arrived. How wonderful the mechanism, some chemical balance within each frond or stem that somehow senses the loss of available production and knows it as the time to let go.

The plants and trees have been doing just this for several weeks, as they prepare for the winter that will arrive in due course. Annuals have gone to seed, and these have fallen to the soil bed. Shrubs and trees have begun to seal off their leaf attachments, creating a thin sheen that prevents the flow of moisture or production from the leaves that have worked so arduously since May. These in turn will degrade, as Chlorophyll gives way, as do the Carotenoids, the greens that fade to reveal the orange, red and yellow spectra within. These too decline, and as the leaf stem gives way the air is filled with the tumble of autumnal colors that slowly accumulate on the ground.

September 25

There was a mild frost this morning, visible only on the tops of the cars that had been left out overnight in the common area beside the church. The lawns and rooftops seemed unaffected, so the temperature must have been somewhere between 33 and 35 degrees.

This early frost comes and goes like a slow moving tide, arriving secretly in the early morning, in the low lands initially before progressing further each day, until it takes hold fast, and we see autumn depart.

After the sunrise, this frost will retreat, leaving wet car tops and dew-soaked grass in its wake.

September 26

The farm truck skirts the edge of the pepper field that lies next to the knoll in front of Anna Maria. In the bed are several worn bushel baskets, each containing a mixture of green, red and yellow peppers to be ferried to the store. As we walked slowly behind, the vehicle descended between the copse of trees and the edge of the plastic bedding, following a well worn two track that arcs around the end of the rows and between a break in the stone wall.

The small hillside that borders the field edge is covered with tall grasses that have gone to seed, their heads bent over from the weight and all moving in the wind like undulating waves. This hillside is now a purple sheen of autumn, as certain grasses within have taken on a hazy auburn color of decline. There are also purple splashes of New England Aster and sere bird's nests of the Queen Anne's Lace that have gone to seed.

As we approached the curve, we caught sight of the truck passing through the breech toward the store, slowing first to avoid a pallet full of orange and white pumpkins on display in front of the entrance. Beyond, there are cut stalks of corn for sale, leaning against the far storage garage that abuts the near field where sugar snaps once grew in June but now is given to fallow soil filled with the cover of Rye.

September 27

The temperatures warmed enough last evening that we were able to keep the windows open and let the fresh odors of the September woods drift softly into the house. Since early summer, we've grown accustomed to this luxury to the point that having the house breathe is simply an expectation or ritual rather than privilege. Soon enough the chill will be here to stay, and we will grow wistful for the fresh air until next May, and knowing this is sufficient to remind us to enjoy what remains.

The air has been laced with earthy scents ever since the thaws of April released frozen remnants from last autumn's decline. The coming of spring was infused with potential, as the recycle of nutrients had given way to new beginnings of shoot and leaf, of turned soil warmed anew by the sun that strengthened with each passing day, and of air that carried the sweet perfumes of pollens.

July and August carried maturity of the season, when the air was filled with the lassitude of humidity and warm water wind that blew across the tired fields, bringing the scent of cattails and pickerelweed, mixed with the smell of cut grass and the volatiles of forest production. Now there are the first hints of wood smoke in the evening and the early decay of leaf tannins from those that have let go prematurely to the ground.

September 28

This afternoon, a town worker drove slowly by in the mowing tractor, using an attached outrigger to crudely thrash the various weeds, brambles and other such undergrowth that populates the roadsides. It is a brutal affair to witness, as the ground beneath is damaged by the rotating mass of angry chain within the maw on the end of the arm.

In its wake lay the matted refuse of summer's wildness, bits of grass stalks and tattered ivy among jumbled vines of reaching bittersweet and dogsbane and the scarred surfaces of newly exposed rocks.

This cutting is late this year. Typically the town sees fit to mow in August, and so at least we've benefited from an additional month of having the shoulder display of the accomplishments of summer. We understand the rationale for cutting; clearing the edges promotes greater visibility, especially along the curbs where line of sight may be compromised by grasses and such that reach upwards of a meter or more. Still, it seems unnecessary to decimate the straight sections on both sides, and it instantly changes the scene from country lane to harsh cultivation. Perhaps I overstate here, but it is rather unsightly to watch, listen and smell the process (the odor of thrashed understory creates its own unique blend of volatile aromatics that carries along the wind, often preceding the actual mower itself by several minutes).

I suspect there is no overarching plan for cutting. No semblance of regard for aesthetics or timing. This would require a consideration for nature that seems frankly absent with the powers that be toward maintaining the state of the town. Rather, the job is likely relegated to some available time in the late summer or early autumn, after the major growth has concluded, and before the leaves have fallen such that their collective presence would render the thrasher ineffective.

Consider the British, who tend to value aesthetics of their country lanes to a notable degree. From the area of Cumbria, which encompasses much of the lake country to the north. The government codifies the manner in which verges (our "roadsides") will be maintained: "Flower rich verges are generally cut later in the year. Other types may require an earlier cut. Every four years a full width cut is made late in the year to prevent woody weeds and saplings from growing. This cut is mainly for scrub control to protect the fabric of the road, but it also protects the flower richness of the verge by removing those plants that would shade them out. On "special" verges, this happens every two years. Over 600 "special" verges have their cuttings removed to reduce fertility and prevent a build-up of mat vegetation, and so encourage a greater diversity of wildflowers."

Wouldn't it be wonderful to adopt such an ethos here?

September 29

Apple cider has been at the store across the road for nearly a week, though we've yet to purchase some. We noticed that Louise had begun placing both full and half gallons on the shelf next to the bins that hold the varieties of the apples themselves. These we've sampled, and thus far the fruit has been relatively small but sweet. The drought has certainly contributed to this.

Early cider tends to be more acidic and bitter than what will arrive within the next couple of weeks. It's remarkable the difference, much in the same way that early corn lacks the flavor of what comes when we begin to eat the crop that arrives in early August. These aren't subtleties mind you! The true cider aficionado knows to wait until September gives way to October.

Our own crab apples were productive too. Again, the lack of moisture seemed to discourage mold and blight and also allow for the sugars to concentrate. It's been several weeks since they fell to the ground, though there remain a few stragglers on the branches that are yet safe to sample. The remainder we collected loosely and put in haphazard piles near the side of the road, making it easier for our neighbors Jim and Barbara to gather a few each day as they walk by. They take them up Grove past Sunset Lane to the split rail fence on the eastern side, where horses graze in a small field.

September 30

The upper blossoms of the Golden Rod are beginning to turn brown while those that lie beneath remain a striking yellow. I suppose that no summer lasts forever, and there have been ample signs around the countryside that one season has now been eclipsed by the next. Indeed, our warm evenings have given way to autumnal chill, as September comes softly to a close. With the arrival of cooler weather and the departure of the laziness that came with summer's maturity, this change in season finds us invigorated anew. Where before we were content simply to sit among the grasses and idly watch the sultry day pass, we now feel the urge to explore old and familiar places again and to see how they've fared these past months.

As the leaves begin to fall, new vistas will open within the woodlands that border our homes and hillsides. Look closely; it has already begun. Apple trees have started losing leaves, and they tumble downward to the ground in haphazard piles of yellow blades that seem strangely out of place. A crisp northwest breeze catches the upper boughs and shakes more of them loose, and these too descend and join the others in a twirling dance upon the ground. We notice the motion. It is something new, these falling leaves and yet familiar that we recall the continuity to seasons past. It is only startling to initially see the

179

changes we knew were soon to arrive. Up high, the boughs have thinned some, and there is new light that passes between the leaves that still remain, and beyond we see through the gaps to the curve of the distant hillside where only yesterday it was hidden by the deep greens of the spreading leaves.

This is the wonder that comes with autumn. All around there is change and decline, as the landscape works to prepare itself for the long dormancy that awaits with the coming of winter. There is too the arrival of color so resplendent, the smell of wood fires, and hoarfrost upon the morning grass, the swishing brush of sere grasses against one another in the gentle breeze, and the opening of vistas we'd nearly forgotten during the comfort of summer's womb. September comes gently to an end.

October

October 1

When the afternoon sunlight angles low enough and
streams through breaks in the spruce line across the road,
it strikes the trunk of one of our corner oaks and makes it
appear as if it were on fire. This is because the Virginia
Creeper that covers the bark and climbs upward in the
fashion of a vine has now turned a deep and glowing red,
where only last week its leaves were still green. These, like
the bladed palms of the Shagbark Sumac, are among the
first foliage to turn and reveal the wonderful shades of
orange and red that have remained hidden beneath the
chlorophyll until now. Why they are among the first to
change, year after year, is a mystery, but we appreciate
looking to the ivy and sumacs as a harbinger of the
beautiful colors that will follow in the rest of the woods.

Poison Ivy is slowly going to yellow, which tends to be the
norm. We have a bank that creeps along the stonewall in
back and has made inroads toward the yard, having
extended out and upward through the trunk of the arbor
vitae we planted several years ago as a visual break from
the access road behind. Once the leaves have fallen away
and turned to brown, it may be safe to do a little cutting
back of the vine – at least enough to shrink it to the berm
side of the wall, whereupon next spring it will reach again
toward the yard in what has been a never ending
conquest.

October 2

Daybreak revealed a misty rain that slowly turned to fog,
and the tree trunks in the border woods stand in contrast
more than they did a month ago. The bark of the oaks,
maples and cherries all are dark, a sort of blackish grey,
where the surface faces the side of the prevailing wind and

mist. This contrasts with the lighter dry surface on the undersides of branches and the leeward face of the trunks.

In the filtered light of the fog, the tree boughs almost reflect an iridescent sheen, and it's plain to see how much deep green has collectively vanished from the canopy. So too the dark trunks and branches stand in contrast amid the nearly yellow-green of faded leaves, and from a distance it is striking to see the angled forms of limbs among the foliage. With the absence of any singular red maple or ash having gone silently to brilliant yellow amid the backdrop of our typical deep green, we don't readily discern that changes have been afoot. Yet this fog, this rain reveal how much these woods have begun to prepare for the coming of winter not too far off. Deep green has given way to lighter shades, and though there are hints in individual leaves of the acceleration of autumn's chill, the progression has been steady but slow.

October 3

This afternoon we noticed Tag staring intently at something on the edge of the driveway. His eyes were fixed on a point, and we could barely discern an object in the grass where his gaze remained. Slowly he lowered his nose, and as he got closer his tail began to cautiously descend toward the ground, much in the manner of a diviner with a stick who has chanced upon some hidden source of water.

At the moment the tip of his tail touched the driveway, his nose brushed against the object. Flick! Up and away a grasshopper jumped and landed roughly five feet away on the asphalt. Tag jumped slightly from being startled then looked in our direction presumably for confirmation that he actually saw something jump.

"Get it Taggie," I encouraged.

He moved slightly to the left and walked slowly to the grasshopper's new location. This time, he bent down less cautiously, and flick!, the insect sprung away to a new location. This back and forth continued for roughly five minutes. Repeatedly Tag would arrive, drop his head, try to snap at the grasshopper, and show what looked like dog frustration when the insect evaded him time and again.

October 4

In the warmer months, we would occasionally see individual crows flying high above the fields or sitting perched in the upper reaches of the spruce trees. We paid them little mind, as the house seemed surrounded with our resident songbirds and summer tenants who all deserved attention with the arrival of the season. Now so many of them have departed, and we are close upon the days when only the winter birds remain. It is only a matter of time before the Juncos arrive, and this will truly signal that the cold is not too far off.

The crows too seem to have changed their behavior. Now they fly in loose groups, low across the fields and announce their presence more insistently than before. They congregate in the mornings in the tall trees of the woods and squawk to one another like miscreants intent on planning some daily mischief.

October 5

The farm has been predictably busy this past week, as the leeks have come into maturity and are ready for harvest. Now foreigners frequent the store and wait patiently (mostly), speaking to one another in some unknown language of hushed exchanges while Fred works to clean and bundle the crop. He stands outside in the passageway between the store and the garage on the rocky drive that leads to the fields where the growing leeks can be seen in the distance poking up through the black plastic rows. In the truck bed are several dozen that he just picked, laying atop one another and waiting for preparation before they are taken away almost immediately in sale.

The leeks are long and thick, with a blanched portion that extends nearly six inches up the shoot from where the many roots branch into the soil. It is interesting to watch him take a harvested leek and shake it vigorously by the shaft. This dislodges the soil free from the filamentous root stock, which is such a curious thing and so unlike the many root crops we are used to seeing as such. These do not go deeply into the ground but rather extend outward in all directions save upward and grab hold the earth with the tenacity of multitudes, like dozens of small white anchor lines. He then washes them clean of leftover debris and applies a quick jerk with a knife to trim the end, cleaving the roots in the manner of a crew cut. Bundled together in a group of three, they make their way to waiting arms.

October 5

For the past week, there has been an emergence of the pretty white caterpillars of the Tussock Moth. We see them mostly on the driveway, as they undulate slowly across from one grassy surface to the next. They are remarkably

185

pretty little things, with fuzzy tufts of white hairs that stand erect in all directions and two shoots of jet black tufts on both the front and the back of their bodies.

The dogs fortunately don't seem to pay them much attention, apart from their occasionally bending low to sniff one in greeting as it walks slowly in accordion fashion along the pavement. I've read somewhere that the Tussock's hairs can be irritating to the skin, and so we'd prefer the dogs leave well enough alone.

October 6

The old access road to Asnebumkit Pond begins off Grove Street a hundred yards or so down from the farm driveway across the road. Though it was maintained several years ago by the town, it has since been left fallow, and the will of primary succession has given way to small saplings and briars where before it was simple a two-track path. Seen from Grove, it is still evident by the absence of tall trees that some passage once existed here and led off into the distance of the descending hill toward the forest below.

The briars are a nuisance only for the first fifty feet, where more daylight has filtered through and hastened its growth. Further on, the way becomes less cluttered, as the track is interrupted only by various field grasses that no longer get mowed or the chance fall of some downed tree. The road angles to the south and divides the higher ground of sparse hardwoods and white pines on the east side with the wetland growth of the vernal pool on the west, before ending nearly a hundred yards further on at the bermed dam of Asnebumkit Pond.

A small trail skirts the ridge of the berm to the east and follows the shore of the lake toward the spillway just

186

beyond. To the west, a path departs from the water and leads upward through the woods where it empties onto the Klingele Fields.

We come visit the water's edge here sometimes and take comfort in the privacy and beauty this vantage affords. To the north, the woods descend slightly in a lower basin and show the effect of both wetter ground and the action of beavers. They conspire to make this area a boggy fen, where the skeletons of trees long gone rise upward as grey and lifeless testaments to the changes the landscape has endured. Here and there some trees on the edge of the bog show chew marks, and some have been cleaved altogether, leaving only the pointed shaft rising to the sky, where the upper trunk has been removed by the beaver and taken to its dam further beyond.

To the south, the expanse of Asnebumskit spreads outward and its deep blue is offset by the shoreline ring of woodlands and shrubs, where now the red and sugar maples show more yellow and crimson among the deep greens of the sheltering pines. On clear and calm days, the water reflects the distant shore so perfectly and creates beautiful mirror images of the oncoming fall colors.

Blue Herons remain here yet, waiting patiently on the water's edge. They walk silently toward the border Phragmites grass and disappear in and out of the tall reeds that have now started to yellow with the arrival of autumn.

October 7

Cooler nights and shorter days have hastened the yellowing of more than just the deciduous trees. The crab grasses in the lawns have gone from vibrant green of only two weeks ago to now nearly brown, revealing the lawn again as a mosaic of the perennial fescue with thin and bare spots of dying crab. The effect of this past drought has rendered itself plainly as the fescue and bluegrasses are fairly thin themselves. Only the spreading violet leaves seem indifferent, and surely they will continue to overtake next year. In the side yard the patchwork lawn is hidden beneath the early fallen leaves of the apple trees, and the front expanse rests below our twin red oaks, both of which hold their leaves well into November.

White pines have browning needles now. Two days ago, I looked particularly to see if the changes had begun, and there was only a dusty hint. Today it is noticeable. Roughly a third of the needles have gone to brown, giving each pine a two-tone appearance until the sere ones detach and fall gently to the ground. The same is occurring in the Rhododendrons. One in three leaves is now yellow and will soon fall away, leaving the remainder to soldier onward through the coming cold, curling and uncurling as the temperatures fluctuate.

October 8

The air temperature drops nearly ten degrees on the descent from the top of the hill on Marshall Street down to the small valley before the entrance to Kettlebrook Golf Course. Near the bottom, there is a misty veil of fog, where the cool air that had settled in from last night condensed above the sun warmed land and flowing water that forms the creek basin. As the morning sunrise crests the tree line to the east, it angles downward to the valley and highlights the fog, making the approach from the top of the hill an ethereal transition into the thin layer.

At the bottom, where the culvert passes underneath the road, the small creek pools before entering the breach. Upstream the water curves away and out of sight into sere

188

blades of cattail reeds, whose tips rise above the fog line and are lit brightly by the daybreak.

The roadside has an old guard rail, the kind where cement forms were placed as posts into the ground and thick strands of cable wire ran between them. Now it is in disrepair, with posts having collapsed and fallen into decay, and only one cable remains in place. It passes through an upper hole of a resistant form then drops away to connect to the tattered remains of another that lies in pieces among the tall grasses and ferns that too line the roadside.

October 9

Today we bid farewell to the screen insert on the front door. It's an old handmade wooden door that has a swivel latch at each corner to lock into place the two inserts we have. For the past several months it has contained the large screen. It seems like only yesterday we decided that the spring had warmed sufficiently to allow us the luxury of including it, letting the earthy odors of renewal breathe into the house and replace the stagnant air of winter's remnants.

Now we have to acknowledge the waiting debt, as the temperatures cool for the long haul and seasonal changes lead to the coming dormancy of winter once again.

It's a simple job to replace one insert for the next. Within a few minutes, the screen frame is removed and the glass one takes its place. And just like that, we have to let go of what has been a simple pleasure and enjoy a month or so of having the glass door permit the angled sunlight into the mudroom. Soon enough we'll need to close the main door as well to ward the cold, and with this acknowledge that late autumn has arrived.

This afternoon was sunny and somewhat warm, with temperatures in the low sixties, and we sat in chairs on the brick walkway in front of the house and simply listened to the fading birdsong and noises from the farm. Then, there was a padding sound, a gentle "thump, thump, thump," and we turned to see the cat reaching with upward with her paws to get our attention through the glass door. Yesterday, she was content to sit and "meow" sweetly through the screen, but today there is no sound of her gentle plea. There is only the silent movement of her mouth and the insistent pawing.

October 10

The early fallen leaves collect on the forest floor, and our woodland trails display a mixture of yellow splashes of color from the beech, elm and birch leaves that have come to rest in random splendor. They catch the light that penetrates more deeply now and are cast in sharp relief against the darkness of the trodden ground, making the going a kaleidoscope of autumn in the forest that is less foreboding and more golden.

So too the white pine needles are beginning to collect on the ground and make a soft carpet that hushes our footfalls as we pass. There are stretches of trail where the combination of angled sunshine and golden leaf reflections makes it difficult to distinguish the path from the remainder of the forest floor, and we are disoriented in the reverie of the beauty of the woods.

Where the boughs of pines overhang the shoulder of the road, brown needles collect overnight in large patterns, and the first passing cars make gentle tracks in their midst. From a distance it resembles a dusting of snow that has been marred. A rising breeze will lift these needles,

190

forming small clumps that blow about the road and collect as tattered masses among the shoulder.

October 11

There was only the faintest hint of dawn at 5:45 in the morning, and it is still difficult to become used to the increasing darkness at both the beginning and ending of the day.

Last evening when we went to bed, there was enough breeze that we'd hoped to avoid the forecasted frost. By morning, the wind had died completely, and there were patches of grass that showed the dusting of white on their tips. We won't know whether or not it was a killing frost until later in the day, as the warming temperatures will reveal its effects upon the basil and tomatoes, whose leaves will collapse and wither.

The dawn was spectacularly clear, with the waxing moon trailing the sunshine well below the horizon making the skies especially dark and the stars crystalline against the backdrop of deep indigo. It looked like a cold air night sky, which is one of the rewards of having the humidity of summer depart.

There on the edge of the eastern horizon sat Jupiter, still within the small band of barely refracted atmosphere so that its appearance was both magnified slightly and made orange by the sun's rays that were far beneath it and yet to rise. Roughly twenty degrees overhead on the ecliptic, Orion stood majestically, and I thought about Jupiter's slow progress through the heavens. Two years ago, Jupiter rested near the Orion's left shoulder near the star Betelgeuse. Last year it was midway between where it is presently and Orion. It's path is slow though steady, arcing through the heavens in a circle that takes roughly thirty years to complete, which means it will return again to reside near Orion some twenty eight years from now. Odds are slim that I will be here to see it like this, but who knows?

October 12

There are still many chores to be accomplished while the fair weather prevails, though we've been spreading out this necessity for several weeks. How different than the coming of spring, when we hastened to accomplish as much as possible in the span of only a few days. No doubt this reflected our urgency to eagerly welcome time with the outside, after so many months spent indoors.

Now we drag our feet in bidding farewell to the warmth, and each task ahead is a reminder that we will soon make the transition again.

Today I took the snow blower out of the lower barn, where it has sat happily forgotten since early April. It was covered in dust and bits of grass and feather, the latter two a sign of the chore ahead. I pushed it up to the front yard, feeling a little foolish in walking behind it on the grass in the middle of the sixty-degree day. Fortunately, only two cars passed by on Grove, and both drivers (unknown to me), gave quick, curious glances.

I muscled it over on its side, knowing the likelihood of what was beneath in the inner housing that is accessible by little drain holes. Access is the key word here, and sure enough there were bits of grass poking out the holes. After removing the four bolts that hold the housing plate to the bottom, I used a long screwdriver to pop the plate from the base. Out spilled a large mouse nest, complete with at least seven juvenile white-footed mice and a rather confused mother, all racing to escape the sudden confusion by running helter skelter across the surface of the grass.

The injury here isn't so much that I have to suffer this cleaning task each autumn (I suppose I should be more sensitive about who suffers). Rather, I suspect that several of these very mice will now find their way into the secret passages that breach the foundation or house sill, and we shall meet again as the temperatures continue to descend.

October 13

The big maple by the side yard is just beginning to lose its leaves. It seems a bit late this year, though it has been unusually warm, and perhaps like us it too is reluctant to let go of what has been a wonderful stretch. Now there are dozens of early fallen leaves on the ground beneath, and the majority of these range from a mere faded green to the first hints of changing yellow. These came down in the windy front of two days ago and have lost their chance at more colorful splendor.

Still, enough have fallen that splashes of sunlight filter through the upper boughs and pass into the windows of the sunroom, and this is a pleasant change from the shade we've had inside since nearly April. Over the next week or so as more descend, the sunroom will be lit in full once again, adding a measure of warmth to what will increasingly become cool days ahead.

It's remarkable how the angle of the sun has changed from only last month. This shouldn't be a surprise, for it's been this way year after year, but somehow it still seems to catch us off guard. The rays come into the windows differently now and reveal new patterns of shadows and light upon the walls and floors. So too outside there are long shadows of the trees that line the access road, casting themselves far across the driveway in the middle of the day, when only last month the pavement was nearly all in full sun.

October 14

There is a well used section of the rail trail in Rutland that begins near the parking lot where the entry road passes by and ascends steeply for a hundred yards before leveling off and turning slightly into the deeper woods. Each year in spring at the bend we look for a small clump of Pink Lady Slippers that grow conspicuously amid the emergent greens of various grasses and weeds and the predominantly dark tones of the surrounding woods. If the light is right, the rays angle downward to this spot as if designed to highlight the delicate blossoms in glowing color. They are simply beautiful. It is also heartwarming to think that hikers refrain from picking the blossoms outright.

Come August we returned to the spot to see if any of the flowers had been successfully pollinated, and sure enough there was one in what was a grouping of roughly ten blossoms which had a strange green pod between the withered flower petals and the long supporting stem. The others simply displayed the dead petals and nothing more.

In early September we came once more, and I removed the pod for my own collection, taking care to cut the stem an inch or so below. (The reader is asked to forgive my admission here. I am sheepish about doing such a thing, but in defense I will point out that the flower derives from the root structure deep beneath the soil. I was simply taking the potential of seeds within the now sere pod).

Today I checked the pod, which has been sitting idly on the windowsill drying further and turning a dark

194

chocolate brown. Along its nearly inch long side, a seam had opened slightly, revealing thousands of tiny spore like seeds inside. These I dumped carefully onto a piece of white paper, making a pile of what must have been truly an incomprehensible number. I then transferred them all to a small, labeled vial and added them to my collection of wildflower seeds.

For the past few years, I've gathered over a hundred and thirty different species of wildflower seeds from within the borders of Paxton, and I now have that many tiny vials within small cubicles of an antique typeset frame that hangs on the wall of the office. Last spring, I took various samples and germinated them, then transplanted the seedlings to a few locations about the yard and woodland. In this way, I feel repentant that I've gathered seeds and pods from so many, believing now that I've also helped foster future generations of many wildflowers.

October 15

Yesterday gave me visions of cultivating a field of Lady Slippers, but here is where certain difficulties arise. Lady Slippers are orchids, and it isn't simply a matter of spreading the profligate seeds willy-nilly to a waiting soil bed. These seeds are nothing more than a tiny embryo, with virtually no endosperm, meaning that there aren't any supportive nutrients to sustain a germinating plant as we typically find in most seeds.

Rather, the embryo of the Lady Slipper requires soil that contains certain symbiotic fungi that work to provide nutrients during germination. Evidently, this partnership is indeed a rare event, and it likely accounts for why Lady Slippers produce seedpods with almost incalculable numbers of tiny seeds. Each has nearly zero chance of landing in just the right soil with just the right symbionts, however there are thousands upon thousands of seeds that spread to the wind. Probability favors that one will chance to grow.

October 16

It felt more like October today. The full Hunter's Moon set below the horizon just as the brightening of the dawn came in the east amid skies that were free of any humidity. The past few evenings have been especially chilly, and there are fewer and fewer insects calling in the morning as temperatures continue to flirt with a killing frost. Sunrise came softly, with only the distant call of crows somewhere far beyond Asnebumkit Pond and with barely a whisper of wind, and this quiet is such a contrast from the constant din of life that is a part of summer and early autumn. Soon we will enter the long quiet, where only the artic breeze through the evergreens and bare trees affords us much in the way of noise beyond the silence of winter.

The calm beginning gave way to a warming sky that turned a brilliant shade of cerulean blue that contrasted well with the horizon line of deciduous trees in peak colors, which ranged from crimson red to deep yellow and the occasional green splashes of spruces mixed within. Even these have an autumn flare; the bindweed and bittersweet we generally disdain are forgiven for a while. They've been steadily climbing within the boughs of the pines and reaching upward in hidden, spiraling ascents. Now the leaves that are a striking yellow and conspicuously reveal their presence in spidery patterns.

Through our own spruce line across the road, the lifting breeze carried tufted filaments of milkweed silk through the gaps and toward the house. The sere plants we know that grow near the lower stone wall must have opened their pods in readiness, for the air is filled with tiny parachutes when gusts come from the open field. Most continue by, carried on the wind that lifts them gently as they approach the front of the house, sending them upward and over the roof, destined for somewhere beyond the lower woods.

October 16

We picked the last of the remaining tomatoes this afternoon from what were fairly pathetic looking plants. Of the twenty or so seedlings I transplanted in early April, we must have enjoyed over a hundred specimens of wonderful red and yellow tomatoes since early July. Now that the temperatures have flirted with the freeze, most have stems and leaves that have either yellowed or withered to brown.

We pulled the plants and placed them into a waiting wheelbarrow, then used a hand plow to loosen and turn the soil in the raised beds. Now they look clean again, as they did in late March when the ground was beginning to thaw for good and we were filled with the promise of spring and the excitement that comes with renewal. It was all the more bittersweet this afternoon, for the day was unusually warm – an Indian Summer in full measure where the sunshine, though angled lower than yesterday, provided enough heat to make it feel as late August. However, this was betrayed by the sepia tones of the filtered sun against the yellowed leaves of the changing woods.

These beds will gather leaves as they fall delicately from the sky, and for a while there will be a pretty mosaic of yellows, reds and browns as these October patterns collect one upon another. They will stick to one another in some passing rain, and slowly turn to faded shades of earthen tones, before becoming brittle and lifeless as November snows bury the ground in an early blanket of white.

October 17

For the past two months, an older gentleman has been walking daily past our house. On those still afternoons, we would hear him approach from up the street, with his wooden walking stick that makes a staccato "tock," each time he placed it intently on the pavement. He walks slowly, simply to enjoy being outside and profit from the exercise and beauty the changing landscape affords. For two months, we've not spoken to him, apart from our giving a brief smile and wave as he passes. In return, he too has been reticent to say anything, though he is quick to respond with his own pleasant nod and smile as he continues onward down Grove.

This afternoon I was once again using the snow shovel to gather acorns from the ground beneath the big oak in front. It is astounding that this tree continues to drop more of them to the ground, when the past several weeks have seen them plummet surely by the thousands. It's been so unusual and alarming that we've joked about the possibility of the trees forecasting some sort of approaching Armageddon. There has been something unusual in the alchemy of temperature, moisture and timing that has contributed to this bounty. We hope it's nothing more than that. Should we face deep snows ahead, I suppose we'll have something to associate.

As he approached, the gentleman paused to watch me push a small pile of acorns off the grass edge and onto the shoulder of the road. I looked up sheepishly, filled with a mixture of embarrassment equally divided between the foolishness of shoveling the yard and the inconvenience of spreading what were essentially hundreds of small diameter wooden marbles onto the road.

He called across the street, "Those smot when they hit."

"I'm sorry?" was my reply, not understanding his wording.

"I got hit by one of those in the head up the street, and it smotted."

It occurred to me that our new neighbor was a New Englander in dialect. "Smarted," I stammered in recognition. "Yes. Yes, they do hurt when they hit."

He smiled again and waved slightly as he continued onward past the house, and I stood in the yard and watched him descend the small hill until he was a hundred yards or so away.

October 18

We planted no mums this autumn, which is fine by me, for I've always considered them an unwelcome advertisement to the ending of the outdoor flowers. I am quite certain I am in the minority, however for me there is something simply too artificial in the appearance of mums within the cultivated mulch beds and window boxes, when the remainder of the plants that still remain show obvious signs of limited time.

Without them though, the bees around our house are running out of options, apart from the marigolds that are thriving yet in the borders of the knot garden and the edges of the brick walkway. Despite their foliage, which looks respectably ragged, the deep orange and crimson blossoms seem to defy the calendar. In any given grouping, we must have twenty or thirty in bloom, and there are a half dozen bumblebees and honeybees that travel between each flower in crisscrossing patterns.

The arduous honeybees reveal themselves, with hind legs that have pollen baskets full to the brim with deep orange dusting that is almost iridescent. We watch them navigate the composite flowers, pushing deep within to retrieve their reward and pausing between to clean themselves free of pollen. The full ones take flight, lifting upward slowly and with purpose toward the spruce line across the road, they navigate in a straight path through the gap and out of sight toward the horizon line across the open field that is now fallow from corn picked several weeks ago.

October 19

Sometime during the still of last night, a sugar maple decided to shed nearly half its leaves, which fell calmly to the ground beneath. As the sunrise of the morning filtered through the thinning canopy of the lower woods, it caught the maple in its path and reflected upon the remaining leaves as brilliant splashes of deep orange and red. Cast against the darker background of the grey stonewall and deep greens of reluctant oaks, the maple truly appeared on fire, and the ground beneath was littered with a perfect circle of fallen orange leaves from overnight.

It was so stunning that it was breathtaking.

For a moment, the light held and the stillness remained, and a gentle dewy fog rose from the moist humidity of the woods and bathed the maple in a diffuse sunshine that tempered the fire of the tree to a softer wonder of orange. Then a breeze lifted, created out of the heated ground and open fields, toward the lower woods where it banished the soft mist and gathered the fallen leaves, setting them about in a dervish toward the wall. It rose up to the boughs and rustled loose many that remained from overnight, making them cascade in the wake of the passing breeze.

October 20

The changes have softened our familiar woods, where only last month the paths we took wound among the deep greens of emerald ferns that thrived in the dark shade of the forest floor. Then, only the upper canopy captured direct sunlight, revealed as incandescent reflections off blowing leaves, seen through sparse gaps of the lower boughs of oaks and maple, pines and spruce. The light that penetrated to the floor was filtered in faded shades of shadowed green, making the way at once both a reverent and secretive escape from the heat of summer.

Now the canopy has thinned, and the floor is bathed in golden light from above, where rays of the more angled sun come softly in comfort through those yellow leaves that remain reluctant to concede to the changes. They dance about in breezes that flow through the heart of the woods now, making the lower branches come alive with movement where only last month their leaves remained silent as sentinels of the woods. They flutter softly until their time to let go. Some do as we walk among the sounds of crispness, where no footfall will be silent as before, among sere ferns that only add to the welcome comfort of this changed place.

October 21

As the darkness settled this evening, two Great Horned Owls begin calling to one another from somewhere deep within the lower woods. We sat for a while on the back porch and listened to their conversation and watched as thin clouds drifted overhead rapidly, pushed by a southerly breeze and illuminated from behind by the gibbous moon. The air carried the scent of fallen leaves, made enhanced by the wetness leftover from a passing shower this afternoon.

We remarked to one another how spooky the evening seemed and felt silly in characterizing it so. Yet, it was spooky, this late October night, where shadows of the thinning trees cast shapes on the leaf-covered expanse of the back lawn. As if on cue, a single fox gave a barking scream from somewhere out front, perhaps the open field across Grove. We both jumped in fright then laughed to one another, remarking how natural such feelings of fright come when the season is just right.

October 22

A torrential rain came through overnight, brought up by a southerly warm front and enhanced with moisture drawn from the ocean. After so many months of drought, it was startling to witness such a deluge. Over two inches must have fallen within the span of a couple hours, and when combined with such an unseasonal warm wind, a great many of the remaining leaves were torn from their stems and brought down to the wet pavement and grass below.

It didn't take long for debris to coalesce in the low spots of the road. Leaves and sticks gathered around the storm drains as the rain enhanced, and within no time huge puddles formed and stretched across the road in several places. There is a particularly bad spot in the dip on Grove between the exit of the parking lot to Klingele Fields and the open meadow that fronts the Anna Maria hillside. Though there are two storm drains here, they rest beneath towering maples whose leaves fall deliberately when it rains like this.

Through the years, we've grown accustomed to clearing these drains, particularly after the spring rains when the left-over leaves from beneath the melting winter snowpack reveal themselves and also during the October rains that bring falling leaves similar to today. We would put on Wellington boots and bring a shovel to the newly formed pond, wade carefully to locate the drain beneath the murky, leaf filled water, and use the spade to scrape away the offending mass to help the water enter the holes underneath in a cataract of swirling debris.

October 23

An early Alberta Clipper pushed downward across the Adirondacks, over the Berkshires Mountains and past the Worcester Hills. In the span of a few hours, the temperature dropped from the upper fifties to the mid thirties as high winds ushered in the coldest air of the season. In the tempest throughout the morning, golden leaves from the big maple in the side yard flew all about, swirling in small tornados of air that caused them to pirouette wildly among one another before settling down rudely against the eddies of the house. By noon, the yard was covered once again, and we smiled wryly to one another. We had just raked yesterday, and the evidence of our work was covered anew.

Out front there is a coating of new debris. The winds set loose the thousands of acorn caps from the big oaks, and now they litter the yard and driveway just as the nuts themselves did so nearly two weeks ago. It's been such a strange autumn. We can't recall another year in which the nuts fell in reckless abandon without their attendant caps. Perhaps the prolonged drought stressed the trees so that the nuts released early. Regardless, the yard is now a mess of caps and small twigs, early brown oak leaves and small spruce needles, all set in motion by the relentless fury of the clipper across the open field.

In the morning I took a walk up the Asnebumskit trails, beginning at the dead end down Belle Arbor where the two track enters the forest for several hundred feet until it abruptly ends in a single path. This ascends the mountain side, rising through a hardwood forest that still has at least half its leaves in place, their yellow and orange hues filtering the early sunlight in warm tones and creating dancing shadows as the trees overhead swayed violently in the tempest. The path was covered in fallen leaves, made slippery by the recent rains, yet as beautiful as the color seen overhead. Near the summit, the wind penetrated through the exposed upper boughs, making a white noise like breaking waves.

October 24

Sarah saw a single Junco this afternoon, sitting happily beneath the side yard feeder tube inspecting the cast offs strewn about from above. Who's to say whether or not this is the first returned from its summer residence? It's certainly the first we've seen, and soon enough there will a dozen or so here to stay for the duration. It seemed perfectly at home in the company of two grey squirrels that also spent the better part of the afternoon foraging beneath the feeder.

Early last month there were at least a half dozen grey squirrels, composed of the two remaining parents and four juveniles, the latter easy to identify on account of their coloring and behavior. They were typical teenagers, all play and scuffling as they'd chase one another around the girth of the big maple, spiraling upward to the thick branches. They'd come to the feeder full of ambition, trying desperately to navigate the baffle affixed midway up the pole. We'd watch and laugh as they'd try all sorts of acrobatics and marvel at their ingenuity and lack of fear.

Sometime as the days turned into weeks, they disappeared, leaving only the original two parents, though occasionally we suspect that one of the offspring does come to pay a visit. Where they've gone is a mystery. Sarah recognized one (with a clipped ear) far across the road in the Anna Maria field, loping quickly to the island of hardwoods perhaps to a new home?

October 25

The frost crept in again overnight, barely showing itself as a thin veil of powdery white on the tips of blades of grass in the lawn. The sunrise temperatures were 31 degrees, and as the rays tracked in their stately arc across the southern sky, the frost remained in the shaded portions of the north side of the trees and from the long shadows cast by the roof lines of the house and barn. There, on the lawn, where the chimney shadow splayed out obliquely toward the road as the morning sunshine struck the house from its now acute degree, the lawn beneath displayed a ghostly white, while the grass beyond melted from the warmth.

The ebb and flow continues, and we know soon the creep of winter's grip will descend upon us for good. It lingers now in the shadows and on the high elevations, past morning and until noon, when enough of autumn remains to banish it away. But it returns again, as the wind settles through the night and the heat radiates upward and beyond. Tomorrow it will gain more ground, hang on for longer in the recesses where fall is content to let go, where the colors once vibrant with the arrangement of orange and yellow upon the ground have given way to muted tones of brown and tan, hastened by their internal decay and the changes that await.

October 26

Yesterday's tone was gloomy, wasn't it? Take stock, there is still enough beauty in the woods to enjoy. The season hasn't concluded just yet, despite that we are obviously past the peak of colorful splendor.

The oaks above still hold russet colored leaves, most with hints of remaining green along the mid vein. When the breeze lifts through the thinning woods, their sere edges scrape against one another and make soft swishing sounds. We can hear this only when we pause from our walk, for the leaves beneath crunch loudly with the passage of our feet.

There is something childish on our familiar paths, the leaves that gather in wind-formed piles. We know the bare trail lies beneath, hidden by the patchwork of maple, elm, beech and birch in colors that still run the range from brown to red. We could tread cautiously and lift each leg up high to gingerly step through the pile, but no. We know this path well. There are no hidden rocks or roots here. No surprise deadfalls either. This is familiar ground, these woods, where we tread childlike through the layers, perfectly happy to shuffle our feet and listen to the gentle rapport of autumn's harvest.

October 27

Where yesterday's skies held the deepest blue between horsetail wisps of passing clouds, the weatherman warned us of the changes that came overnight. This morning looked ominous and more like late November, with a uniform blanket of low leaden clouds that hinted of a coming storm.

The remaining leaves of the maple were strangely vibrant in the filtered grey light, though it was a matter of contrast against the darker backgrounds and not of color, which seemed leached further by the dreary day.

Something had tipped the birdbath over last night, perhaps out of frustration. The temperatures dropped to the mid twenties with the coming of the front, and the water inside the concrete bowl froze. This morning it was tilted over on its side, and a hemispheric chunk of ice discharged to the ground, where it lay throughout the remainder of the day. Two colorful maple leaves that must have been in the bottom when it froze were stuck to the whitish ice and looked rather pretty as a temporary sculpture.

By noon small flakes of snow came gently downward. This was no tempest. That is to come tonight, as the temperatures climb enough to warrant rain. Snows of October are this way, gentle things mostly and ephemeral. They melt as quickly as they settle. They are only a hint of what will come in earnest soon enough.

Within an hour the snow changed to a light rain.

October 28

The maul axe has been in the same place since early June, when I was full of an early summer exuberance that eclipsed both experience and common sense. It still rests in one of the sections of a maple we felled in May, blade embedded a quarter of the way into the edge of a log with the fiberglass handle extended upward to the sky. For several months we've ignored that both log and axe have sat near the edge of the woods where we first rolled the big sections, all exposed to the elements of summer and now fall. The handle weathered fine, and though the blade is covered with peppered spots of light rust, it too is little worse for the exposure, though leaving it thus is not something to admit.

It didn't take long in June to rediscover the difficulty of splitting newly felled sections of hardwood. I think I must have done a dozen or so before conceding to common sense that such tasks are better accomplished in the cold, when the wood tends to crack apart explosively in vertical fissure rather than separate reluctantly in the moisture and warmth.

Now the season is upon us, and it is time to split the maple and put the sections in the barn. They'll go to the rear, behind the hardwood unused from last year, the maple, oak and hickory that have seasoned well for nearly eighteen months. These we'll ferry as need requires to the basement, where they will stack and warm inside, waiting their turn to woodstove upstairs.

October 29

In the predawn darkness of this frosty morning, yellow leaves in the side yard crunch beneath our feet. They make the only noise amid the calm, for the insects have perished from the recent cold, and the remaining birds now wait until the building light to come quietly to the feeders. There are no calls like those of late May, when joyous noise filled the air with the sounds of returning life and growth.

The quiet is peaceful though and not unwelcome, and our breath makes pretty clouds of condensing vapor that rise up and briefly obscure the few stars we see through the thinning branches of the trees.

From somewhere we catch the hint of wood smoke and are reminded again of the season, when such things are done as much for ambiance as they are for necessity. We are still in the midst of transition and take pleasure in fallen leaves, hot apple cider, potato leek soup, thick coats that smell slightly of moth balls from storage, and the tang of wood smoke in the air.

A chickadee comes in early from somewhere in the lower woods. It alights gently on the feeder tube, not five feet away from where we stand and regards us quizzically in its own way. It is so quiet that we clearly hear the shuffle of it's tiny feet upon the cold metal of the feeder perch, and it emits a stoic greeting "chick a dee, dee, dee" before deciding we are an unthreatening part of this October morning.

October 30

The farm is officially closing today, which is another indication of the season. Last week the peppers in the front field still had rather vibrant dark green leaves that sheltered the dangling unpicked fruit of green, yellow and red. With the heavy frost three nights ago, the plants now look done. The leaves are wilted and resemble cooked spinach, and the peppers have dark spots on their surface.

Work still goes on, of course. The boys will continue to pick leeks until the crop runs out, and there are still potatoes in the lower field that may have survived a penetrating freeze. Then there will be irrigation pipes to organize and plastic to pull before the ground freezes. Regardless, things are coming to an end.

Fred may yet find time to use the new no-till seeder. It's a bit late in the season, though with luck we may have a stretch with temperatures that will cooperate. He's been short handed this year and not able to put down the cover crop in those fields that have been left fallow since the vegetables ran their course. The new seeder needs no plowing and so may save time. It would be nice to see green shoots of rye in the fields, even if they would be destined to freeze and yellow soon in the coming cold.

October 31

October has been bittersweet and typically mercurial. We've experienced warm and cold in fluctuation, with no steady periods of either the entire month. Such is the nature of turbulence and indicative of transition.

One season evolves slowly into the next through the succession of things. Summer gives way to the beginnings of fade even as it reaches its nadir in July. We just don't notice the changes as readily when there is so much to experience. The same is true with autumn. The lingering warmth of September often comes on air masses that are drier, and the diminishing sunlight catches us off guard when we notice the lengthening shadows at midday.

This October has been more punctuated in its evolution. One day was cold and the next warm. One day was dry and the next with rain. It's difficult to mentally let go of autumn and prepare for winter when things have been in such fits and starts. Still, the days are progressively getting shorter, and the color in the landscape is slowly fading away. These changes are steady and provide the most assurance that November is around the corner.

November

November 1

There are no wildflowers left in bloom, not even straggler asters. It seems as though the color is being slowly leached away as the landscape increasingly turns from yellow to more earthy tones of tans and browns. Puffy heads of the golden rod still linger in the roadsides, but their color left some time ago as petals gave way to miniature balls of tufted seeds. They resemble dandelions this way, and we sometimes slap them quickly to watch the small parachutes lift upward and beyond. Next year's golden rod perhaps.

The irony is how certain trees stand out more now than they have in months, and we will look to them increasingly in the weeks and months ahead for the promise that such color will once again predominate after the long dormancy. The arbor vitae especially are deeply green and healthy. We paid them little attention last month, hidden as they were among the oaks, maples and other deciduous understory trees. So too the white pines we'd nearly forgotten in the deep woods. See how they contrast brilliantly in the fading light of the afternoon?

The sun angles through the woods in golden hues, and it is lighter in even the deeper hollows, down where the ground is moist from seepage of Asnebumskit and where green moss covers portions of large stones that stick above the leaf strewn floor.

November 2

In the front garden, a ladybug was tucked within dried brown sepals still attached to a leftover seed cluster of a Rose Campion. We noticed it only because the afternoon

213

sun's rays shone directly on the spot and set apart its tiny bright red and orange carapace from the drabness of its hidden retreat. It must have decided that the small recess would provide enough shelter against the oncoming cold.

Soon enough more will move into open fissures around the window frames, if they haven't done so already. Here they will wait out the winter freeze, content to let things take their course until such time that warmer weather gives them the impetus to emerge once more. In some ways we envy them.

At some point during the season, perhaps if January is kind enough to release his grip (he being Janus, after all), we'll enjoy a stretch of relative warmth, and we will open the windows briefly for the shear pleasure of having fresh air. Inevitably we will discover dozens of ladybugs tucked beneath the window, rudely awakened by our interruption and moving slowly about in confusion to escape the incoming cold. It's a pleasant surprise to come upon them in this way, a visual reminder of the last growing season during the middle of our own indoor hibernation.

Ladybugs evidently can withstand a freeze. I've come upon several that have wandered out from some hidden spot in the rough siding of the barn on a sunny winter day, when the sun's rays strike briefly upon their place of hiding. They stumble about in torpor until the light shifts and the wood is in shadow once again, whereupon they go still and remain so for a while, until gravity pulls them loose to the ground. There they'll remain through the thick of things. Most die, especially if the temperatures decline too low, which is the norm in January. I've rescued several seemingly stiff from the hard freeze and brought them inside, letting them thaw within a terrarium next to the windowsill. After a time, they begin to move again, revitalized in every sense from winter's grip.

November 3

For no specific reason, the oak leaves began falling one after another in the afternoon. There was no hard frost last night. In fact, it was rather mild. This morning, the leaves were notably brown, where yesterday they still had a yellow tinge, and a slight breeze brought them down in remarkable succession.

Out front, they gather briefly below the two red oaks, until the wind comes over the field across the road and sets them tumbling toward the house. Most come to rest in the thick Vinca that borders the foundation, though some get entangled in the long grass of the lawn that I should have mowed some time ago. It's too late now, and my inattention will make the leaf raking that much more difficult.

It's been challenging enough this year with the acorns that still adorn the yard by the thousands. When the maple leaves came down, I spent the better part of an hour clearing them with the rake to the periphery of the yard where the border woods lies. I'm embarrassed to admit that I fell more than once by slipping on the acorns as I raked; they act like small ball bearings on the firm ground, and comical as it may seem, I did take several tumbles.

Biologists describe the liberal seed production as a mast year, which is nature's way for the trees to periodically tip the balance in favor of their progeny surviving. Every few years, oaks will generously put forth acorns to such a degree that they oversaturate the supply and as such guarantee the likelihood that many acorns remain unmolested by the rodents and mammals (including us) who would gather them away. This costs the tree enormous resources to accomplish, which is likely why mast years only happen periodically, and I for one appreciate fewer hazards in the yard.

November 4

Now that the yellow leaves have fallen to the ground, the bittersweet vines stand out distinctly among the trees within the border woods and along the roadways. Their many berries display themselves in spiral patterns that rise upward through trunks and outward across branches, giving ornaments of yellow and crimson to the woodland.

Its yellow casing displayed first a few weeks ago, though it was hidden within the remaining foliage. Now it has become conspicuous and also altered, having split open to reveal the crimson berry that lies within. For those evergreens like our arbor vitae near the berm, where bittersweet has invaded and taken hold, there are dozens of small yellow and red splashes of autumnal color, and it is difficult not to appreciate the unique beauty these invasives provide.

However, it is growing late in the season, and some have begun to shed their casings, brought down by strong breezes of Canadian air across the Berkshires. Look beneath the vines, and soon there will be small scatterings of yellow shells, strewn like corn kernels among the remaining blades of the adjacent lawn. These mix with newly fallen oak leaves and will be raked when we have the time.

November 5

We heard the sound of the tractor this afternoon and caught a glimpse of it through the dark trunks of the spruce trees that line the road. Now that the understory of vines and juvenile poplar have lost their leaves, we are once again able to see across the fields and to the horizon of woods far beyond where the stone wall divides the upper from lower rows of the farm.

This familiar sound means beginnings in April, when the field is clear of snow and the ground is dry enough to allow it to be turned over in preparation. It is the signal that soon new growth will begin, and we anticipate the look of rows where small seedlings appear as if by magic behind the slow chugging tractor and the trailing transplanter.

This is also the sound of maturity in July, when there is time between planting and harvest that requires cultivation. We watch the slow pass as it makes its way down the rows with bladed tynes behind, turning the soil in the fallow troughs between the beds to break the roots of the growing weeds.

This is the sound of endings too, come November when the work of harvest is long past and the store is closed save for those customers who know there are still root crops and potatoes for sale. We see the tractor again, along the same rows of spring and summer, pulling long horizontal bars behind it to dislodge the plastic enough so that the field hands that remain can release it from the soil.

November 6

Sure enough, in the stiff afternoon breeze we saw billowing plastic across the road, as the boys worked to lift the windward edges of the bedding so that mother nature could assist. Upward, the long rows of tattered black would go violently, throwing loose soil skyward where it would catch the breeze and make light brown clouds that moved swiftly in the air.

Beneath lay exposed the mounded rows of darkened soil, save for the stubble of whatever provender remained from the harvest of weeks ago. The plastic kept light from penetrating and held moisture within the Earth for the growing plants. These now naked rows contrasted starkly with the weed-filled troughs between, where pigweed, clover, dame's rocket and pepperweed still held supreme, among other perennials that would overrun if left unchecked.

The exposed soil will dry quickly, of course, but for now it resembles the appearance of the newly-turned ground we see in spring. In this sense the land has come full circle, as have we who've watched the succession of the growing season, the life on the farm, and the simple rhythms of this year.

November 7

We turned the clocks back for daylight savings yesterday, and apart from the benefit of gaining an extra hour of sleep, the adjustments are less rewarding. The morning sky shows the hint of the approaching dawn slightly before six o'clock, which is fine for us early risers. However, the sunset takes place near four thirty in the afternoon, and by five o'clock it is notably dark.

Daylight savings aside, it is remarkable how much less sunlight we now have compared to several months ago. Such is the payment we owe for the leisure of June.

Of course, the savings are our own contrivance, and the adjustments must be made by our own motives. Animals have no such consequence, aside from those that must share our time schedules and as such adjust their own in concert. Our dogs, for example, do not do well with

218

"daylight savings." Their internal clocks for waking and feeding, the latter being more critical, are remarkably precise. This has made their confused adjustment our own difficult one. What was normally the morning breakfast at 6 am is now 5 am according to their circadian drives. And the evening five has been replaced by four. It will take weeks to get them accustomed to what is ostensibly *our* new rules.

So too the wild animals don't adjust. They continue on as before, their behaviors governed by diurnal schedules that wax and wane but not with retrograde degrees we artificially impose.

It would be simpler to leave well enough alone. Besides, we aren't saving any daylight at all! It keeps diminishing day after day until late December. We should rather call it "Daylight Adjustment" time instead. I think the few remaining farmers would be just fine with that.

November 8

A vixen fox cut through the side yard this morning, passing beneath the old maple now bereft of leaves. It paused momentarily to mark its territory near the base of one of the tube feeders and then proceeded rather casually to skirt the stonewall toward the lower woods.

We assume it was a female, for several minutes later another fox with slightly darker coloring followed nearly the same path. It (he?) stopped to inspect the spot beneath the feeder, and he too walked in a leisurely route to the lower woods, entering the trees in the same place as did the vixen.

Both were beautiful shades of orange and brown, with tufted fur along their tails that ended in small white splashes. Their den must be somewhere within the woods, perhaps down near the outlet stream of Asnebumskit where it follows the shallow valley toward Streeter Pond a quarter of a mile down Grove.

Sometimes in the early morning before dawn, we'll hear the strange barks and cries of the fox, which never fail to stir feelings of fear. Their calls are eerie and a little frightening, which add flavor to those dark autumn evenings when moonlight casts stark shadows on the newly exposed branches and the periodic sounds of Great Horned Owls come from far off in the woods.

November 9

The winds shifted to the south today, which brought the afternoon temperatures into the low sixties. An hour before sunset, I sat on the large stone rock that fronts the house and allowed myself what might be the last pleasure in doing so for several months.

The light is even more golden now than last week, and it angles so acutely at this hour that the late afternoon seems sepia toned as an antique photograph. Even the experience of sitting here feels out of place, or out of time given the month.

Some small hatch must have happened in the warmth, for several tiny insects floated by, backlit in the sunlight from my position. So too came loose strands of webbing from some spider; they floated upward and back down, coming in and out of view when the light reflected within them. These things are ephemeral, as they will be gone soon and not return until May.

The sun started below the tops of the woods across the road, and shadows cast obliquely up the side house. The temperature cooled quickly, and a lone chipmunk called its chirping cry atop the stone wall.

November 10

It is a pleasant mystery that some maples see fit to hold out against the changing season. Our own grand sugar maple in the side yard is nearly bare and has been so for over a week. Its brilliant leaves adorned the yard in wonderful shades of yellow and red until we summoned the stamina to rake them to the side berm, where there that sat in loose piles succumbing to further decline. I see today that their color has diminished toward the russet end of the spectrum, and the leaves are notably dried.

Yet, traveling home from Holden on the town road, there are many such trees that still stand resplendent in the midst of autumn color. There is a rather fine example that fronts the old Van Wyck house at the corner of Grove and the Holden Road. It's boughs reach skyward and out toward the road, and its branches spread to such a degree that the afternoon sunlight shines through layers of bright yellow leaves, each capturing the rays and seeming to glow with incandescence. Seen from below, it is simply wonderful.

November 11

A fifth of a mile downhill past Robinsons on lower Grove, the small bog on the east side of the street shows off its winterberry now. Within the nest-like appearance of wetland shrubs, there are splashes of brilliant crimson. These festive berries will remain for several weeks, if not more, until the deep snows hide the more accessible pickings and the remaining birds get desperate for some daily fare.

Mixed within are hold out leaves of the burning bush. Most have now dropped to the ground, but here and there remain single leaves of crimson that dangle loosely in the gentle breeze, making shimmering patterns against the rigid grey stems of the surrounding shrubs.

It's been a wonderful year for the burning bush. We have several in front, and all turned color slowly and in fits and starts. For two weeks, there has been a mixture of deep red, bright yellow and still green leaves on each bush, and in fact these three colors even exist at the same time on single leaves. How atypical from the traditional transition to uniform yellow then red. This scattering of autumn hues has been a reward for the prolonged drought, particularly when we expected nothing in the way of traditional color.

November 12

Small skins of ice lay on the surface of portions of Kettlebrook where the water shallows near the shore. In the stillness of last evening, they formed delicately as the temperatures fell below freezing, revealing themselves in the morning as smooth ice interrupted by small ridges of crystalline expansion.

By eight o'clock a breeze had risen with the warming of the land by the lifting sun, causing small waves to form on the northwest side of the reservoir and travel toward the shady places where the ice still remained. The water lapped gently over and wore away its foothold, and after an hour or so the ice was completely gone, melted away for the time being thought likely to return again tonight.

Across the reservoir the sunlight cast the far shore in sharp contrast, setting apart the deep greens of the spruces and cedar from the surrounding browns of dormant trunks and the earthen tans of their decaying leaves that lie below on the shoreline.

Two brilliant splashes of orange moved slowly in the distance, skirting the tree line along the shore. These must have been hunters, for the season is upon us now, and we are reminded of the caution we must take in exploring the woodlands for the time being.

November 13

The canopy of trees over the road offers far less shade now that the leaves have fallen away. Overhead, branches crisscross in spidery patterns that were hidden for months within the comfort of the soft boughs, where street level the pavement was shaded and the air was markedly cooler.

It is cooler still, though not because of the shade of summer. The angled sun makes its way through the thinned forest, and it is remarkable how far we can see deep into the fell from the street, where only a month ago the ferns and shrubs made the going difficult, let alone our line of sight.

Overhead the sky is impossibly blue, and the dark branches move in parallax as we pass beneath. Here and there, reluctant leaves still hang on, dangling by some hidden connection between petiole and stem and moving in gentle twists in the breeze that passes high above.

Some things stand out uniquely from this perspective, like the cones of the yellow birch, which look strangely out of place when seen with leaves still attached. Bare twigs of this deciduous tree have clusters of cones, and we are momentarily confused by this circumstance. There are several birches here, in these lower woods, where the cedar and white pines also have cones to offer.

224

November 14

It is easy to become melancholy now, as we bear witness
daily to changes that suggest endings of so many things
we've come to enjoy. I suppose the same is true of spring
and summer, though autumn so wondrously caps the end
of life and growth. The maturity of July gave way to the
harvest of September and October, and we were filled with
the satisfaction of seeing the promise of spring fulfilled
from the flower to the seed of tomorrow's rebirth. It is no
wonder that we may be wistful in taking stock, as the color
continues to fade, and the animals recede one by one into
dormancy.

No season lasts forever, and we must look to the simple
pleasures of what remains and the comfort of rest that
winter will provide. Without these things, I doubt our
wonder would be as profound. We know too well what we
shall miss these next few months, which makes the
appreciation all the sweeter.

It's pleasant today sitting here on the back porch, and
though the woods have lost much of their splendor, the
golden light filters through warmly. This and the absence
of wind make it tolerable here with just a light jacket. Plus,
I have a cup of hot tea held between my palms. The heat is
enough to warm my hands and body that the chilly air
isn't bothersome but rather pleasant. Small wisps of steam
rise upward from the tea and mix with the air,
disappearing on small currents that eddy somewhere out
of sight. It is beautiful here. There is still much to enjoy.

November 15

The full Beaver Moon hung spectacularly over the western
horizon before dawn this morning. As it descended it took
on a slightly orange hue, it's reflected light passing

through the haze of thin clouds far away and its spectral blues refracted so that the yellows and reds predominated.

According to astronomers this was a super moon, meaning that it was particularly large in the sky. We're to understand that the slightly elliptical orbit of the moon shifts, and there are relatively rare times when its heavenly dance brings it particularly close to Earth coinciding with its position opposite that of the sun. In short, the full moon was actually at its closest point to Earth by nearly thirty thousand miles.

An hour earlier, it was higher in the dark sky and brilliant white, almost painfully contrasted against the inky black beyond, where the pinpoints of stars seemed less distinct because of its luminescence. This was a late autumn sky, absent of the dust and humidity we associate with spring and summer. It was clear and cold and stark, this Beaver Moon, looming large in the mid-November morning.

November 16

The sky darkened midafternoon, and shortly thereafter came a deluge. Truly, it rained the likes of which we've not seen for several months.

It happened with such force that the oak leaves were stripped nearly clean from their stems, and for several minutes at the outset it appeared as though a snowstorm of falling brown leaves was taking place. The consequence revealed itself as the rain abated slightly; the yard was covered layers deep in oak leaves as were the pools of water in the low depressions of the driveway.

Runoff gathered strength from the open fields to the south and also across the road, quickly creating small rivulets that merged into an impressive flow of water at the side of the road. This came with such force that it cut a path through the fallen leaves on the roadway, lifting them in the torrent and carrying them down Grove toward the lowlands near Robinsons.

By late afternoon the rain ended, and we surveyed the front lawn. To think that we'd spent hours already raking the maple and apple leaves! Now the second round is upon us, this final tidying of summer's production, which will be gathered in piles within the border woods to await decomposition next spring.

November 17

Along the southern edge of the lawn, the grass has increasingly gone to moss. This has been a curious thing, particularly this year with the drought, however it continues at a slow pace. Who knows? Too much shade, acidic soil, high moisture, or neglect? Some combination of all, I suspect.

It is conspicuous now that we have raked the leaves once again to the edge of the woods. The ground here is emerald green and spongy underfoot, with blades of bluegrass and fescue poking through in a losing battle against the inevitable. While the remainder of the lawn has been slowly going dormant, this border moss is thriving in the late November transition.

Sometime during the night a skunk must have visited, for the moss is pocked in dozens of places where small claws dug through to the soil beneath. Given the moisture, they must be in search of earthworms or perhaps grubs, though the latter seem to prefer the open lawn where the tender roots of young grass reside.

November 18

The male goldfinches have lost nearly all their color since
the striking yellow of early August. It is surprising that we
still have so many around the feeder this late into autumn,
but there they are, loitering as nearly a dozen on the
perches in the tube. The stragglers seem content to rest
patiently on the shepherd's hook, waiting for one of the
cohort to abandon the post. We wonder if there is some
established pecking order, or if it is merely first come –
first served.

How distinct their behavior from the resident chickadees
and titmice, which prefer to come and go to the woods
with their seed. The chickadees alight within the spruce
boughs or the bare maple branches nearby and call in
greeting, then swoop gently to the tube to take a single
seed. This they carry off to the safety of the forest edge,
where they will carefully open and clean the contents of
the small black sunflower prize. Then it's back again,
quickly this time for they are used to our presence nearby.
No need to call, apart from a slight chatter to announce
their intent.

As one they suddenly scatter, taking flight to the forest as a
shadow passes overhead. Somewhere above a falcon or
hawk makes its presence known, and the woods go
strangely quiet for several minutes until furtive calls begin
anew.

November 19

We keep an old-fashioned barometer on a shelf in the
office and occasionally check to see if current conditions
outside match the descriptive text on the face. Presently
today is characterized as "fair," which aligns well with the
rather atypical warm temperature and clear skies this late

in the month. When I tapped the glass, the needle jumped noticeably to the counter clockwise direction, signaling a move toward "changeable." If I were to tap it again soon after, there would be no movement, however I suspect that several hours from now it would indeed jump again in the same fashion.

According to the weatherman, a large cold front is coming from the Midwest, where it has there already dropped temperatures by nearly twenty-five degrees and unleashed both heavy rains and snow in the higher elevations. In short, this is the first major storm of the season, though it is likely to bring only wind and cold our way by tomorrow.

Winter storms often arrive this way, on the crest of powerful fronts that race in quickly to displace the current calm. In the absence of modern forecasting, we would be in ignorant bliss today of the tempest due only tomorrow, save for the barometer that portends something in the air. Perhaps it is better expressed as something not in the air, for the pressure is dropping steadily, and I suppose technically this means fewer molecules of gas in a given volume.

Nature won't abide this change, and soon the winds will undoubtedly increase as she strives to equalize the pressure differential. The lower the "glass" drops, the worse the storm will likely become.

November 20

By dawn, the winds had increased to a steady breeze, causing the scattered oak leaves in the front yard to twirl wildly, lift and dance toward the front of the house. Up above in the branches of the big oaks, the hold outs that still clung tenaciously to their stems all strangely aligned with the wind direction like dozens of brown miniature weathervanes. Sarah remarked that they looked like schools of fish that sway back and forth in formation.

An hour later the wind picked up notably, and unfortunately had become forceful enough to agitate the piles of leaves across the road and carry them over and onto the yard. Within ten minutes the yard was fairly well covered again with the same leaves we raked several days ago. All we could do was sigh in exasperation.

By noon the first flakes of the season began to descend, carried forcefully by the gale of the incoming front that also dropped the temperatures into the mid thirties. The day had gone from amusing, to frustrating, to alarming all within the span of a couple hours.

The first snows are ephemeral things, and this will be the case with the dusting we received today. The ground is too warm yet to allow us the pleasure of more than a few hours with grassy surfaces covered in white. By tomorrow the front will have passed, and while the chill will settle in for several days, the snow will be only a memory for now.

November 21

The north side of Asnebumskit hill looks now as if autumn has given way completely. In the afternoon sun, the deciduous trees are almost all bare, making the evergreens stand apart from the vantage point where Grove meets the Maple. It's been a rather typical transition, I suspect, though it feels as though the slow change from early to late autumn has come in punctuated progression. Only a month ago we remarked how the hillside was bathed in golden hues that contrasted beautifully with the crisp blues overhead. Surely, we thought, it won't get more spectacular than this.

We were overruled, as the yellows gave way to the coming of varied colors. Deep reds and russet browns offset the fading sunshine of the hillside, making the landscape more alive in its maturity, with the vibrant greens of the white pines and eastern spruce providing evidence that nature holds on to production even as the remaining trees let go brilliantly to the season of growth. Again, how wonderful the view, and how certain we were that the best was now at apex.

Now we view these same hills, laid bare with branches bereft of leaves and colors that speak of muted tones of earthy browns and greys, where skies once the color of cerulean blue have given way to changeable moods of leaden cold. And how far we can see through woods, to the arc of some distant hillside that was hidden only last week. How liberating this period, amid what is understandably framed as decline, and this may be true as far as colors and life, sounds and warmth, but our vision expands to horizons we'd forgotten during the leisure of our greener months.

There is beauty now of a different sort.

November 22

The road surface now has a white sheen, made so from the liberal use of salt by spreaders of the Department of Public Works. At some point yesterday the trucks must have canvassed the streets, winnowing salt crystals to the ground in anticipation of a storm that ironically never materialized. The salt dissolved nicely with left over water from the melted snow of two days ago, and in the cold sunshine yesterday this mixture evaporated. The salt remained behind as a thin coat of dry, powdering film, making the roads appear as though they've been covered in a delicate layer of powdered sugar.

I almost wish this were the case.

I detest the salt. Truly, there are few other subjects about the governance of the town that raise my disgust more than the excessive use of salt to make the roads more navigable in winter weather.

It wasn't too long ago, perhaps only six or seven years, that the town still used sand when the roads became treacherous. Sand is messy. Sand isn't as effective, for it helps with traction only modestly, and it has little effect on melting. Sand is labor intensive in the spring, for the town obligates itself to spend more time sweeping the road clear of the winter accumulation.

However, sand isn't corrosive. Sand doesn't alter the pH of the surrounding soil. Sand doesn't adversely affect the water uptake of roadside foliage or trees. All we need is to look upon the burned needles of the evergreens along the heavily salted routes to appreciate that something is amiss with its use.

November 23

The dusting of snow from a few days ago has largely melted, apart from the shaded areas of the back porch, where the air underneath prevents the warmth of the ground from conduction. In other places, there are small puddles of water from the melt held within depressions of the cupped boards. Now the sun is too weak and the air too cool for them to evaporate, and so they remain throughout the day and night, freezing over as the temperatures descend by evening and melting slowly in the attenuated daylight.

A couple weeks ago we cleaned the stone birdbath and set it on its side to dry before putting it in the barn for winter storage. To compensate, we placed a large plastic basin on an old stump near the side porch and filled it with water, not worrying about damage from expansion or contraction as the freeze and thaw took place.

The birds seem to have adjusted just fine, though there are interesting moments in the late mornings when they first arrive to the edge of the basin. Overnight a thick film of ice builds on the surface, and the first arrivers to the basin (typically the chickadees) appear impatient for the initial melt to occur. They perch stoically on the edge and test the lip for signs of liquid then fly off to the big maple and then the woods. As the sun strikes the ice it slowly melts, initially as a transparent film of water on the surface, then fully as the day progresses. Birds return throughout the day and take turns, before the skim forms as dusk arrives.

November 24

Until today, I had forgotten about the small patch of Trailing Arbutus I transplanted in late spring to a shaded area of soil near the stone wall in the back. This morning, I happened to be standing on the back porch when one of the few remaining oak leaves from a nearby tree let go and drifted softly downward, coming to rest on a small pile of similar leaves over the spot where I'd transplanted. So I walked over, leaned down and used my hand to scrape away several wet layers of detritus. There beneath lay the Arbutus, it's healthy deep green waxy leaves among the vine-like stems.

When I transplanted it, there were nearly a dozen pale pink flowers protruding from the ends of several stalks, each nestled among the ivy-like leaves and the surrounding moss in a small carpet of boreal growth. These flowers would have emerged early in spring, signaling the transition toward warmer days ahead and a harbinger of the beauty of returning life.

Of course, the flowers were long gone, yet there beneath the leaf cover, the Arbutus survived. And, in several places new buds had formed, now closed tightly to protect themselves against the coming cold and to await the proper conditions that only spring can deliver. How wonderful to see it so.

We tend to think retrospectively on this day of thanks, and I am grateful for the small yet profound experiences this New England life affords. I keep a transient list of favorite things in my head, and when I am feeling a bit blue I remind myself how fortunate I am to experience the everyday little things throughout the year. Seeing this Trailing Arbutus so is another reminder of the beauty of this life.

Binding these experiences is the assurance of the cycle of the seasons - that those things we cherish dearly will come again as one day gives way to the next and as months stack upon themselves in the succession of the Paxton year. There is a promise in the Arbutus buds beneath the leaf layer, that one day not too distant from now the cycle of wonder and growth will begin anew.

November 25

We finally opened the fireplace room, feeling somewhat like Howard Carter in opening the door, peering inside and smelling the cooler stale air. It is true, though difficult to believe, that we haven't used this room since roughly early April, after having spent nearly every day last winter seated on the couches nearby the wood stove.

Our house is what is termed a 1700s Salt Box, with a massive chimney that extends up through the middle of the house and thrusting centrally beyond the wood shakes that line the roof. If the house were viewed from above in schematic, there are essentially four large rooms on the first floor; each having one wall in common with what is the chimney, though in three of the rooms we have wainscoting and lathe with plaster to hide the brick. Only in the fireplace room is it exposed, with nearly one whole wall given to both the Rumford maw and a small Beehive oven next to it. Around the other three walls are darkly stained wainscoting and white plaster, with 24" wide plank pine on the floor that abuts to the extended brick of the hearth.

Within the maw, I placed a large woodstove and insert, connected to the flue opening and capped on either end to prevent drafts. This arrangement is far more efficient and warm than the traditional fireplace, which tends to draft all heat upward through the flue in remarkable rapidity.

Today I cleaned the woodstove, first pulling the stovepipe from the rear and using a vacuum to remove the creosote. Then out went the old ashes from the basin, those leftover from the final fire of mid spring. After reconnecting the pieces, we were ready for another winter.

The first fires of the season are pleasant ones, nostalgic in many ways. We sat today in our favorite places: Sarah and I on the couch, the two dogs and the cat on the hearth, dangerously close to the heat of the stove. We will use this room nearly every day from here onward till sometime in March, and the nostalgia will quickly dissipate, replaced by acceptance that this form of heat is messy and a chore but worth it as we wait patiently for the coming of spring.

November 26

With dense clouds overhead, daylight filtered weakly through the lower woods, and with a slight fog that formed over the wet basin, the trunks of the trees contrasted darkly against the grey veil.

By midday, the mist remained despite the strengthening sun somewhere above. The light increased enough to reflect more acutely through countless microscopic water droplets in the air, making the entire basin strangely glow.

A slight breeze passed through and moved the fog closest to the ground, making visible eddies of water vapor. These trailed downstream and revealed in clearing a small hillside full of beech trees. Their light brown leaves are almost translucent, and they reflect the filtered light strongly against the grey.

November 27

Soon enough we will lose the front yard to the snow,
perhaps for several months. Though the grass has gone
dormant from the cold, it still looks like autumn on the
lawn, with stray oak leaves caught in the blades of taller
sections of grass that avoided the late season mow.
Overhead is something altogether different; the trees
themselves are almost universally bare, apart from the few
dead leaves that continue to resist the pull of the wind and
cold.

The ground is hard in the morning, having frozen in the
cold temperatures overnight and taking until midday to
thaw again. Each evening the frost increasingly gains the
upper hand, and soon there will be no ebb and flow from
the cold. It's best to simply enjoy what little time we likely
have with these conditions.

The squirrels seem to have taken this to heart. Several
greys spend more time beneath the big Red Oaks in front,
taking whatever leftover acorns they can scavenge from
the ground beneath. One keeps a nest in the upper
branches of a large maple that borders the yard near the
road. It carries a large nut in its mouth as it bounds from
the middle of the yard toward the road, then ascends in a
spiral path up the telephone pole out front until it gets
high enough that it can jump across to one of the studying
maple branches.

November 28

A quarter mile past Robinson's approaching Pond Street,
the forest on either side is fairly thick, and the land is
recessed enough to prevent the cold crosswinds from
gathering strength here. It's for this reason why we often
take the dogs for an afternoon walk in this direction. At

our house, the prevailing northeast winds come across Cournoyer's fields with some ferocity, and there is little in the way of foliage across the road to buffer their approach. The spruce line has grown mature to the point that the lower branches, those that ten years ago were thick with evergreen needles right to the ground, have become bare and lifeless with the passage of time.

It was 28 degrees late morning, and we made the turnaround where Pond Street intersects lower Grove. On the return, we were treated to direct sunlight, noticeably angled low in the sky yet aligned almost precisely with the direction of the roadway for a short stretch.

Within the upper boughs of the bare trees on either side, we listened to the white noise of the winds, interrupted occasionally by the sparse forest chickadees and such. Despite the noise, there wasn't even a whisper of breeze on the road as we walked slowly, making the most of the late autumn sunshine on our faces and enjoying what little sounds to be heard as winter approaches.

November 29

Shots ring out well before dawn, from deep within the lower woods, sounding closer than is likely the case. The stillness of the morning and the cold air surely enhance the rapport.

A city-dwelling friend of mine noted her curiosity in the number of trucks parked in what she thought to be "the strangest places." By this she meant the shoulders of roadways that border any large patch of woods. I could only nod and agree that this may seem a little odd.

We have to be a little cautious these next few weeks, which is why our outerwear wardrobe includes more in the way of reflective vests and fluorescent colors. I'm to understand that the resident deer aren't able to sense such colors, and as such the only alarm will be to the area hunters, who are out with notable frequency.

November 30

November comes to an end, as does the last of the autumnal colors, when only a few weeks ago the woodland was still afire with the magnificence of varied hues.

Now the same leaf litter that once suggested something magical in its ending lies in nearly uniform russet tones where life has ebbed. We will become accustomed to these new colors for a while, until the deep snows arrive and blanket the landscape in the fresh brilliance of winter's arrival.

We've already begun to forget the deep greens that dominated in summer. Day by day, the last remnants in the yard have gone to dormancy, fading slowly to a mosaic of yellow green. It is only the rascal thyme within that provides stark contrast to the decline. These small islands of green are much the same as they were two months ago, though then they were well hidden among the production of the grasses. So too the mosses at the border show emerald green, looking strangely out of place in their surroundings.

December

December 1

Two nights ago we shared dinner across the road at the farm house with friends. Now that their pace has come comparatively to a halt from the days of planting, cultivating, harvest and sale, we look forward to the fallow that winter affords when we are able to meet socially and talk of the small things this place provides.

Apart from leftover turkey from the week prior, the meal consisted of vegetables entirely derived from the soil of the farm. It is impossible not to appreciate the wonder of eating dinner that is locally grown in every sense.

With each ingredient, we'd remark about some anecdote from the past eight months:

> "I remember when we helped transplant these peppers,"
> "The leeks made out fine despite the drought."
> "Tomatoes did well this year, all through October."
> "The squash was ravaged by the deer, but we harvested enough."
> "We're still picking potatoes even this late in the season."

Dinner passed with conversation and laughter, and afterward we made our way home across the road, feeling fortunate again to know such friends.

December 2

Sometime in October, when we were beginning the process of cleaning the back garden in preparation for winter, Sarah left a large plastic pot on the edge of the side porch next to where we step down to the yard. Over the course of the next several days, it would catch any stiff breeze and topple over then roll about the porch and generally get in the way. So, we set it upright again and finally decided to take one of the smaller pumpkins and place it wedged into the top of the pot.

There both pot and pumpkin remained, largely forgotten as one of several background items on the porch (which includes an old metal stool, an antique and rusty child's wagon, and a few large rocks with interesting patterns).

In the interim, the pumpkin slowly decayed and shrunk down within the inside of the pot, leaving only the very top and the stem sticking out. This afternoon, we watched as one of the grey squirrels repeatedly bounded to and from the plastic pot from within the protection of the upper branches of the large maple in the side yard. It would reach gingerly to the lip of the black plastic and pull itself up and over, coming to rest inside and partially on top of the soft orange of the pumpkin.

We watched it move its jaws rasp like across the surface of the pumpkin, digging deeply into the now soft outer skin

to the fleshy pulp within. After a short while, it would raise its head to look about, revealing its muzzle covered in a mess of orangey goo. Then it would retreat to the safety of the maple, ascending in spiral fashion to some nest far out of sight, before repeating the process in several minutes hence.

December 3

The weatherman professes that we are in the beginning of
the meteorological winter, which is the three-month period
designated typically by the coldest months of the year.
Anyone who's lived here in central New England for a few
years or more knows full well the inaccuracy of this
declaration, despite that historical records seem to bear
this fact. March is typically no peach in terms of weather,
and I suppose the forecasters mean well; it's always nice to
believe that you have a good head start on something that
is to be endured. The solstice is still a few weeks away, and
even then it isn't a safe bet that the astronomical winter
will conclude a mere three months henceforth in late
March.

This is New England, which means that winters are long
affairs, followed by the interminable period of "almost"
spring.

It's best now to muster resolve for the long haul ahead and
to take stock in the austere beauty that winter does deliver.
Soon enough the snow will arrive and blanket the ground
for weeks if not months on end. For now, we enjoy that the
ground is still bare, the leaf-strewn trails are still passable,
and the roads are clear of salt from the rains of the past
week.

December 4

In the morning I took the dogs for a walk around the
periphery of the fields across the road, which is something
we haven't done in quite some time. They are getting on in
age now, and what was an easy jaunt only a couple of
years ago is now almost too long for Kipper to manage.

This fact of aging is cruel, particularly since his spirit still demonstrates the desire to walk the trails of his youth.

Fortunately the cold air seemed to rejuvenate him, and both he and Tag ran ahead almost playfully down the two-track road that skirts the field edge along the border of the stonewall. They'd get fifty yards ahead and stop to smell something in the grassy patch between the tracks then sense my footfalls as I approached and begin to bound ahead once more. I lost track of the present moment while watching them so, for their movements reminded me of countless times over many years we'd walked this same stretch.

Down near the lower field, where the two track descends slightly as it reaches the corner where the stone wall angles ninety degrees to the south, we stopped for a while to enjoy the shelter of the enclave of surrounding trees and the morning sun coming directly to our location. There, next to the wall in a protected spot exposed to the sun, grew a yarrow wildflower, still barely in bloom. It was partially hidden among fallen leaves and yellow grasses far past their prime, but somehow despite the odds it held on to its green color and tiny white flowers.

December 5

Where the woods begin on the north side of Anna Maria's campus, the land descends into a forested valley that leads toward the shores of Pine Hill reservoir roughly a half mile away. Here, cultivated ground gives way abruptly to a forest that still shows the scars of the ice storm of nine years ago, where large deadfall limbs litter the floor and make the passage difficult.

The lower field of the farm abuts to the east, bordered by a seldom-used grassy road that skirts the forest edge before entering the woods and out of sight near far the corner of the open field.

In the afternoon, the sunlight angles across the campus and through the trees, casting the border field in golden sunshine. Here, within the raised middle of the old road stand the sere remnants of golden rod and milkweed, their presence an indication that this thoroughfare had no traffic for many months.

The stalks of both are mostly grey and brown, with vestigial leaves that dangle loosely on the stems and flower heads that have mostly lost their precious seeds, save for a few here and there that have yet to let go. We pulled the silks from the large pods of the dried milkweed and threw them rudely to the air, watching them catch the light brilliantly against the blue of the clear sky and drift slowly to the east toward the upper field until they caught some unseen eddy and lifted away.

December 6

The first measurable snow arrived silently sometime during the night, revealed by the street light that reflected off the white lawn and illuminated the inside of the house. We knew without looking out the window that everything was covered in fresh powder.

In the beam of the corner floodlight by the porch, hundreds of large flakes drifted lazily downward to accumulate on the masses that already lay beneath. An inch of fluffy snow covered every surface by dawn, and we looked out the sunroom window toward the lower woods, where the green boughs of the evergreens began to collect small drifts of white on their upper surfaces. The leafless branches of the deciduous trees showed themselves in beautiful crisscross patterns of white and dark, transforming the morning woods from what was solemn yesterday to simply lovely now.

Small footprints on the porch told the story of some early visitor, a mouse or vole having come to the bird feeders to steal cast off seeds now hidden beneath the new blanket of white. The tracks displayed a dainty path, following the outer wall of the house and dropping off the porch into the small pile of deadfall leaves that have a dusting of new snow.

December 7

As the temperatures fall below freezing, the rhododendron leaves begin to curl. They loosely follow linear relationship to the falling thermometer. At thirty degrees, they are still mostly full. At twenty-five, the outer edges have begun to turn under, and by twenty all the leaves have started to turn into themselves. Colder still, they form tight cylinders of deep green.

At the corner of the house, we suspected two robins had built their nest this past spring somewhere deep within the recesses of the rhododendron. It seems like long ago when we'd watch them travel back and forth to the nest in search of food within the yard for the babies that remained hidden in the bush. June gave way to fledglings and then again to their departure, leaving the nest fallow and forgotten as July slipped into autumn. Now in the cold afternoon the curling leaves slowly reveal the inside scaffolding, and the nest comes easily into view, giving us a glimpse of what may arrive next May when the warmth builds and life returns with the pulse of spring.

December 8

The air pressure is dropping once again, signaling the coming change that has been forecasted for several days. I tapped the glass this morning, and the needle jumped noticeably lower, which means the coming front is close at hand.

Of course, we knew this to be the case well in advance, and this is a privilege of our contemporary circumstances. The weatherman's images on the television two days ago depicted the circular movement of the building low pressure far up in Manitoba. Some alchemy of experience and simulation allows rather precise predictions to be made, taking into account all sorts of factors that lead to the strong conviction that what began as a small disturbance far away will coalesce into the arrival of wind and cold here this afternoon.

This brings to mind the parable of the butterfly's wings, when flapped gently in its flight some thousands of miles away causes such cascade of changes to the winds and weather that typhoons emerge in another part of the world.

I suppose we have become so reliant on contemporary forecasting there is no real need to be attuned to local indications that a storm is on the way. Such was the nature of things long ago, before television or radios or even barometers. New Englanders were more facile in interpreting the subtleties of changeable skies or behaviors of their resident animals.

Above now, there is a grey wall of leaden skies building on the western horizon, ushered in by the slightest breeze that has risen in the tops of the spruce trees. Activity at the feeders has increased noticeably, as the chickadees, titmice and juncos know somehow that challenges arrive soon. So too the cardinal pairs have come more brazenly, as do the jays and our big red, all quickly taking what they are able in preparation.

December 9

Last weekend we stretched clear plastic film across the inside molding of the windows, creating an air space of several inches between the exterior glass and the plastic. The film attached to self-sticking tape that was placed around the edges of the window frame, and we applied hot air to its surface to shrink it tightly across the opening.

Now that the December winds have arrived in earnest, it is remarkable how the film helps minimize the drafts through the sill. This is particularly true for the west facing windows, which tend to receive the brunt of oncoming fronts that descend upon us from somewhere out past the Berkshires.

The view is affected slightly, though in one respect it is more authentic to what would have been typical in a 1700s saltbox. No glass pane two hundred and fifty years ago would have the clarity that ours possess. There are some homes in Paxton that still retain one or more original panes of glass within the glazing of rather ancient windows. These antiques demonstrate the true character of pane glass, where even the most exemplar possessed distortions and even bubbles such that any view through the window was altered.

Such is the case with our plastic film, where the world outside is transformed slightly to one of historic distortion.

December 10

We awoke to the coldest morning of the season, with the thermometer outside the kitchen window reading fourteen degrees at five o'clock. I glanced out the porch door to see the feeder tubes swaying gently in a light breeze, which meant the wind chill must certainly be close to zero.

By daybreak, it was so cold the birds were reluctant to leave the shelter of the small spruce tree next to the berm. They preferred instead to stay puffed up within the windbreak provided by the network of green needles, whose branches swayed gently as small gusts of wind passed by the side of the house and down toward the lower woods.

A lone male cardinal looked out stoically toward the house, his brilliant red plumage contrasting festively among the surrounding deep green, making him an ornament of holiday color in this cold morning.

December 11

Yesterday's cold continued through the day and into the evening, with temperatures dropping once again to the single digits among skies that couldn't possibly be clearer.

Venus is as bright as she will be in her position as the evening star. She reached the apex of her inclination sometime in early November, and now she begins slowly to descend each evening from her highest point in the heavens. Her orbit around the sun lies within our own, and as a consequence she moves more quickly in her nearly circular pirouette compared to Earth's more sedate orbital velocity. This means that Venus is bound to pass us by roughly every nine months, and during those weeks that precede the time in which she overtakes our own position, she becomes brighter with apparent magnitude.

Paradoxically, as she brightens upon approach, we see less of her surface, for like our own moon, Venus exhibits phases. She takes on the crescent shape as she nears Earth's position, though she lowers ever more in the evening sky, until she becomes lost in the afterglow of the sunset. Like our new moon, Venus too passes between the orbit of the Earth and the sun and so becomes "new" herself until a few weeks hence she rises again before the sun and assumes her mantle as the morning star.

December 12

A thin layer of crusty snow still remained in the woods up Asnebumskit hill, though the ascending trail itself was clear, apart from the clutter of brown leaves that covered the track. The morning sun angled over the top of the summit and shone golden through the thinning canopy near the peak, shining down the ascending trail and reflecting off the sparse snow holding on within the shade of the large trunks.

Where snow remained, it was pocked as though a rain shower had briefly passed through, despite that the skies have been cold and clear for a few days. It must have been the melting snow from the overhead branches, warmed enough by the sunlight yesterday to turn to liquid and drip gently downward to the forest floor.

December 13

The Cold Moon

It stormed again during the night, and by morning the ground was covered in six inches of dense snow. In the hour predawn, the outside was unusually bright from the reflected light of the descending full moon that sat roughly ten degrees above the horizon to the west. Evidently, whatever storm passed during the night took with it the majority of clouds that brought the snow.

A thin haze of indistinct fog also rose above the tree line, slightly obscuring the moon so that its reflected rays diffused downward to the land. There was also a chromatic ring around its circumference, as its light refracted through the haze, making a slight circular rainbow.

I took a short walk up the road to enjoy the new snow and the surrounding skies. The town plow had yet to pass our netherworld of existence, which was fine with me. It felt fitting that the road still harbored its covered look, free from the scarring of the blade and the cast-off deposit of the newly lain salt. Apart from a singular track from some early departed car, the road may have as well been abandoned, save for my footprints that receded toward our driveway some hundred yards behind.

Without a hint of breeze, it was perfectly pleasant to shuffle along in the moon lit morning, where refracted light from above cast sharp shadows of the overhead trees onto the fresh snow on the road and field.

December 14

There are times when the transition to winter is especially lonely, as in the wooded hollows at the break of day, when there are few outward signs of life and the sounds of any activity have yet to muster. In the windless cold, the snow crunches softly under my feet, which break through easily to the clutter of fallen oak leaves hidden beneath. They rustle when disturbed, and the effect is one of repeated "crunch, swiffle" as I walk among the lifeless trunks of the deciduous forest.

When I stop to listen, and my breath calms to the point that it is silent, the woods become almost painfully quiet. There are no stirring sounds of some creature awake nor curious pips from a transient chickadee come to investigate my presence, nor gentle breeze that blows unseen through barren boughs. I am alone and still, save for the upward lift of my clouded exhalation.

This vapor rises in shifting form, through the lower branches and still visible though indistinctly in the diffuse light from the nearly full moon. Sometimes I hold my breath altogether and remain perfectly still, listening intently for any sign that life persists, my eyes open and looking skyward up through the canopy of skeletal forms to the dark and star lit heavens.

December 15

Yesterday's feelings persist, this melancholy of nature's decline. It is tempting to wish winter away, much like the animal that descends to the earth in torpor or hibernation.

Yet, we need remind ourselves of the value this transition affords. We must, as with all things, see endings for what they are, not necessarily as something final but rather as diminuendo. December gives way to the new year, and with it we rest in order to gather strength for the rebirth that follows, cycle upon cycle as winter one day gives way to the coming of spring.

December 16

A thin coating of ice has formed completely across the expanse of Asnebumskit Pond. This will likely remain until the real thaws of early spring, and so we had better get used to seeing it as such.

At the shore's edge, dried Phragmites grasses thrust upward from the surface of the blue-white ice through small holes that are resistant to a complete freeze. When a breeze hails somewhere on the expanse, it pushes gently on the surface and causes the water underneath to invisibly respond. We see a gust of wind far across in the upper boughs of spruce trees that ring the shore, and shortly thereafter small splashes of water burst upward through the holes where the grass reeds poke through. It is wondrous; this power of nature that sometime affects unseen.

Down Holden Road, where it reaches the valley and crosses the causeway over the reservoirs on either side, ice too has crept slowly over the surface though not completely. Near the bridge, there is flow underneath, as the water moves eastward from one reservoir to the other, ultimately to drain on the far side where the gothic-looking stone folly keeps sentinel to the spillway nearby. Even in the coldest winter, the reservoir near to the spillway rarely freezes over, as the flow is enough to hinder its change to ice.

December 17

The house began creaking during the evening, as temperatures fell below zero in the midst of an arctic clipper. We sat pitifully in the front room, each of us pretending to read though really listening intently to the fury that was building beyond the wall.

Out the window, the spruce trees across the road were clearly visible in the light of the waning gibbous moon. They shook so violently that small twigs of evergreen kept breaking loose and plummeting downward to the yard. Powerful gusts would strike the house a second after coming through the breach, crossing Grove in an instant and hitting with such force that the plastic covering inside the glass windows rattled slightly. All the while, the house creaked in protest, and doors shifted back and forth, catching on their antique latches and making small clinking sounds throughout the house.

December 18

The storm left as quickly as it arrived, and by daybreak the sun shone brilliantly across a cold landscape. We spent the better part of the morning sitting quietly in the sunroom, enjoying the direct rays that came in between the trunks of bare trees in the near berm forest. This is a pleasure of winter, when our sunroom is aptly named. From spring until the leaf fall, little sunlight reaches inside through the large side windows, apart from that which comes from above via the skylights.

What a contrast this day. Last evening we sat together with a mixture of awe and fear, listening insecurely to the tempest that continually reminded us of the harshness that winter sometimes delivers. This morning we sat in peace, and watched calmly as the dooryard birds returned to the feeders from whatever place they chose to ride out the storm.

We are not so different, really. We too huddled close and listened and watched powerlessly to the forces of nature that battered the house. We too waited patiently for the tempest to subside, when after we sought to enjoy the beauty delivered in its wake.

December 19

It warmed substantially this morning, brought in by a front from the south that sent temperatures up past fifty degrees for several hours. This hastened the melt of the snowpack, which has been modest thus far and now severely diminished from the warmth.

The fields became foggy with the melt, so thick that it was nearly impossible to see much further than a few dozen feet beyond the roadside. Small rivulets of water poured down in the natural depressions where the two track comes over the rise and across the front. These pooled into small ponds of several feet, where frozen ground beneath resisted any moisture from penetrating below.

By later afternoon the winds shifted suddenly to the northwest, pushing the warm air quickly aside and ushering in an arctic front. So suddenly, the fog was stripped away, revealing the landscape, the bare earth visible again in places where the snow melted nearly complete. Temperature fell through the twenties, causing the slow running water on the road to freeze in beautiful layers of icy flow.

December 20

The lower woods still have several inches of snow, despite the wonderful reprieve of yesterday's melt. With the refreeze, what had been lovely powder only a few days ago had now become a crusty affair, making our footfalls harsh as we navigated the old single track toward the low basin.

This year we decided out of nostalgia (and admittedly frugality) to cut our own Christmas tree from among the choices that had grown near the outlet stream that runs from Asnebumskit down the valley toward Streeter. In truth, the pickings aren't all that favorable here; most of the forest is composed of deciduous hardwood, and what few evergreens that have established a foothold are still relatively young. Several white pines do rise rather majestically here and there, perhaps eighty feet or more, and while there are dozens of offspring within their sphere, they are mostly saplings of a year or two. Strangely no adolescents seem to thrive. This is no matter, of course; white pine isn't the preferred Christmas tree anyway.

There are Eastern Spruce near the stream, but even these are relatively small, apart from parent stock that once again grew too tall to be of our particular use. We did manage to find a few we thought to be between seven and ten years mature, using the yearly growth of radial stems as an estimate. From these, we selected one that grew within the enclosure of a spot in the forest where the canopy had opened from some past disturbance. Here the open access overhead gave the tree enough light so that its growth was more aesthetic.

I took the saw and cut through the base. In truth this was a fairly minimal affair. The tree had a girth of less than three inches and was no taller than five feet high! No matter. We carried (not hauled) it back through the woods, up the access road across the crunchy snow, and set it up nicely in the sunroom, our own little Christmas tree to celebrate the Holy Days ahead.

Winter

Rest

December 21

It is counter intuitive that on this day the Northern Hemisphere is at its closest point to the sun in our annual orbit that we define as the year. Astronomers call this the *perihelion*, which derives from the combination of two Greek words, Peri (for "around" or "near") and Helios (for "sun").

Of course this is counterintuitive! After all, it's cold outside, and we understandably reason that being closer to the sun should, like bringing one's hand nearer to an exposed light bulb, provide us with more radiant warmth. However, this is not the case. While we are technically closer in perihelion, the orbit of the Earth is nearly a circular ellipse, with the sun at one of the foci. What this means is that the distance from the sun to the Earth in perigee is roughly 91 million miles. The aphelion (furthest distance) is 95 miles. The difference between the two is approximately 4%. This is like holding a hand 100 feet away from a light bulb as in summer and moving it only four feet closer as in winter – not enough to make a difference.

Today at 5:44 am we also call this the winter solstice. This is the official transition when our orbit leaves perihelion as Earth moves slowly in its yearly dance toward we will embrace soon enough as the coming of spring. Now the days begin slowly to accumulate more light as the axis of our inclination begins to tilt back toward the sun. Each day, the sun rises slightly higher in the sky. Each day, the rays become that much more direct, and this accounts for our seasonal variation.

As I type this, the sun just crested the lower woods. It is 7:35 am, and it shines golden through the tops of the tallest spruce trees and through the sunroom window to where I sit, waiting peacefully for spring's return.

December 22

I wore a headlamp in the hour before dawn as I walked the paved road that leads into Moore State Park. The air was perfectly still, the skies clear, and the temperature of thirty one felt strangely warm after the past week of rather artic cold.

It is curious how we adjust our tolerance to the cold as the season progresses. When the first hints of cool air arrive in September on the heels of the sweltering summer, we worry how we'll manage as the temperatures dip into the fifties overnight! Now the thirties feel decadent, which indicates how far we've come.

Where the two stone pillars stand as sentinels for the road as it descends slowly toward the pond and the spillway, I stood silently and allowed the beam of my light to shine ahead, illuminating the bare trunks of the deciduous trees on either side of the road. Those nearest reflected the light strongly, and as the forest retreated from the beam the shapes became less distinct until there was nothing but the darkness out beyond where no light penetrated.

As I walked slowly ahead, I turned my head away from the road and shone the beam into the thick of the forest, and from a place deep within, two distinct points of silvery light reflected back. I stopped in surprise (and a little fear) and watched for several seconds as the eyes of some unknown animal continued to monitor my presence, their luminous orbs blinking occasionally as the two pinpoints would vanish and reappear.

December 23

An acquaintance remarked about the lack of holly berries
in the woods. He and wife typically gather boughs from
the evergreens to make Christmas garland, using small
sprigs of holly to add little splashes of bright red. They
spent the better part of an hour walking the familiar trails
that lead from their back yard up into the trees that line the
lower slopes of Asnebumskit. In all the familiar places, not
a single holly could be found. Of course, there are
scattered bushes of winterberry, and while these will
suffice for the effect, it's a curious thing that the holly has
all but vanished.

I've another friend who thinks the rise in the wild turkey
population is to blame, as they tend to forage on low
browse, and the red berries are notably attractive.

We have two rather large holly bushes next to the house,
safe enough from wild turkeys but not from the rabbits,
who will go after the bush if things become desperate. A
couple years ago, during a particularly rough stretch when
the snow piled at least three feet high in all directions,
unbeknownst to us a rabbit had taken refuge under one of
the large bushes, which was entirely buried by snow.

Come spring, after the snow finally receded, the holly was
revealed stripped almost bare! The rabbit had eaten nearly
every leaf and berry to survive and had left piles of calling
cards behind.

December 24

It was especially quite this evening, with not the slightest
breeze and the absence of any traffic on the roads.
Sometimes in the stillness, particularly when the cold air
seems its most dense and thus conveys any noise easily

from even the most remote places, we hear the background pulse of passing cars from over a mile away or the strike of the town clock upon the hour, or sounds from some conversation down the road.

Tonight was breathlessly still, as if all life waited quietly in observance of this Christmas Eve.

December 25

Sarah thought the sun seemed to rise a little further to the north this morning. Doubtful it is noticeable yet, though it is true we both anticipate the stately movement of its progression away from the solstice. The first few weeks of winter won't see much appreciable gain in daylight, but by this date next month it may be enough to foster hope.

It is one of the ironies of the beginning to winter, that the days have begun to lengthen and will continue to do so in an accelerated fashion through nearly April. However, though we rightly want to correlate this welcome change with advancing warmth, we have yet to experience the prolonged cold that assuredly January and February will provide.

The light is quick to respond to Earth's changing inclination, and though each day we receive ever more direct and lengthy radiation, it takes what seems Herculean power to overcome the inertia of the settled cold, much as the difficulty in turning a massive ship and expecting it to alter course suddenly when the reverse engines are initially engaged.

No, nature will continue on its path toward winter for a while longer.

December 26

I spent the better part of the evening reading a book I received for Christmas. It is titled, "Hedgemaids and Fairy Candles," and describes both botanical and folklore aspects of the most common North American Wildflowers.

The author introduces nearly eighty well-known species and does so according to the timing of their flowering, meaning that he begins with the earliest of blooming flowers (Skunk Cabbage) and continues through the late Asters. Reading this is the next best thing to experiencing the wonder of the passing seasons firsthand, and it makes me anticipate the coming of the spring colors.

We feel much the same when the seed catalogs arrive, as we peruse the colorful pages of summer's bounty, longing for next year's growing season. Sarah by tradition gave me several packets of seeds (tomato and pepper) yesterday,

ordered from a catalog source that arrived weeks ago. Within the paper packets are next year's promise, staying dormant through the next few months until I can begin seeding indoors, well before the frost line has yet to recede.

December 27

And just like that a warm front came through today, sending temperatures well into the low fifties and hastening the melt of the remaining snow pack. By late afternoon, the front yard was nearly clear, revealing a smattering of twigs and small branches from the red oaks that must have been set loose in the winter storm of last week.

How strange it is to have this reprieve, and we incautiously have feelings of spring fever. It's one thing to experience such a thaw in the midst of February, but it's quite another so soon into winter.

Even the piles of along the roadside, the ones made by the plow from the action of its advancing wave of tumbling snow, have thinned to the point that they are nothing more than small piles here and there among the showing dormant grass. On front, where the road cuts low against the berm of the yard, there are places where the plow blade took edge of the earth and deposited them up and over onto the shoulder grass. These clumps sat atop the several inches of older snow beneath, and as the warmth took its action through the day, they acted as insulation, so that they now rest above small pillars of white.

December 28

The temperatures returned to normal today, and we are largely relieved. Too much hope for a prolonged period only strengthens our disappointment when winter returns in full measure. It's rather selfish to get angry at things when it's thirty two outside and sunny in December after all.

The cut oak logs near the barn need attention, and perhaps we'll tackle this in the afternoon. These have sat since early May, after we felled the tree, sectioned the wood, and rolled the logs down the hill to the edge of the yard. They've benefitted from several months of summer warmth to remove the moisture and season the wood. Oak tends to a density that requires more than what we've allowed, though it should be enough that it will burn sufficiently.

We tried splitting in September using the eight-pound maw. This was an arduous chore, as the warm log resisted even the most forceful strike. Now I suspect the chore will be much easier and even rewarding. The cells inside the grain have become more rigid in the freeze, and the split apart quickly with a resounding crack, so different from the dull thud of last autumn when we tried in vain to divide the logs.

December 29

Our little red has returned, content to be among its brethren greys, which have dominated the yard for several weeks since the chipmunks went to ground. It comes in quickly from the woods on scurrying feet, fearing nothing but its shadow, standing jittery on the porch, furtively regarding the birds that come and go above.

Little red jumps upon the stool, where Sarah placed a bowl of hot water earlier today, though ice has formed a skin on top, made thicker each passing minute now that the sun has angled lower.

It rests its haunches on the edge and puts its forelegs out across the lip of ice, waiting as its weight tips the skin low enough to dislodge enough liquid beneath that it has water

265

to drink. We watch it from the window. It is unaware that we wonder in his ingenuity and beauty.

December 30

Another storm came through and caught us off guard. There was no preceding front or dropping pressure to signal the changes that were to arrive.

Big flakes began to fall last evening, dropping softly straight down from above, so unlike the wind-delivered tempests that winter typically delivers. The flakes were so clumped together and so large that they cast moving shadows in the air as they passed beneath the corner light of the house. We stood inside the sunroom and watched in wonder at the scene, so truly a snow globe of falling white, collecting quickly on the ground.

By late evening, the storm had deposited six inches of heavy white, sticking to every branch and evergreen needle, bending in protest at the gathering weight.

December 31

Snow drifts pile a foot deep or more behind the back porch where the wind sweeps through the side yard and makes and eddy as it passes by the big maple. It has hidden the evidence of the small stone garden there, which now must wait who knows how long before conditions reveal it once again.

Somewhere, insulated by the snow, rests the trailing arbutus sprig we planted last June, its small green leaves awaiting the coming of the warmth. So too the several buds, now closed tightly, will one day put forth their tiny pink-white blossoms to signal that the new season has begun.

There is no ending in this cycle of the seasons, though we naturally think of this date in those terms. One day slowly gives way to the next, and we marvel in the succession that each day brings through awakening, growth, maturity and rest. The arbutus that sleeps beneath the snow will be resplendent once more in its diminutive beauty.

Our gift is that we can see these things for what they are, the wonder of the enduring patterns of nature in this thing we call life here.

January

January 1

Nearly everything outside is coated in brilliant white, brought by the recent heavy snows that stuck to the surfaces of even the smallest twig or lingering blade of brown tall grass. In the clearing morning, sunlight filtered through the bare trees and reflected off each crystal so that the forest became incandescent with daybreak.

Small clouds of backlit snow came cascading down within the woods, dislodged from above by the motion of squirrels that use the highways of branches to travel. For a while, we could follow their progress from far away by seeing the wisps of snowfall through the trees.

It is so beautifully white outside and so illuminated with reflected sun, it is difficult to believe this land is one and the same as the verdant woods that soon will reemerge.

January 2

The wind arcs across the crest of Davis Hill Road where the open fields on either side descend to the woods below in both directions. Snow drifts across the open space and lifts like a living thing in the breeze swirling in brief tempests above the field before passing across the pavement. The windward side has formed small waves that look as though they might crash downward onto the street, but they remain in place, with only the tops casting the spray of new snow outward and across.

January 3

An acquaintance today showed us pictures of her hoop greenhouse, lit from within so that from afar it glowed like a rising moon against the dark night sky. This prompted our curiosity. "Are you growing something now?" we inquired, thinking reasonably that the season ended nearly two months ago.

For our friend, there is no definitive end to the agricultural year, so to speak. She keeps the small greenhouse sufficiently warm with an oil burner through the night and relies on supplemental overhead illumination to foster growth of the "greens," as she indicated. I suspect she meant lettuce, kale and such, which tend to tolerate the cooler growth and lower light conditions. It is winter, after all, and my sense is that no amount of forced warm air will keep a greenhouse sufficiently temperate for much more than "greens."

This reminds me of the pleasure in stepping into a hoop greenhouse in mid winter, when outside the ground may be covered deep in a blanket of snow and temperatures remain below the freeze. Sometimes, if the angle of the sun is just so, midday conditions underneath the plastic resemble a pleasant autumn day, and it is disorienting to enter into a world of dirt floor and dried grasses, where earthy smells still linger pleasantly in the air.

January 4

A brief thaw came on the heels of a shift in the winds, sending temperatures strangely into the low fifties for several hours, before they tumbled nearly twenty-five degrees by late afternoon.

The path we've compressed through the deep snow out the back porch and to the feeders receded enough that only a thin layer of icy footprints remained, save for the places beneath the feeder. Here, the cast-off dark casings of the sunflower seeds formed a thin blanket atop the snow, giving insulation from the warming air temperatures. Now the squirrels travel easily across the ice-pocket footpath to the small mesas snow where the sunflower sits atop, easy for them to reach and yet remain alert for unexpected approach.

Juncos alight on newly exposed provender. They descend in a small flock and scurry about, paying no heed to the other residents. So too comes big red from somewhere deep within the lower woods. He lands cautiously on the suet cake, which sets to spin upon his action and reveals to us his brilliant red crown and black back, speckled white. He spins around and again, having difficulty gaining purchase to obtain what little suet remains within the cage.

January 5

We received a light dusting of snow, enough to give a fresh coat over the exposed areas from yesterday's thaw.

A lone set of tracks cut across the side yard and up toward the driveway. They were too large to be those of some wandering housecat overnight, and the prints were too scattered unlike a cat's. These must have come from our resident fox, which we've seen in the evenings making its rounds along this same path. Now its evidence is clear enough, and I followed the trail in the building light of the morning.

It traveled down the driveway to the street, turned left, and loped casually up the shoulder of Grove. It passed the fields, then Streeter, and continued up toward Cheney's. It didn't waver from its route along the side, past Camp Street and up the hill toward the old Van Dyke farm on the corner, where it finally veered to the west toward the thick woods and beyond.

January 6

In the far corner of the fields across the road, where the land descends until it meets the old stone wall, there are several bee boxes kept here. We haven't been this way for a many weeks, perhaps longer, for my recollection is that the honeybees were still active.

They remain inside now, enduring the winter cold by forming a shifting aggregate, where inner bees within the core benefit from a respite of cumulative heat, while those on the periphery wait their turn. In this way, the hive can survive even the most brutal cold snap.

The owner of the hives wraps the boxes in black waxy paper, presumably to capture as much radiant energy as the winter affords, adding whatever nature can offer in addition to the activity of the colony within.

Inside they will remain, living off the reserves from last year's collection, waiting for the warming melt of spring's deliverance. It's a long way off yet for us to anticipate, and we still cling to the nostalgia of the images and sensations from last year, when these same bees foraged so distantly across the green fields to our summer flowers.

January 7

Across the street from the Cheney farm, daybreak hits the top of the tall pines next to the road and slowly descends as the sun rises higher in the morning sky. Sometimes here the Guinea Fowl roost high up on the lines that stretch between the poles. They ascend to perch at the coming of dawn and remain to enjoy the direct sunshine of the new day. As we pass beneath, they reveal their presence above through pips and clucks, and we smile in wonder at their choice of roost.

The Cheney's have kept fowl for many years, and we've grown accustomed to their antics throughout the seasons. They are either brazen or dim-witted, having no hesitation in crossing the street regardless of any person or oncoming car. There is something particularly bucolic in having to brake to stop so that the Guineas are able to complete their traverse.

As they congregate above, the wires bend notably. They often select to perch on the main power line, which is of no consequence as long as they don't ground themselves in any way. As they gather together too closely, the wire lowers near to the others that pass beneath, and should they accidentally touch, it is likely more or more of the birds would meet their end.

January 8

Several inches of snow fell overnight in the midst of a cold air mass. There was little moisture associated with this storm, making the flakes light and fluffy and prone to drift.

Cold snow, very cold snow, doesn't respond to pressure as we expect. A skater's blade exerts tremendous pressure on the ice, changing it momentarily from its solid form to liquid underneath the blade. The skater glides on a thin layer of water, which freezes immediately again in the wake of the passing blade. In this way, water is unique. Its solid form can become liquid with pressure alone if conditions favor.

However, temperatures too cold counter the effect. Ice that is too cold doesn't succumb as easily to the pressure of the blade, and the skater's glide is notably lessened. So too the effect of our walking upon snow that is frigid, as it is today. The pressure of our boots only compact the granular crystals and do not cause any liquid transition to muffle the sounds. Hence we experience the strange sensation of walking on sand-like snow that squeaks with the friction of our passing.

January 9

How different these still mornings than those of our overwhelming spring, when the woods and fields are as alive with sound as possibly can be, and we feel the kinship pulse of life that celebrates its return.

The storm passed in the night, and its wake left predawn as still and cold as what must surely be the most solemn church. I stood outside beyond the pale of the corner light, where the snow covered side yard lost definition. It was painfully quiet, and only the sound of my own exhalation marred the absolute stillness of the star-strewn sky and calm beginning.

From somewhere deep within the lower woods came a started chuff of a deer, followed by the distinct sound of hoofs that breached the crusted snowpack. I waited and listened for several minutes, following the movement of the animal through the deep woods as it traversed along the frozen creek basin down toward Streeter Pond below.

January 10

Today is my fiftieth birthday, and it is understandable that I am particularly introspective. Forgive me this.

What is fifty years worth in the scheme of things? Not much really. Cosmically, it is nothing more than the blink of an eye. It is slightly more than the period of four Jupiter years, which makes me feel particularly youthful somehow. Uranus takes eighty-four of our Earth years to complete one of its own, and if I were born on the new Uranian year, my paltry fifty would have me only 5/8 around the sun, not likely to live long enough to complete even one year on Uranus.

The ancient Ptolemy introduced epicycles to the Aristotelian model for better explaining the movement of the planets through the heavens in the Earth-centered universe. Epicycles are curious things. Imagine the Earth at the center of your paper, and you begin to draw a large circle that arcs around it. As your hand moves, you would occasionally introduce a small loop attached to your growing circular arc, making the orbit look something akin to a child's drawing of a sunflower, with fat, circular petals attached to the main center. But I digress.

I think of epicycles now and then, when I reflect upon the cycle of the seasons. Our lives are like the large circular orbit. We are born, we live, grow older, and ultimately decline, once around the circle. Through this wonderful journey, we are blessed to experience the cycles of the seasons year in and out, repeating upon each other, the beauty of growth and maturity, harvest and rest. These are the epicycles for us to see time and again as we move forward in our slow singular pirouette that we call life.

January 11

The strangest front blew in violently last evening from the south, lifting temperatures throughout the night. By daybreak, it had risen past the upper forties as clearing skies remained in the wake of receding winds.

This must be our January thaw, for it is to continue throughout today and well into tomorrow, with temperatures near fifty amid sunny skies and light winds. By midmorning, the air had become nearly still, and the yard was alive with the joyous sounds of chickadees and titmice, which must certainly be confused at this sudden change. All throughout the woods we could hear them singing as if proclaiming the arrival of spring, and as we stood in the sunshine on the back porch to listen, it was easy to become swept up in the false hope of their song.

January 12

The thaw continued through last evening and into today, with temperatures moderating well into the mid fifties. Since yesterday, the snowpack in the front yard has completely melted, revealing the grass again, which is littered with the detritus of red oak twigs and acorn caps.

In the afternoon, the dogs and I were perfectly content to stand in the leeward side of one of the big oaks, positioned so that we were protected from the cool breeze that came across the remaining snow near the woods. Both Kipper and Tag sat peacefully nearby in a slightly elevated patch of lawn, dry and in full sun as if it were a pleasant autumn day. I stood with my back against the oak, turned my face to the sun, and closed my eyes, content to enjoy the warmth of this unusual thaw.

All about were false signs of spring. Water trickled within the near woods and birds called to one another from about the yard. It was so pleasant that we stayed nearly thirty minutes, the dogs sitting calmly among the soft lawn and I happy to allow the infusion of angled January sun into my body.

January 13

We were given one more morning of warmth, before the temperatures fell drastically in the afternoon and the return to normalcy.

After breakfast, I walked the access road to the falls at Moore State Park, curious how the melt of the past few days had affected the flow. Where the road descends from the parking lot toward the reservoir, the rhododendrons that line the way were in full leaf. How different from their tight curls of only a few days ago, when the temperatures were in the teens.

The shaded woods on either side of the road still contained a sizable snow pack, and with the warmth of the morning sunshine it formed a condensed layer of fog that spilled out onto the pavement. The fog thickened with the approach to the reservoir, and the way was marked only by the reaching forms of the rhododendrons on both sides and the pavement beneath my feet. Everything else was shrouded in a white out of misty cloud.

January 14

New fissures have opened across the road as the warmth of the past few days hastens the movement of the frost heaves.

Three years ago, the college contracted to have a new water line run up the length of Sunset Lane, and this necessitated further work along Grove. The road was dug up, and pipes were put down, including new lines that crossed the road to the houses on the west side of the street.

Of course, this work was done in the late summer, and when all was finished, new pavement was placed the length of the road.

Each winter since, above where the cross pipes were placed, the pavement buckles with the coming of the frost heaves, lifting the road sufficiently that any vehicle which traverses makes a notable "bump, bump" as it passes by.

We can only speculate why this has taken place. Perhaps when the new lines were put down, the workers neglected to sufficiently compact the surrounding soil, thus allowing enough air spaces within to collect moisture. This of course is the villain of the heaves, as the water expands and contracts during fluctuating periods of freeze and thaw, with impressive force to buckle even the most pliant of asphalt (winter hardness aside).

On the southern edge of our property, not fifteen feet from the side of Grove and just within the border woods, is an old well. It is nearly hidden, having been covered years ago by a flat and large rock to discourage would-be lookers from investigating. It is a rather impressive thing, nearly four feet in diameter, with smooth walls that run almost ten feet down to the water below. The well is situated nearby a conglomerate of large foundation rocks within the woods, which are largely hidden by the trees that have grown tall in the years since it was once a stable for horses. This was over a hundred years ago or more.

Diagonally across Grove from the well, again within the berm of the border woods that divide the road from Cournoyer's fields, is another foundation. It too is barely discernable, though at one time it was a small house. Tucked within the base of the foundation and pointing in the direction of the well across the road is an old pipe. This same pipe enters the well roughly two feet below the surface and presumably crosses underneath Grove.

Each year, a small frost heave buckles across the street at the spot where the pipe runs beneath.

January 15

With the retreat of the snowpack from the thaw several days ago, a bounty of discarded seed now lies beneath the feeders in the side yard. This is a boon to our resident community of squirrels and birds, who now feast with reckless abandon in the relative mildness of this interlude between storms.

Blue jays have returned again in large flocks from wherever they wander, and they seem to take delight in teasing the other birds. One sits presently below the feeder, keeping a wary eye on two of the ground squirrels nearby. It hops sideways a few inches closer then reaches quickly downward to devour several cast off black sunflower seeds. The twitching of a squirrel's tail sets the jay to panic, and it screams in protest and hops twice in withdrawal.

January 16

At 11:20 the sun shines directly down the length of the old access road to Asnebumskit. We walked from the house to the lower woods then up the road toward the pond, enjoying the sun dappled woods strangely devoid of any snow. We know this won't last much longer, as winter is bound to remind us soon enough of the season.

The vernal pool on the west side of the trail is still frozen, though beneath the layer of surface ice the small volume of water must be warm enough to permit the grasses to retain a measure of green color. We stood for several moments and watched the movement of air bubbles underneath, seeing them follow the contours of the ice along with the slow flow of water, moving toward the small outlet stream that cuts across the old road.

Up ahead, where the road rises to meet the grassy dam that holds back Asnebumskit, tall sere heads of Phragmites are backlit in the opposing sunshine, and they sway gently from the breeze that cuts across the expanse beyond. From our vantage below, we watch them move against the backdrop of deep blue sky, their feathery edges so illuminated to be incandescent.

January 17

At midday the sun retreated behind a bank of building grey clouds that ushered in a return to winter. So much for the respite that has been the past few days. Admittedly, we've enjoyed the ease of walking along the bare trails and seeing the dormant lawn.

The slow chugging sound of a tractor across the road interrupted the stillness of the pre-storm morning. This, combined with the lack of winter scenery, was momentarily confusing, as if somehow we'd been transported to late autumn when the last of the harvest chores remained to be accomplished.

Even the morning skies had a decidedly October look, with brilliant sunshine and no humidity, making the green of the passing tractor contrast markedly against the brown Earth and distant deep blue.

By evening, the coming front gave way to sleet that made a transition to snow. All we could do was sigh in resignation.

January 18

The storm that began last evening lasted through the morning, though by the time it wound down, we only received two inches of heavy wet snow. This was enough to return the landscape to winter. We know in the scheme of things this is as it should be, however, I admit to feeling grateful for the possibility of a mild winter. The past few have been traditionally cold and snowy. What's wrong with a periodic respite of warmth?

Kipper feels the same. He's content to sit idly on the sunroom couch and watch the squirrels beneath the feeder, huffing and growling occasionally largely to remind himself of his authority. He no longer has much impetus to explore when conditions are wet and cold, and frankly I can't blame him. We both are sliding slowly into maturity.

January 19

In the lower woods, there are fresh tracks of all sorts in the snow. Tiny vole prints traverse the surface before they enter a patch of exposed leafy grass on the lee side of a rather large tree. Nearby are distinct marks of wild turkeys, two or three birds who've come this way from the direction of the hill across the stream that runs south to north from Asnebumskit.

January 20

The cold settled in again. An arctic air mass descended calmly from somewhere beyond northwest Canada, bringing a return to daytime highs in the teens.

Our wet snow of the past few days hardened fast enough, making passage through the back trails more difficult with the crusty pack. Our footprints from yesterday's walk had compressed and melted slightly only to refreeze and harden with the cold. Now they are a hindrance, forcing us to go carefully with our eyes on the trail rather than scanning the woods and horizon.

January 21

The cold has brought the Junco's out in a frenzy to the feeder. I am fond of these winter birds, for they remind me of a well-dressed diner, who is content to browse on the ground for his fare.

The juncos are a harbinger of winter, normally arriving in late November as they leave their summer breeding sites up in the mountains of New Hampshire and Vermont to settle for the winter in our neck of the woods, among other places.

They frequent the feeder area, usually in larger groups, and are fairly sociable birds, though not quite as gregarious as the chick-a-dees. They tend to hop and scratch more than chick-a-dees will, trying to dislodge seeds below the snow or soil. When startled, the juncos are clear warning signs of an intruder, like a passing falcon or red-tailed hawk. As if in unison the Juncos scatter in all directions, quickly vanishing to the underbrush or forest to escape a threat. I suppose the markings that so nicely camouflage them in the summer are a liability in the snow cover, as the darkened tops are more easily distinguished against the snow.

January 22

We keep a birdfeeder just outside the sliding door of the sunroom, set on the end of a shepherd's pole that is driven into the grass. Each morning my wife Sarah fills the tube full of black sunflower oil seeds and puts any excess in a little pile on the edge of the porch.

After weeks of this daily practice, the area around the feeder is littered with the cast offs that birds pull out of the feeder and drop on the ground below. It gives the snow a deeply peppered look.

I am watching around the feeder today, only because we have this jittery red squirrel whose antics around the porch are irresistibly comical. The red squirrel is one of among several resident squirrels that consist of roughly five ground and our singular red. We also have flying squirrels that live among the trees, but as they are largely nocturnal, we rarely see them and only occasionally hear their calls.

Our red typifies the petulant manner that Beatrix Potter so aptly describes in several of her children's stories. He darts about defiantly often stopping to posture with two legs pushed forward and head held upright, chattering his warning call and briskly flicking about his tail.

Defiance will just as quickly give way to retreat when a passing shadow or sudden noise startles this mercurial little thing.

He is a hoarder that one, like all such rodents, and I suspect that the easy pickings of the sunflower cast-offs provide a ready supply of energy. This is particularly true as I believe the red may have forgotten more buried caches than he can remember, and what's to worry when food is provided?

January 23

In the afternoon sunlight across the road, wind gusts lift the snow in the field and push plumes from one side to the other. For a moment, we are reminded of the drought days of mid July, when the breeze carries clouds of topsoil toward the forest line to the east. The wind comes now in harsh oscillation, the calm of moments ago interrupted by another burst of whiteout, traveling as a wave until it hits with full measure against the spruce trees on the far edge. Their shaking boughs disappear in the crystalline fog for a several seconds then reemerge in the sunlight after the gust has passed.

January 24

A squall arrived overnight, down from the northwest with arctic air that buffeted the house in the early hours. Lying in bed I heard the muffled sound of the hurricane chime by the barn clanging away and knew the wind was fierce.

For all the fury, the morning revealed only a couple inches of powdery snow had fallen, though it was enough to freshen the landscape and remind us that we are firmly within winter's domain. When the daylight brightened sufficiently, the chickadees and juncos began to arrive in earnest at the feeders, soon followed by our group of squirrels that behave like juvenile teenagers who have overslept and are hungry for the cast offs beneath the tubes.

The first chickadees landed on the large bell-shaped baffle we put on the shepherd's pole several years ago to deter the squirrels from climbing upward and jumping onto the feeding tube. Their hopping about dislodged fragments of new powder, creating miniature avalanches that slid down the baffle and sprayed to the ground below, disrupting the balance of the bell and causing the birds to hop about in reaction.

Beneath, the arriving squirrels seemed content to dig beneath the powder to find the leftover seed from the past several weeks, though it is amusing to watch their puzzled heads turn as the dislodged snow from above rains down.

January 25

At four o'clock this morning, the full wolf moon sat roughly 20 degrees above the western horizon, seen from our house through the spruce line and hanging just above the Cournoyer's barn. I took the dogs for a walk well before sunrise, onto the two-track lane that sports the perimeter of the fields across the road. The snow fall from yesterday combined with the brilliant moon overhead made the going easy, to the point that I had no trouble spotting the dogs' figures bouncing ahead though the slight drifts.

On occasion, they'd stop to smell the evidence of some animal passerby, whose fresh tracks across the expanse bore witness to their travel at some point between yesterday and this morning. We found dogs' prints, cat, deer, mice of all sorts, and the impression of what looked like a coyote, though admittedly it may have been another dog of some kind. I'd like to think that the wolf moon brought out the feral relative in the coyote, strolling across the field and hunting for mice or rabbits. We hear them from time to time, usually in the dead of night when they call to one another in the yipping manner of a delinquent pack. Rarely the howling call of the coyote that we remember from our time in Colorado, but still the cries here are enough to raise the hairs on the backs of our head in primal concern.

January 26

A strange warm front came through overnight, and we awoke to the sounds of running water dripping falling from the roof eaves as the melting snow gave way to the rising temps. Perhaps this is the January thaw at last, or at least we'll accept it as such to give us something to cling to as hope that one day the cold will recede for good. In a few months, the tinkling of rain will be nothing too special, simply part of the symphony of background noise that makes spring worth experiencing. Now, it is something altogether new – and we don't mind the simple pleasure of listening to the pitter patter as the drops fall onto the ground below.

Later in the day, as I was passing through the sunroom, a brilliant shade of emerald green caught my eye from atop the barn in the backyard. It seems the snow melted sufficiently from the north facing roof to expose the shingles underneath – or at least lay bare the mossy covering that blankets this portion of the roof. Set against the still drab background of the grey and brown woods, the moss is almost too verdant to be believed. Who knows? Maybe the covering of snow from the past several weeks provided just the perfect environment for the moss to grow, shielded from the harsher temps and yet covered with a source of moisture. Now exposed, there are shades of vibrant greens, the likes of which we won't see in full measure until the spring arrives and the deciduous trees make their return. For now, this small patch is a welcome change from the browns and greys.

Several years ago I took a small patch of the roof moss and brought it inside, placed it in a glass terrarium with a little soil, sprayed it with water and closed the container. I'm happy to report that it is still going strong, with tendrils of green moss and other filamentous producers that colonize the terrarium. They wax and wane depending on the temperature and sunlight within the room, and once or twice a year I remember to open the glass and spray water inside. When the winter gets really long, I sometimes open the glass and look at the growing moss within, smell the earthy smells of the backyard in my container. It's enough for now.

January 27

There is water running quickly over the spillway of the dam at Moore State Park. A friend and I took a predawn walk down the road from the main entryway and through the tunnel of rhododendrons on our way to the dam, and we first heard the muffled sounds of splashing water coming from downhill near the spill. It is strange to hear this harbinger of the spring melt while we sit squarely within the grasp of winter (at least by the calendar). This year has been blissfully kind, in contrast to the last when we endured storm after storm of heavy snow and biting cold. How decadent it feels to be about so early with only a modest jacket and gloves, walking on the clear road that we illuminate with flashlights. Neither of us wanted to comment on the conditions, for fear of awakening some New England deity who would remind us that it is January after all.

Even the shaded two track that was once the main route to the Mill Site within the park, Old Brigham Trail, was nearly clear of snow, save for pockets of ice where no afternoon sunshine penetrates through the covered boughs. This is one of my favorite places to hike, regardless of the season, and we easily trudged the gentle uphill for a third of a mile to the park gates that mark the exit to civilization. We didn't even need the flashlight, content to allow our eyes to adjust to the muted tones of trees and road, illuminated enough by the waning Wolf Moon that was filtered so by a thin canopy of cloud.

Without any wind, the forest was exceptionally silent, peacefully so, and we stopped several times simply to listen to the distant rustle of deadfall leaves and the occasional call of a Great Horned Owl somewhere over the hill toward the reservoir in the park.

January 28

Even our side yard next to the porch is nearly free of snow now, save for the darkened ovals beneath the bird feeders where the cast off seeds from the tubes above provide insulation. Move the pile slightly with a shoe and there is snow underneath. The squirrels seem to enjoy this arrangement, as they forage eagerly in the pile of seed then switch ever so often to scoop up bits of exposed snow to put in their mouths. I sometimes wonder if the birds are somehow in cahoots with the ground feeders, for they (and in particular the titmice) seem determined to spill three times as many seeds from the tube as they consume.

The insulation is amazing, really. When the snow is deep, the plows lose sight of the road edge, and invariably one will catch the blade too close to the berm, causing a clod of dirt to lift and curl over atop whatever piles already line the side. Thereafter, snow will inevitably fall enough to cover everything with a fresh coat, and we will forget the disturbance of the earth. That is, until the season gives way to spring, when the snow melt comes in full measure, and the road side is nearly exposed to last autumn's leaf fall, save for odd clumps of snow that have "caps" of earthy sod – those cast offs from the plow which insulate the snow beneath from the rising temps. These remain well into May, even when the daffodils and tulips have begun to wane.

I suspect several of the older homes in town have remnants of ice houses or basements, and the principle is just the same. Large blocks of ice cut from nearby ponds, like Asnebumskit or Streeter, would be ferried to homes and placed within the cellars or ice houses, then covered with sawdust or some other insulating material. These would last well into the summer months and beyond.

January 29

Two bobcats strolled casually across the backyard this
morning, up from the tree line behind the raised beds and
past the north side of the house. First came the kitten,
running playfully ahead then stopping briefly in the
middle of the yard to look back for its mother, who
emerged more furtively to inspect for danger. The kitten
mewed twice, loud enough for us to hear its call from
inside the sun room, where we sat motionless watching in
wonder at the pair reunite in the yard. They say together
for several minutes, content to warm themselves in the
morning sunshine that must have felt good through the
calm air of what is continuing to be an atypical January.

They behaved just like cats, which I realize is a silly thing
to express. Mother sat patiently, licking the back of her
paw and using it to wipe her face, while the kitten rolled
about on the ground, occasionally swatting at some
imaginary demon before leaping about to cozy up next to
the adult. Our indoor cats behave just the same,
particularly when they spend time in the direct sunlight
that streams through the sunroom windows this time of

year – unhindered by the surrounding trees bereft of leaves.

January 30

The sun rose through the far woods as a warm orange ball, looking more like the hazy beginning of a July morning than what we normally expect of mid winter. We keep thinking the "big one" is around the corner, when feet of snow and bitter winds remind us of the price we must pay for those idyllic days of midsummer. Things now feel unsettled, this winter that has been tempered and we hope content to remain so for the next several weeks.

Even the birds seem strangely sanguine. A lone titmouse sat perched atop the arbor vitae next to the berm road, singing intently at the sunrise. This was no winter call, meant only for warning and devoid of pleasure. Rather, its song was the light praise of a morning sunrise that seemed to herald the transition to spring.

January 31

The moss atop the barn has reverted to more normal shades of darker green, less brilliant and alive than only a few days ago when it was first liberated from the melting snow. To see it now inspires no special glance, apart from the hopeful acknowledgement that the roof is clear and perhaps for good. It has all been out of sorts this past month, our January that has looked more forwardly with its face to the vernal feel of the coming spring than backward in its Janus way, holding fast to the bitter chill.

Our New England norm is to tolerate this month at best, requiring that we take stock of the inner comforts of home and look for beauty in the austerity that winter typically provides. January relief is usually a fleeting thing, like a brief change in the wind that hints at something we remember from last year.

The verdant moss was too buoyant to continue, too much a symbol of real growth that will assuredly come when winter finally relaxes. Not yet. Soon enough.

February

February 1

The receding snow in the woods has exposed the leaf fall from last autumn, muted now as a mosaic of brown shades that carpet the ground. The exception is the beech, which holds fast to its papery golden leaves having yet to fully release them to be recycled back to the soil. They are beautiful now, in the afternoon sunlight that streams across the town fields and through the narrow break line of woods that separates the access road beyond.

The deep forest is a mixture of all sorts, though the deciduous trees have receded into the background and allowed the greens of the pine and spruce to dominate. Only the beech stands resolute among the conifers, with its golden leaves cast in sharp relief against the darker tones around, highlighted all the more by the oblique sun that filters through and illuminates them like paper lanterns.

They are not alone, of course. The oaks and sycamores tend to hold leaves nearly until spring, though they've long since turned an opaque brown, curled and dull, a reminder of endings rather unlike that of the beech, whose color seems softer somehow. They are golden.

February 2

Regardless of what happens to the groundhog, I have mixed feelings in seeing my own shadow this afternoon while walking the perimeter of the fields. Things are still out of place, with this January thaw that has decided to extend into February, and walking with only a light jacket is indecent, made more so on the two-track that should be many inches deep in snow. The fields are nearly clear, and the rutted path that would normally be frozen (and snowed in) has softened in the sunlight. Between the tracks, where the grass grows unmolested, there is evidence of lighter green at the base of each sere blade, hardly noticeable unless you take a closer look. Yet it is unmistakable, the slow response to the warming days and increasing light, the reawakening of life that has lain dormant for so short a time this winter.

The forecast is for colder temps to arrive in a couple days, to what the weatherman declares as "seasonable," though I wonder if that means much these days. We've been spoiled, plain and simple.

February 3

The big maple next to the sunroom started dripping this afternoon, and we are reminded that there are stirrings in the ground unseen but manifest in the slow changes that unfold. The nights have been cold enough, and with the warming days it is no wonder that the sap has started to rise. I amend. It is a wonder, really. All the sugars of last year's production, sent down deep into the roots far below for such a large tree, now begin to rise slowly but purposefully outward toward the sky. Surely the botanist could explain some facet of the inner workings, perhaps even to the degree of the chain of chemical events, and while this reduction is fascinating in its own way, it eclipses the mere wonder of it all, the larger sense of purpose and cycle.

I feel the warmth on my face in the afternoon sunshine and sense within my own stirrings of anticipation – for growth and rejuvenation that assuredly this spring will bring. I know that winter will give way to change, that the acceleration of life both within me and beyond is something worth the dormancy we have needed to endure. This is a wonder that I know.

But the maple has no sense of expectation, does it? Does it feel the coming of spring in the same way or anticipate the living pulse that comes with renewal? Surely it must be more than just some measure of chemical changes, made so as the sugars rise to its furthest branches, fostering the renewal that will soon enough reveal the swelling of the buds.

February 4

For several days, we've had a small meadow vole come to visit our porch in the afternoon. It makes an appearance from a small hole near the corner where the cedar shingles of the house meet the clapboard of the sunroom, and admittedly I do not want to consider the possibility that this exit hole is also one and the same the principal gateway to the house for the various deer mice loafers we tend to harbor when the autumn chill arrives.

Seen on the outside of the house, this little vole is simply endearing. It bursts frantically from the shelter of the hole, scurrying alongside the cedar wall until it finds shelter underneath the toy wagon (the red metal antique we leave on the porch), whereupon it sits contently beneath and calmly searches for seed cast offs. The latter come from the work of the squirrels, who profit from Sarah's good heartedness when she places a handful of sunflower seeds into the wagon each morning as a gesture of benevolence. Our eastern greys have no trouble jumping into the wagon and making a mess of things, casting seed aside in gluttony as they use their forelegs to dig.

The little vole sits on its tiny haunches and serenely places a small sunflower seed between its forepaws, working slowly to chew it open and find the reward inside. It remains hidden from preying eyes above, the hawks and falcons who frequent the yard, not to mention the occasional owl. I'm sure they would appreciate the little vole as much as I.

February 5

Just outside the front door we have a small enclosure, made so by the border of the house on one side and the garage on the other. It is here that snow piles deeply most winters, often to the point that the front door becomes blocked entirely with drifts that reach five feet or more. This winter has been so mild, that even the holly bushes that border the house, the ones we usually bid farewell until the spring melt, are fully exposed in the afternoon sunshine.

Around midday, roughly a dozen robins descended to the front yard from somewhere across the field. They spent the better part of several minutes meandering about the grass, looking for some semblance of provender though likely confused by the ground that has remained frozen despite its being bare. We've grown accustomed to the presence of robins throughout the winter, seeing them less as a harbinger of spring as they once were years ago. Still, so many robins seeking food in the yard is a pleasant reminder of what will be more normal in a month or so.

At some point, they discovered the holly berries, and en masse they flew into the enclosure and attacked the bushes with what can only be described as ravenous vigor. Truly! The bushes never saw it coming, and in the span of only a couple of minutes, the hollies were stripped clean of what was before a covering of dozens of bright red berries. Such gluttony could only be marveled at, and then, they lifted off as one and flew onward.

February 6

The titmice and chickadees have been in a frenzy at the feeder all day, and the activity portends the storm that is to arrive tomorrow. It is curious to wonder if they do have some inner forecasting sense, for we do notice more traffic in the hours before bad weather moves in.

At one point in the afternoon, we glanced out the window and noticed two chickadees sitting stock still while perched on the feeder tube, so completely immobile it was as if time had stopped. A minute or two passed without any movement, and it occurred to us that there must have been some predator nearby. Sure enough, up high in the branches of the maple sat perched our area falcon, which was busy looking about for something to eat. Even when the breeze picked up just little, and the tube feeder rocked gently back and forth, the two chickadees remained immobile.

In time, the falcon glided away across the yard and toward the lower woods, disappearing into the trees. Several moments passed before the chickadees begin turning their heads and reaching once again into the feeder tube, content that the danger had passed.

February 7

Winter returned this morning, and in the span of just a few hours the landscape changed from what had seemed like an extended autumn to a blanket of deep white snow. I suspect now we've seen the last of our front yard until the melting warmth of spring arrives in full measure, which thankfully doesn't seem so far away. How unlike last year, when the deep snows came in early January and lasted well into April, and we longed so for some relief from the endless dark and cold.

Today felt like a spring snow, full of moisture and so heavy, coating the bare branches in the woods three inches high or more on every twig, so that the forest sky is a mosaic of lines that go from white to dark. The pine boughs sag from the added weight, our arbor vitae in the back bent over so notably that it seems as though they will surely break in two. Somehow they will recover, as they did last year when the heavy snows arrived, doubled over from the strain they still stand resolved to endure until light and heat help restore them to their proper state.

February 8

The midday sun is as strong now as it was in early November, and the change in elevation is enough to help the driveway and back porch melt free of the cleared snow from yesterday's tempest. As the day progressed, small patches of drifts on the deck began to melt, creating little pools of water in the places where the boards had cupped slightly from years of exposure to the elements.

In the afternoon, a pair of juncos shared a small feast of a handful of seed that Sarah had winnowed onto the porch. They each would open a few seeds and take of the nut within, then move cautiously to a small puddle of water nearby and drink quickly, taking advantage no doubt of the easy water, rather than having to spoon snow to quench their thirst.

February 9

It was bitterly cold this morning, following a clear and still night where the stars shone brilliantly through the absence of any haze. Just now, in the hour before dawn, we are treated to a celestial wonder, made enhanced by the conditions and lack of interference from the moon that is close to its new phase.

Up from the eastern horizon and toward the south, rising in an arc through the sky, five planets align closely within roughly 45 degrees of view. From my vantage point in the middle of the town fields, Jupiter leads the parade, seen just to the south and high in the sky; it's yellow fire shining brilliantly against the black velvet of the night. Next is Saturn, off to the left as the arc spans toward the east, and Mars sits patiently with its reddish glow. Venus hangs closer to the horizon, and she will disappear soon as the morning star as she swings around the backside of the sun. Last is Mercury, barely visible in the orange glow that precedes the dawn; a small pinpoint of light that is difficult to spot at first.

Winter mornings such as these offer their own beauty, and though certainly austere they are worth the expense of bundling up and standing in knee-deep snow to witness them.

February 10

At some point last evening, our resident cottontail must have finally emerged from beneath the porch, for this morning there is a fresh trail of what looks like rabbit tracks through the new 5 inches of powder that fell sometime overnight. We've adopted this rabbit, at least unofficially, having watched it grow since being born last summer and surviving the trials of its youth around the side yard and near the berm next to the access road.

Last June, as the coreopsis grew tall enough to create a shady cool mass of nested stems, a mother cottontail used the location to deposit a brood of five tiny babies. We didn't even know they were there until we caught Tag sniffing around the flowers in an unusual way – the way terriers do when they suspect some fearsome creature, like a squirrel or chipmunk has invaded their domain. Sarah pulled the dog away, and I reached in to part the mass of flowers, revealing five brown babies that were no bigger than small potatoes.

Of the five, four either perished or migrated as the summer progressed and gave way to early autumn. Only one stayed and began to habituate the side yard, near the bird feeders and tall grass, where the shade from the big maple provides plenty of cover and allows the plantains to grow with reckless abandon. We'd watch the young rabbit eating plantains one after another, pause, and then jump about in the manner of a teenager, before heading in a frenzy for the safety of the space underneath the porch. And so, we named it Porch and have watched it all throughout these past months.

Evidently Porch has survived its first few storms and is still around the yard.

February 11

Near the intersection of Grove Street and Sunset Lane,
there is now a slight rise in the road, made so by the early
workings of the frost heaves that soon will do their
mischief throughout town. The road here lifts just a little,
so that the asphalt has begun to crack with the stress,
barely noticeable on foot but certainly so when you drive
across.

At some point early this morning, the town truck must
have gone down Grove and used the spreader to put
granules of calcium chloride onto the road in preparation
for the slight thaw and refreeze that is to come in the next
24 hours. Just after Sunset Lane, there is a small pile of the
blue crystals, beginning just after the bump and extending
as a large strip for twenty feet or so down the road. My
sense is that the loader hit the frost heave and discharged a
mass of crystal from the hopper then left a trailing of the
stuff as it continued onward down the hill.

I can't remember when the town switched to this latest
concoction. Four years ago? Maybe more. The blue crystals
appear decidedly foreign, and though the color dissipates
as they work their magic on the ice, it still gives me a bad
feeling to see it nonetheless. I miss the simplicity of the
sand they used to dispense. Though less effective, it
seemed environmentally better. Plus, there was something
pleasant in pretending that we were driving on a beach in
the middle of winter, in contrast to the blue salt that
evokes a feeling of unnaturalness.

The ice melts, and the blue turns to slurry, slowly drifting
away in rivulets and runoff that drift to the sides of the
road, carrying the collective mass of water and salt to
places unknown. Maybe places like the roadside soil,

ultimately, from which our pleasant wild grasses and flowers, weeds and seedlings make their appearance in May. Hopefully.

February 12

It snowed again last evening and through the night, putting down three inches of a light powdery snow that accumulated gently on every surface. The railing of the back deck was perfectly covered in uniform fluff in the morning, though this was not to remain with the coming of the dawn, which signaled to the area birds that it was time to visit the feeders. Soon, the house finches and titmice arrived, tentatively at first and then in larger numbers as they realized we had filled the tubes with fresh sunflower seeds. The chickadees flew in closely behind, and within the span of only five minutes the area around the feeders was busy with twenty birds, most waiting in queue for one of the precious spots on the tubes to open.

Visitors would swoop in close and alight on the rail, settling softly in the powdered snow and causing it to gently dislodge in a cascade of evanescent dust, backlit from the morning sun and sparkling as it descended to the decking. One after another, we watched the activity, the birds sitting patiently on the rail until a perch on the tube became available, then flying off for their reward. Twenty minutes of such comings and goings, and soon the section of rail nearest the feeders was clear of the snowy covering from last night.

February 13

A furious wind blew across the fields all day long, born somewhere northwest of New York and swept down across the Berkshires toward us as an arctic clipper.

Plumes of crystalline snow keep lifting off the expanse across the road and blowing through the spruce line before hitting the house with a force that momentarily blocks the full sunshine and buffets the windows. There's been a constant white noise since the morning, interrupted only by the occasional clanging of the hurricane chime out by the barn.

This front came with a bite, as temperatures began near 20 degrees at dawn then steadily dropped into the single digits by afternoon. I'm certain the wind chill is well below zero now, as we sit here in the front room looking out the window at the front yard, covered twelve inches in snow that lifts and swirls about in the tempest. In the rare lulls, the sun shines brilliantly, set against the winter sky that is nearly cobalt.

February 14

The thermometer read minus twenty one degrees this morning at 5:30, and there was a decided breeze from the west. It must have been thirty to forty below with the wind chill. The snow around the bird feeders crunched audibly, and our footsteps would squeak as we crossed from the porch to the tubes. This is dangerous cold, where even the slightest intake of breath initiates a cough, and exposed skin to the wind is quickly subject to numbing pain.

Last night, I had left the water running in a slight trickle from the faucet in the spare room above the garage. This morning, the hot line was fine, but the cold line was frozen somewhere. The weatherman claims we won't get above two or three degrees today at best, and so I'll have to wait for a change before the pipes thaw.

The sun began as an orange glow, seen through the trees of the back woods and off toward the barely visible white

expanse of Asnebumskit pond. It rose brilliantly, casting
the surrounding woods in patterns of light and shadow,
the rays hitting the east facing wall of the porch, where sat
a titmouse as if in waiting. It was puffed fully to expanse,
perched defiantly on the edge of the toy wagon on the
porch, waiting for some cue that would signal the
appropriate start to breakfast. There too sat one of the
eastern grey squirrels, its tail arched up an over its body,
providing an insulating coat to ward of the extreme cold.

February 15

One good thing about the extreme cold is that it makes
quick work of splitting the wood. The back barn is filled
with portions of an oak tree I felled last spring; it came
from the lower woods, not too far outside the edge of the
yard within the stand of trees that are mostly a mixture of
upland hardwoods. There was nothing particularly
noteworthy about this particular oak, apart that it was just
about the right size (and not to mention distance from the
barn) to devote itself to a cord of wood for our use.

Dropping the tree was straightforward enough, as was
cutting the sections of roughly eighteen inches. A
wheelbarrow made easy the transport of the pieces to the
barn, where they've been sitting within drying these past
ten months.

Just two months ago, I tried to split a section using the
large maul, when temperatures were in the forties and the
December sunshine came barely across the expanse of the
lower yard. Miserable work. That section resisted nearly
all attempts, and I came away tired, angry and frustrated
in one fell swoop (pun intended).

Today is altogether different, as they crack apart when the
maul strikes, calving beautifully as though they had been

precut to do so. Up goes the maul. Down comes the head. Crack. Another piece breaks away cleanly. It's almost fun. Almost.

February 16

The seasonal novelty of the wood stove has long since December worn thin, and though we largely regard its use as routine now, we appreciate its heat and character all the same. Ours is a traditional Jotel stove with no frills, apart from the glass door in the front. It is rectangular, with a single black pipe that elbows up through the damper and out into the gaping maw of the chimney.

Our house is designed as a traditional 1700s saltbox, typified by a large central chimney that extends upward through the center of the house and out through the roof. There are four separate pipes that feed through the chimney, and of these the one to the fireplace is rather large, perhaps eighteen inches square. This is nearly a pipe that Santa could descend into the wide opening of the Rumford fireplace below (assuming the flue was open). The fireplace is an impressive thing – large enough to stand in the hearth and complete with a separate bee-hive oven to one side (which feeds to another pipe in the chimney). Years of use, prior to our owning the house, are detailed in the blackened bricks that line the rear of the hearth and extend upward to the wainscoting above the mantel.

That first year, we enjoyed the fireplace too, at least decoratively. It didn't take long to realize that a roaring fire caused nearly all the heat to move upward through the flue and out the chimney. The flow was so pronounced that we could feel the draft of air coming from the kitchen and into the room, as the house literally breathed our warmth away! The solution was, of course, the wood stove, placed perfectly within the hearth. And our daily winter ritual has been to clean the ash box, place the tinder and logs, light, and wait until things have settled. No draft, just heat to stave the winter cold.

February 17

Kipper is laying on his side in front of the hearth with eyes closed and tongue lolling out gently to the side. He rests peacefully with the warmth of the fire not more than eighteen inches away; the orange flicker through the smoked glass door casts moving shadows on his white coat. He is unaware of the tempest outside, where through the window that overlooks the front lawn, snow falls quickly to the ground and is accumulating in the glazing.

This is the weather for the wood stove, when winter has redoubled her efforts to close us in and remind us of our vulnerability. The fire burns onward for a time, and we sit comfortably nearby in our chairs, listening to the slight crackle of the new logs as the moisture within expands to release.

Every so often a large gust roars outside, causing the draft within the chimney to pull more insistently and making the fire come alive for a moment. This awakens Kipper, who lifts his head momentarily in concern as he regards the transient flare of yellow and red within the stove. The wind dies, as does the stove, returning to the dying glow of logs that have begun to dissemble into ash.

February 18

Overnight a southerly wind shot the temperatures into the fifties, and the wind buffeted the house well into morning. The daylight revealed the front lawn nearly gone of what was over six inches of snow just yesterday. In its wake lay strewn about various branches from the two red oaks that dominate the front yard, and in the afternoon sunshine it felt decadent to walk about the grass and gathering them into piles.

It's been several weeks now since we last saw the lawn, which is now yellowed and matted from the snow cover. In the warming sunshine, small filaments of some fungus began to form on portions of the yard, resembling cloudy grey patches. It is amazing that this should happen so quickly, considering that yesterday was a tempest of winter weather. Today is altogether different, with signs of regrowth plainly evident, even though it is of the decomposer variety.

In the depressions of the yard, over by the knot garden and near the area where the old apple trees once grew, a small lake has formed from the melt. It has nowhere to escape, and though the ground is spongy on the surface, it is certainly still frozen just an inch or two beneath. The lake is really a large puddle of water, perhaps eight inches deep and twenty feet across. We just call it a lake for something fun; our own private pond for today, though assuredly it will freeze tonight when the temperatures drop.

It will freeze, though not all the way through, and the water beneath will take its time absorbing into the ground beneath, slowly, but in time leaving behind an air pocket below the skim of ice that forms the surface of the pond. In a week or two we'll come out and put our feet on the ice, easily breaking through to the air and ground beneath.

February 18

We look for signs now of change, of those subtle things that signal the transition from one season to the next. The light is more golden yellow in the afternoon, where just a few weeks ago it was paler and seemingly distant, it's angle lower in the sky and filtered by the bare tops of the side trees that line the access road. Now it rises above, arcing higher in its journey toward the western horizon and sending its rays more directly to the ground.

It is high enough now to shine through the windows of the sunroom in the afternoon, bathing the wood floor and part of the old chair in brilliant light and heating the sunroom naturally for an hour or so before it descends just so. We'll enjoy this pleasure for nearly two months yet, till the leafing of the big maple casts everything in shaded tones of earthen green.

February 19

The air returned to a frigid breeze all day, blowing steadily and hard from the northwest. Though the sky was a crystal blue, and the sun came directly enough to provide some warmth, the winds conspired to keep the chill in the mid 20s even at midday.

A light snow must have happened overnight, and the steady wind was enough to drift the new snow across the fields, through the spruce line and spill onto the roadway. I took the dogs for an afternoon walk into the fields, though the footing was more precarious than I had anticipated.

The snowpack of perhaps 6" deep had formed a crust on the first inch or so, covered then just slightly by the light snow that drifted throughout. To step in our familiar trail was an adventure of step, hesitate, and wait to see if a boot would break through the crust to the downy snow beneath. The dogs had more success - their light weight staying secure on the crust as they moved quickly through patches of more heavily drifted areas.

February 20

For just a moment this afternoon, I thought I heard the cry of a red-winged blackbird down in the tall rushes bordering the berm that runs across the east end of Asnebumskit Pond. It was only a juvenile blue jay, perched atop one of the mid white pines just within the woods on the border. In fairness, I don't know if it was a juvenile or not, but its atypical squawk ran on in a trill that sounded strangely similar to the "per-deee" we will hear soon enough when the black birds do arrive. I suppose the jay was just being a little cheeky, enjoying seeing me jerk my head around to locate what I thought was a welcome harbinger of spring. No so.

There is activity enough in the low woods below the berm, down in the wetland bog. Among the hardwoods that have survived the waterlogging, those on the periphery of the swampy area, there are several that look to have been chewed upon recently. A few trees are now only pointed stumps sticking forlornly out of the mire, their fate determined by the chewing action of the beavers, who must have an impressive den somewhere downstream closer to Streeter Pond. This wetland has expanded over the past few years, likely due to their workings.

Birds call among the forest in the afternoon sunshine. Jays, chickadees & titmice predominate. Their songs have changed slightly from a month ago, now laced with melodies of renewal that suggest the promise of spring is around the corner, perhaps arriving soon with the coming of the red wings.

February 21

Wouldn't you know, in the midmorning light that warmed the area near the feeders, two male redwing blackbirds walked tentatively on the ground among our resident winter birds. Both looked a bit thin from the winter, and the plumage was yet the dull black of the season, but each had the unmistakable yellow epaulet showing just beneath its wings as it moved about the yard searching for cast off seed.

These are the first arrivers I suppose, coming well before the females who should follow in a few weeks. The males will begin to scout nesting territory somewhere near the wetlands down by Asnebumskit, which means soon we might begin to hear their strident calls throughout the day. It's a welcome sign that spring is around the corner, like seeing the tentative tips of the snowdrops and crocuses push their way through the retreating snow pack out front or the subtle fattening of the buds on the lilac and forsythia in the side.

Soon the bird calls will be a cacophony of territorial advertisement, to the point that it is overpowering in the coming of the morning light. Soon the hylas will begin to advertise, tentative peeps at first when the nights remain warm enough and the gloaming of the evening comes later to the lower fen. There are signs all around now of reawakening, slowly but surely as we progress ever onward toward the promise that spring will bring.

February 22

The snow has nearly all melted, apart from the shaded areas where the sun's warmth can't establish any degree of lengthy foothold. Across the road through the spruce line, there are rows of snow that make it appear as if Fred has laid down new white plastic in preparation for transplanting. The troughs between last year's rows have sufficient shade and protection from the wind to keep this winter's snow lingering, making the illusion complete. It is disorienting to see such order, when about the yard the retreating patches of snow form uneven mosaics of dormant grass and thinning white.

The melt flows onto the driveway during the day, creating small pools in the depressions of our old asphalt, carrying the detritus of last fall with it, like a retreating glacier pulling the vestiges of boulders and debris. These pools collect old pine needles and tattered maple keys, which then freeze over when the temperature drops at night, trapping them within until tomorrow's warmth sets them free again.

February 23

The edge of the front lawn that borders Grove Street is now clear of snow, revealing a swath of loose sand and small sticks in the yard. We've come to anticipate this each year - the cast offs that are deposited by the town plow as it lumbers down the road, lifting the snow and curling it over onto the roadside. It is a pleasant thing to tidy, giving us a feeling of early spring cleaning as we work with the rake in hand, moving down the road and sweeping the mess back into the street where the run off from rains yet to arrive will take it downhill.

In short order the lawn looks remarkably clear, though decidedly yellow and patchy with the growth of certain fuzzy molds that proliferate briefly in the moisture of the receding snow. We have to remind ourselves that it is still February. The fickle month of March is still to come, and likely we will receive several more storms that will cruelly displace these feelings of an early spring.

In the border of the knot garden, where the soil has been exposed for several days and has lifted and cracked from the cycle of freeze and thaw, there are hints of the shoots of the snowdrops and the crocuses. Nearby the daffodils have been up for over a month, emerging prematurely during the lengthy warm spell in early January. They were soon covered in snow and have only recently been exposed again. Their blades look burned on the edges, the tentative green that poked through in January having turned a tired yellow in the covered freeze. They will survive just fine and none the wiser – though the yellow tips will remain as proof of the long thaw when the daffs do grow in earnest in the sustained warmth of the real spring yet to come.

February 24

Freezing rain this morning turned to plain old rain around midday, and the temperatures never rose above 34 degrees. Everything was coated with a thin layer of ice that not even the rain could remove by evening. Dreary, cold and unspring like.

Despite it all, a chipmunk emerged from somewhere near the old stone wall that borders the access road. Sarah caught a flicker of movement and watched the small creature climb gingerly on the ice that covered the stones. It sat silently looking about as the steady rain continued from above then made its way tentatively downward and across the yard toward the feeder poles for the cast offs.

This is the first chipmunk we've seen since last December, and for whatever reason this little one chose a decidedly cold day to make its debut into the world. I for one would rather stay in bed and wait for something more inviting. Some urge must have impelled it forth, perhaps cabin fever too overpowering that no degree of inclemency would change its mind.

It stayed for several minutes beneath the tube, gorging on seeds not taken by the birds. It would bend down quickly, locate a suitable candidate, then rise up to open it while looking around furtively for signs of trouble. Up, down, up, down in rapid succession, before bolting away for the safety of the wall.

February 25

In the knot garden, underneath the leaf litter that we left
undisturbed from last autumn's raking, the first snow
drops have emerged and are beginning to display their
delicate while blossoms. This is further evidence of our
mild winter, and the balmy temperatures of the past week
have hastened these first arrivers to push upward. I
commented to Sarah that the snowdrops have been up for
a few weeks in England, according to the news reports.
She replied flatly that Paxton "isn't England," and I admit
that it's a bit disconcerting to see things this far along in
late February.

Last year we were several feet buried in a near historic
snowfall, so much so that we didn't see the yard at all until
nearly mid April. This year feels out of place for the
opposite reason, as the lawn shows tentative signs of
greening as the red winged black birds and grackles have
increasingly congregated about the side yard, calling in
voices that are decidedly more vernal than winter.

February 26

We lost a dear friend not two weeks ago, and I've been
reluctant to write of his passing, but not to do so seems
wrong somehow. He more than any other inspired us to
see the simple things, those that are just outside the
dooryard and in the common places where life seems to do
just fine.

There were bluebirds in the bare trees this morning along
the northwest wall of his fields, resting gently with their
faces toward the east as the sunlight came over the crest of
the hillside. The ground had refrozen last night, and the
dogs seemed to prefer the hard dirt of the two-track, in
contrast to the softer muck that the last few days had

created. They didn't pay any mind to the bluebirds overhead as we walked stoically south along the wall toward the small break in the diagonal of the field where the track angles through and downhill toward the lower plot of land.

He would have been out here this morning, pulling any remnant plastic from atop the rows of soil used to grow last year's harvest. Or perhaps he would have been driving the tractor across the field, slowly with the bucket lowered while Fred walked ahead picking up any large rocks that mysteriously made their way to the surface. He would have stopped to watch the bluebirds too and would have told us about them later in the day, had we not already walked this way.

We remember him in the passing of the day, in the rhythms of the seasons that display the beauty of living and dying. We have lost such a dear friend, and yet we are so much richer for having known him.

Life goes on, with one day, one season turning slowly into the next.

February 27

According to the Farmer's Almanac, skunks should be mating about now. This coincides with the odor that greeted us this morning as we stepped out to take the dogs for a walk. There's no mistaking the musky smell of a recent spray, and this must have been close by, for it was so powerfully strong that we could almost taste the scent. Whew!

It's difficult to imagine that the scent itself is part of the attractive display. Perhaps in seeking a mate, the would-be suitor is discovered by some other animal or startled by a passing car, and this causes the defense mechanism to occur. Nonetheless we are all assaulted, and it all the more jarring when we so desperately want to smell things again outdoors as the Earth begins to shift from dormancy to spring.

February 28

The snow has been nearly gone for several days on account of the warm spell last week. There are a few desperate hold outs in the hollows of the woods and on the north side of the barn, but these small drifts are the remnants of the powdery snow of two weeks ago.

The exposed grass is rock hard in the morning, which makes it easier to rake the accumulated piles of sunflower cast offs from beneath the tubes. All about the side yard are strewn seeds and concentrated in large piles underneath where the birds pull them from the feeder in what seems like reckless abandon.

I used the broom to sweep the seeds into two large piles and then took the coal shovel to scoop them up into the wheel barrow, filling it nearly to the top. There must have been thousands, maybe tens of thousands of seed casings. This the fodder from several months of winter feeding, now sitting in a compost pile by the berm after having been transferred and dumped there.

Directly below the tubes, there remained small frozen piles of seed, protected from melting by the covering of shells from above, insulated remarkably from the warming trend. Now exposed, the sun should make quick work of them, and we'll tackle the remainder tomorrow or the next day. After all, we have to leave some pile for the squirrels to root in.

February 29

February at an end, uniquely somewhat as it is the leap year, and we've been rewarded with a day that is more typical of April than February.

In the afternoon, the dogs and I simply sat out in the front yard, I with my back propped against the trunk of one of the big red oaks and the dogs content to flop onto their sides to absorb the late winter sunshine. We've been spoiled so far, and this day continues the streak of calm and sunny skies.

All about on the ground lay strewn the remnants of detritus from the storms of late fall through winter, and it was pleasant enough simply to sit and casually examine the bits and pieces. Here were seed casings from the bittersweet vines that grow across the road among the spruces, their paper red coats and yellow caps faded yet festive looking in the muted greens of the dormant lawn. All about were the caps of acorns from the tree above, with the nuts having been molested from the activity of squirrels and mice these past few months. Pieces of the spruce tree lay about, small branches that must have blown off in one of the winter furies from January.

Even a small beetle had made an appearance, walking gingerly down the base of the oak and onto the grass, passing close by where we three sat. It resembled a lightning bug, though certainly it must be something only similar in appearance. (I gently picked it up to have a peek underneath, just to see if abdomen had any sign of the yellowy translucence that the true lightning bugs possess. No such thing.).

How wonderful it is to sit idly with eyes closed, face set toward the afternoon sun, the sounds of the titmice calling to one another in the distance, and the slight smell of warming Earth carrying the scents of spring that can't be too far away.

March

March 1

Today is the beginning of the meteorological spring, as
claimed by the television forecaster who defines seasons in
tidy three month bundles. This may work just fine for the
rest of the country, but New England rarely feels very
spring like in early March. Even when the astronomical
variety comes near the end, on the equinox, do we
typically feel all that vernal.

There are signs of change, regardless of the weather. Fred
is out across the road in fields pulling plastic, and this is
welcome activity after several months of having the
landscape fallow. It's windy out which helps, and he starts
at one end of the row by pulling up the plastic so that the
wind catches it underneath and helps lift the entire thing
into the air. If the breeze is just right, the whole row nearly
comes up, flinging dried earth and sere plant material high
into the sky as the loosened plastic flutters in a long strip
across the fields.

This means plowing can't be too far away, should March
cooperate a little and not come in angrily with snow. I
must have spring fever, wanting desperately to see and
smell the turned Earth. I should know better. It's March
after all, and we're likely to see the lion again soon.

March 2

The ice is starting to recede on the reservoirs. Down at
Kettlebrook, along route 56 toward Leicester, a cold wind
blew down the expanse of the lake, which is divided
roughly in half with ice on one side and exposed water on
the other. The breeze is strong enough to build the wave
action as it moves toward 56, causing them to break on the
edge of the ice and spill water onto the frozen expanse.

The temperature is cold enough that the spill freezes in thin layers, one after another, until small spreading patterns form on the surface.

The thaw has opened the spillway at the southern end of the reservoir, where the pretty cement bridge arches gracefully across the flow of water that leaves to go down the sluice toward the lower reaches. I stopped briefly here to watch and listen; the ice sheet ended just before the spill, and small bubbles of air would appear from underneath and move grudgingly toward the open water. Downstream the sound of the flow in the sluice is still foreign after the quiet of the past three months. In several weeks we will see the first signs of new growth along the banks, where skunk cabbage first thrives and then the ferns come in.

March 3

The morning began at 50 degrees, with the sunrise showing only as a hint of pinkish hue through leaden clouds that suggested change. Sure enough, the wind shifted to the northwest and built quickly to a steady breeze, as the temperature dropped just as swiftly. By the time I had returned home from taking the dogs for a walk around the fields, the thermometer read 38 degrees and continued dropping. At three o'clock in the afternoon, the skies had cleared, though the wind continued to blow constantly and the chill sat at 29 degrees. This felt like March, come fiercely across New York and over the Berkshires, bringing the winds of the Great Lakes across New England and toward places east.

The wind has whipped through the bare trees all day, making a white noise that doesn't cease, interrupted here and there from the clanging of the hurricane chime that hangs from the corner of the barn. Stray brown leaves from last autumn's litter occasionally break free from the piles in the side of the yard and across the road, taking flight then bouncing quickly across the front. They either stop when they hit the house straight on or pass by the side, tumbling toward the back and the lower woods beyond.

This feels like a cleaning wind, as if Mother Nature is content to blow the accumulated dust and debris of last season, now exposed from the snow cover to the open sky.

March 4

Two Canada geese flew in this afternoon from the somewhere in the direction of the knoll on the east side of Anna Maria's campus. They passed over up high, announcing their arrival to each other in the distinctive honking as they proceeded over the house and toward Holden's direction. A minute later they had returned, flying lower and descending toward the bare field, almost touching the tops of the spruce trees across the road before dropping rather ungainly downward to the earth, flapping their wings backward to slow before putting their feet tentatively on the soil.

These are the first I've seen since last November, when the last of the large flocks were still making preparations to migrate southward. In the weeks to come there will be more, and the numbers will rise (as will their chatter). If the weather holds, I would expect Fred to be out plowing soon to get the fields ready. This will turn the soil and loosen the remnants of last autumn's crop, stubble and cast-offs mostly, but once turned will make interesting fodder for the arriving birds. It's fine to have them congregate this time of year, apart from the noise that becomes grating after a while.

March 5

I heard it again this morning, down near the spillway on the far side of Asnebumskit Pond. Somewhere in the sere stand of *Phragmites* a red-winged blackbird sang its unmistakable "prrr deeee." I could only stand still and smile, listening to this sure harbinger of the coming spring.

It must be an optimistic bird, for the pond is still frozen over, and the surrounding berm and woodland is yet covered with at least 2" of snow. Yet there it perched within, hidden inside the tall fronds grasping a single stalk, swaying gently in the morning breeze.

I stayed several minutes just to listen; the bird called and paused perhaps a dozen times, and I couldn't help but wonder the purpose of its call. The females aren't due to arrive for nearly a month, so my sense is that this bird might simply be proclaiming this territory to would-be male rivals.

March 6

Drive along the roadways, or walk the back woods and you will notice the willows starting to yellow. If the light is just right, they even seem to create their own glow. The red and swamp maples are also starting to color in the stems.

Down on route 122 out of town, in the low area that forms a wetland that connects directly to the small lake inside Moore State Park, the road passes over a large culvert that provides passage for the wetland. On either side, but particularly on the eastern portion, swamp maples predominate around the low land.

They are starting to awaken so noticeably now, as if someone has painted on the stems a bare reddish sheen.

March 7

Given the recent uptick in bird activity, I thought it best to inspect the bird boxes we placed in the periphery around the feeder yard. All told, we have two wren houses and a large traditionally shaped birdhouse that has been home to chickadees the past several years.

This has become a spring ritual, to open each of the boxes and clean out the nesting material of last year's occupants. Admittedly, I always feel a bit ashamed at doing this, because I suspect (and hope) that the soon-to-be arriving tenets will be one and the same from last year. I feel guilty in so easily removing the engineering concoctions of twigs, moss and grass knowing that the same birds will likely spend hours rebuilding.

The two wren boxes had typical wren nests, overly packed and notably large for such a small little bird. The chickadee house gave me a start just as I began backing out the screws that held on the wooden base. The screws made a screeching sound on account of friction with the wood, and this caused the entire box to resonate with a high pitch as I removed them.

After a few moments of this I paused, because the box itself was making a deep vibrating sound within, and for the life of me I couldn't explain it. The vibration stopped. I started on the screw again, and no sooner did the vibration begin in earnest.

At this point, a child-like fear took hold of me, as I began to invent all sorts of irrational bird-box demons that were waiting to attack the moment the floor dislodged. Curiosity eventually overruled, though I admit to jumping back quickly as the last retaining screw released its grip and the floor dropped to the ground.

Wouldn't you know, in the midst of all the nesting material of grass and twigs and bits of dryer fluff – a queen bumblebee had made her overwinter nest. She drunkenly buzzed about just within the nest ball, awakened rudely from her hibernation.

March 8

It snowed all night and several hours into today, with a driving wind out of the east that is typical of a nor'easter low that sits off the cape. I took a ruler out to the back, in a spot that isn't subject to drifting too badly. Nineteen inches of new snow since yesterday afternoon and at least 6" more is forecast.

The drifts in our front dooryard are nearly four feet deep in spots, and the front entryway is completely blocked.

Just before bed last night, we checked the back porch to see if our surrogate new pet opossum had visited. She's been regularly coming now for the past two weeks, foraging under the feeders for discarded sunflower seeds. Sure enough, she was sitting right on the porch, using her front paws and long snout to push aside the snow that accumulated around her, oblivious to our watching her from only a couple of feet away.

Where she goes during the day is only a guess, but we've seen tracks that seem to lead across the access road to the neighbor's garden shed. And, when we first discovered her, the dogs gave chase while she ambled in that direction. (I kept hoping that she'd perform the coma-like seizure and drop dead, only to see what the dogs might do.) If she comes again tomorrow, JD wants to name her Pat.

March 9

The storm of the past two days is now gone, and the skies shine clear, though the wind remains fierce.

Sitting in the sunroom watching the birds return to the feeders in earnest, the wind must be out of just the right direction, as the hurricane chime in the front keeps sounding.

It's a fairly large triangular chime that I fastened to the corner of the front barn. Its weight is heavy enough so that only a fairly strong breeze out of the north will cause it to sound.

It is a deep and pleasing metallic chime, reminding me of the sound of the harbor channel markers that sit off Woods Hole in the Vineyard Sound. The intermittent "clang, clang" I am hearing just now is oddly out of place amidst the snowpack and winter scene. In my mind, I see seagulls hovering just above the boat, and warm water wind blowing spray from the tops of the crests, sounding the big red channel buoy as it pitches in the swells.

March 10

The killdeers have returned to the farm. We heard their distinctive trilling "tee tee tee tee" this morning and caught glimpse of a pair walking briskly across one of the raised rows in what was the tomato plot of last summer. They must be looking for a nesting site among the small rocks that collect in the troughs between the rows.

Soon enough, the female will lay her small, stone colored eggs within a cluster of similar rocks, making the entire affair nearly hidden from passing eyes – and certainly camouflaged from us as we walk nearby. Within a week or two, we will be alerted to a likely nest by the behavior of the attending parents, who feign injury close by so as to divert our attention. Sure enough, when the killdeers act this way we know their must be a hidden nest. And soon enough, we'll see the little puffball babies making their way frantically, running across the peaks and troughs of the rows as they chase their parents.

March 11, 2016

It's been unusually warm the past two nights, so much that we've had the windows cracked a little to allow the fresh air of the early spring to breathe into the house. There is a humorous anecdote in the writings of John Adams, who described an experience he had when traveling with Dr. Benjamin Franklin one early spring in the latter part of the 1700s. Adams recalled that he and Franklin argued about the beneficial health of fresh air when sleeping, Adams being in support while Franklin considered such air the potential for carrying harmful disease and insisted upon sleeping with the windows closed. It wasn't uncommon for people to believe that ailments such as colds were caused by "bad air," and in fact the root of our word Malaria reflects such a view. Of course, this was well before the understanding of germ theory, and so disease was attributed understandably to such things as bad air, a displeased God, imbalanced humors, and so on.

Adams had it right of course, or at least he did not subscribe to the notion of colds being caused through the circulation of the night air. For our part, it is a blessing to open the window now, decadent really, as it is only March 11th. To smell the earthy changes as they waft inward, made more so by the dampness of the rain from earlier in the day, is rejuvenation itself.

Note: Spring crocuses are blooming in the knot garden, as are the snowdrops.

March 12

The air was warm again at 5:00 this morning, and as I opened the porch door there was the unmistakable trilling of the Gray Tree Frogs from somewhere down by the vernal pool. It seems early for this to happen, but we can't deny the unusual warmth this winter. Things seem to be advancing toward an early spring, and the calling frogs are another harbinger of the changes that are just around the corner. If these temperatures hold, my guess is that we will hear the tentative "peeps" of the *Hylas* soon, beginning as sparse calls in the early morning and after the evening dusk, but building through the weeks to a constant din of mating calls that signals spring for all to hear.

Last autumn we discovered a Gray Tree Frog perched rather nonchalantly on the flower box that affronts one of the windows in the vestibule area of the house. It sat motionless in the faded light of the November afternoon sun, soaking up the warmth no doubt. It resembled a speckled mixture of greens and grays, with a splash of egg-yolk yellow on its underneath and feet that ended in splayed pods of sticky toes. Why it chose the house to rest, I haven't a clue.

In another month, the vernal pool will be alive with the sounds of the tree frogs, wood frogs, spring peepers and even the bulls. Their calls begin in the gloaming of the morning and persist throughout the day, building in the evening as twilight descends. These are the sounds of spring's arrival, the joyous notes of life renewed as winter has given way.

March 13

The flower garden bordering the driveway is mostly bare now, save for the shoots of daffodils that are nearly six inches high and reaching earnestly in these unusually warm days. The crocuses are the only real splash of color, and we presently have several large groupings at the edge that is exposed to more sunlight during the day. Their colors are brilliant white, lavender, and a pale primrose, each blossom opening in full as the day warms, revealing the saffron delight of pollen within.

In the warmth of the afternoon, a lone honeybee (*Apis Melifera*) came to visit the crocuses, buzzing first nearby the bright yellow splash on my jacket and deciding that I offered nothing nutritious. This bee must have come from Scott's hives across the road, nestled in several tiered boxes at the north end of Cournoyer's main field, where they live and forage and help pollinate the growing crops. Soon, as

330

more crocuses come, and the grape hyacinths finally make an appearance, we will have more scouts arriving daily. Thereafter the flowers will be visited frequently for many months, as workers ferry back and forth to the hive.

March 14

The willows are yellowing on the twig, filling with their own renewal of the pulse of things as they progress toward budding. The trees now have a sheen all their own, signaling the change that is soon to arrive. I expect the red maples will begin shortly to display their own reddish hue, followed in a couple weeks by flower and catkin. Things are several weeks earlier this year than normal.

There was activity across the road in the greenhouse just visible through the spruce line, and so we decided to pay a visit. Inside, Moose the cat was sprawled prostrate on the table in the middle of the building, basking in the 95 degree warmth of the sunlight and heat, trapped within by the glass walls and ceiling, making the room smell earthy and summer like. Sometimes in the winter, on the cold and clear days when the angled sun still reaches the greenhouse enough to heat the air within, we will trudge through the snow and step inside to feel the warmth and smell the ground, to remind us of the growing seasons and the promise of what will arrive when winter finally ends.

Fred was filtering soil for planting, using a screen to separate the small twigs and clumps from the cover bedding he will place on top of the leek seeds that Louise has placed in the small cells. Thousands of leeks and several hours of work, all being made ready for germination and patience until May, when with good luck they will be large enough to transplant into the waiting soil outside.

331

March 15

Thinking of yesterday's leeks reminds me that it is time to seed our own tomatoes; if we hope to have large enough plants to put in the garden come May. Several years ago, our neighbor down the road Gary Monfreda gave me a homemade germination box that he had no further use. It's nothing fancy – just a twenty-inch wooden cubic box with a sliding glass panel and a mounted socket for a light bulb in the rear. Despite its rudimentary austerity, it has worked perfectly through the years, with the addition of a rheostat switch so that I can adjust the intensity of the single 45 watt bulb inside.

I frankly enjoy this late winter task, as it is my first hands-on connection with the promise of growing and harvest that will one day occur as the seasons evolve. We've been receiving the seed catalogs for several weeks now, and they have been resplendent with images of idyllic crops of all shapes and sizes, flowers, trees, fruits and vegetables of every imaginable variety. We look forward to the catalogs in early winter, when we are just settling in to the prospect of the long, dark haul. Receiving them in March is another story, for now we are raring for a change, impatient to get outside and renew our own feel for the land, desperate to watch and feel and smell the pulse of life that the next season delivers.

Tomatoes are usually the first step in this direction, and though it is a small accomplishment, it is satisfying to fill the cells with potting soil and plant the various seeds within. Place the flats into the germination box, turn the bulb on dim so that the temperature inside is in the upper 70s, and wait. Soon enough we will see the tiny seedlings emerge, signaling the beginning of the long, welcome stretch of growth and renewal.

March 16

There are Coltsfoot shoots coming up in the lowland roadsides. They are unremarkable now and resemble the emerging greens of a dandelion. I wouldn't even recognize them for what they are, except that I've grown familiar with their annual appearance in certain places. There is a good patch down at the end of Grove Street, just before it makes a turn to become Pond Street, on the north side of the road and tucked within the sunny spots of the berm.

They seem to like the mixture of exposure and proximity to the wet marsh that abuts just beyond, where the cattails will rise upward along with the ferns as May gives way to June. There is another patch I know on the old Brigham Road, past the rear entrance to the trails of Moore State Park and just down the hill a ways. Again, you'll find them on the side of the road thriving in the poor mixture of rocky soil.

In a couple of weeks, you will think they are dandelions. They look similar, with the striking composite yellow head atop the single stalk, though look closely; the stalk of the Coltsfoot is braided, notably so.

It's a funny thing. I admire these early spring weeds and look forward to their splash of yellow against the changing browns of the sere plants and grass that accompany them. These dandelion looking flowers are fine with me, where they are, by the roadside. Soon enough, the green shoots of our real dandelions will appear in our yard among the mixture of grasses and weeds that are emerging from dormancy. These dandelions are invaders, unwelcome, and scorned. Actually, our yard is such a mosaic of field grass and weeds at this point that it's silly to stand on principle, yet I was taught that dandelions are the enemy, and such views are difficult to change.

March 17

The folks at Robinson's are busy, readying the flowers. Two weeks ago the greenhouse was nearly empty, and now there are hundreds of pots with soil, waiting for germination. In another week, we'll see the seedlings of what will be dozens of varieties of flowers of all types, and each building will be awash in what is almost overwhelming displays of color. It is all the more striking this time of year and particularly when we get a cold stretch in late March. Outside still looks like very early spring, with the ground yet mostly dormant despite the hint of tinges of green in and among the blades. The buds on the trees are fattening, and we've had the first show of crocuses and snowdrops. The roadside weeds and grasses are only just arriving and nothing to speak of. It really looks more like November than spring.

One only has to walk down to the greenhouse and go inside. On these cold and sunny days, the heat of the air and the varied colors are jarring and wonderful at the same time.

Notes: First sign of starlings at the feeder.

March 18

The water is flowing quickly down the cascade that runs beneath the descent of South Road as it drops toward the reservoirs. It is worth taking a walk to the place where the pavement flattens and watch the creek tumble from above, moving through the moss covered rocks and through the culvert toward the forest ravine on the other side.

Sometimes in the early mornings I will come here, as the first hints of daybreak show through the still bare trees as a pinkish glow from across the expanse of the water down below. In another month this place will begin to fill in with the new leaves of spring, and the ferns will return to the banks of the stream, nearly hiding the water altogether as they become thicker with the passing season.

The sounds too change here as March gives way to the maturing spring. The rush of water now is forceful from the melt, falling quickly across the large rocks. With May it will subside, and apart from a rainy shower to recharge the flow, it will be nothing more than a trickle until drying altogether in the heat of the summer that is to come.

March 19

It's been a week since I planted the tomato seeds in the cells, and I am starting to worry that the house temperatures have been too cold for them to germinate. Surreptitiously, I decided to walk across the road to see how things have progressed at the farm, as Fred spent the better part of last weekend doing just the same, though he must have seeded a thousand plants or more. This makes my paltry twenty cells seem insignificant in the scheme of things, but I'm invested in them nonetheless, because they are my seeds and will be transplanted in my garden, diminutive as they will be.

Inside the greenhouse lay dozens of flats basking in the afternoon sunshine, each containing the tiny deep green cotyledons of the newly emerged tomato seedlings. Darn. That seals it. The air inside the greenhouse must be a least eighty degrees, where our house has hovered around sixty five at best as we've negotiated this cool stretch the past couple of days.

Mine may yet germinate in the cool, but it will take at least another week or more I fear, plus there's the worry that the seeds might simply rot. I'm impatient to get things going, as each day brings things closer to May when I can transplant. Plus, seeing Fred's veritable forest of small seedlings in the verdant enclosure of the greenhouse fills me with jealousy. I'm not proud of that, but I'm willing to put pride in my pocket for the sake of the growing season.

www.ingramcontent.com/pod-product-compliance
Lightning Source LLC
Chambersburg PA
CBHW070104290526
45789CB00005B/1914